Lucifer Dreaming

Marcus Rian

Mozart & Reason Wolf

Sarasota 2009

Aknowledgments

Lucifer Dreaming is a work of fiction. Names, characters, places, and incidents are the products of the author's imagination. Any resemblance to actual persons, living or dead, businesses, locales, or events, is entirely coincidental.

Version 4 (Abridged)

Cover photograph from Swan Point Cemetery, Providence, RI, by Merissa Depasse.
Sky-diving angels make-up art on back cover by A. M. Caratheodory & M. Depasse
Author Photograph by Merissa Depasse
All poetry by A. M. Caratheodory, with permission of MRW, Ltd.

Published by Mozart & Reason Wolf
      8051 North Tamiami Trail, No. 51
      Post Office Box 1551
      Tallevast, Florida 34270-1551
      mozart@reasonwolf.com
      editor@3musesbooks.com

Publisher's Cataloging in Publication Data
Marcus Rian 1950-
  Lucifer Dreaming

  1. Fiction.
I. Title.
PS
ISBN 978-0-911385-36-6 0-911385-36-3 (paper)

Book Design by Rian Garcia Calusa
      Design@RianGarciaCalusa.com

  Printing February 2009

Printed in the United States of America
10 9 8 7 6 5 4 3 2 1

Lucifer Dreaming

Contents

Dedication

To Margaret Ryan, a reader extraordinaire, who encouraged me to read and then to write. And, to my late friend, Lena Nieman, a writer extraordinaire, who challenged me to write this and to finish it before she finished her own novel, *Oyster Bay*. "Ha!" she said.

Chapter 1. The Others

Small particles of dust, some brought by the solar wind, triggered water vapor to cool and condense, and become rain drops, falling gently and briefly over a clearing in the park. One drop seemed to become a crescent. The crescent became a bird. Fully extended, the wings touched vertically. As the hand wings, with their stiff outer primary feathers, drove down, each feather twisted to drive the air behind. The secondary feathers of the arm wing were kept slightly tilted to provide lift. The stroke moved the wings down and forward, stretching in front of the head and body, almost touching. With the start of the upstroke, the upper hands rotated the feathers twisted open like blinds, and the wings were thrown back vertically, tips flexed. They were drawn backwards and upwards strongly and extended until they touched above the back. Then the stroke moved forward to complete the cycle.

The body was tilted down. The bird moved over the park and angled toward a bench in the sun. The seat of the bench was occupied. Several feet away, the wings were held horizontally. The glide path dipped below the wooden back rest. Then the wings and body were lifted; the final yards were covered in an upward glide, losing speed. The tail feathers and alula were spread to slow the approach further and reduce stalling speed. The landing was absorbed by strong legs. The wings were folded, and the bird regarded the human stretched out below.

* * *

The memory of what they had done to him was more painful than the actual cutting. Afterwards, still before dawn, they had tied him facing east; he could see several of the ships in the Harbor. He felt leather holding his head straight, stone against his back. He watched the first tentative rays of light appear like a high curtain before dropping slowly lower. After the sky became lighter, he knew that it would be pink, then red, orange, and white. He watched the change with consuming interest. As it became white, he knew that he would not see it for very long.

"Regulus," came the boast, "the sun will be up soon. Are you ready to gaze directly on its power?"

He did not answer. His eyes itched already from dust and teared slightly. He would give them as little satisfaction as possible. He stiffened his back, pulling his shoulders back. Carthage was a bad place to be a Roman, worse to be a Roman general, and far worse to be caught as a spying Roman general. They had beaten him; six had held him immobile while his eyelids were cut off. Someone had cleansed the blood off his face as he was tied to a post to face the sun. He would gaze on the sun, he would be blinded, but he vowed that he would counsel another Roman army on the task of leveling this impudent city. Then let the sun gaze on the dead rubble that he would transform from a living city. At first, the light was gentle and red. His eyes itched more. Then, he felt every ray pushing into his eyes, crowding in. He shifted his glance down to the trees and ramparts, noticing the texture of leaves and stone, the colors. The sun was higher; he could not look away. Rivers of light ended in the caves of his eyes, spilling out. The beauty turned to heat, and pain. Light filled every part of the sky, flooding down through the city and into him. He grimaced to avoid crying out, feeling chilled.

He gazed into its metal heart, his lips shaping words: "God. The sun is a god." Then, he cried out.

* * *

There was a loud clap as the pigeon took off, the wings thrust up and pulled explosively down, accelerating the body up, air rushing into the space where the wings had been, a vortex of air shed by the tips of the wings. Muscles sent blood to the wings, laden with oxygen needed to burn fat to power the lift. Walker fell off the bench seat, startled by the noise and motion, opening his eyes to see the pigeon six feet above him, turning to escape something. The memory receded.

He sat up, noticing a gray feather by his feet. He picked it up and examined it. The vaned feather was mostly a hollow shaft, the web made up by hundreds of barbs, each barb having hundreds of filaments having interlocking hooks. He thought he could still hear the air rushing through the feathers. The sky was not lifeless, like the space between stars. But birds and insects had handicaps to overcome to fly. Only wings, that had to move up before they could move down, gave them the air. Many men knew how hard that was.

He knew it had been a dream, but he couldn't remember it. He never could. Then, he remembered why he was waiting in the park. He hoped that it wasn't one o'clock, yet. As he hurried out of the park to look for a clock, he heard other people's voices. He couldn't miss this interview; good jobs were rare in Honolulu.

He saw a clock. It was 12:50. The appointment was set for 1:00. He wouldn't have time to eat before walking to the bank. Just as well; his teeth would be cleaner, and he might feel more like eating afterwards. A bank, how sad, he thought. He hadn't minded using computers in his last job, since he had been expertly trained in astrophysical research—his ex-job, anyway—but he couldn't get very excited about operating one for forty hours a week. Some kinds accumulated a lot of down-time; that made deadlines harder to meet. He didn't doubt that bank deadlines were more urgent than research deadlines. He felt the slight stubble on his cheeks; his razor was too dull to cut anymore. His hair felt a little greasy, too. He hoped that no one would notice these things.

The receptionist was attractive and polite; very clean and well-dressed, also, dark hair, dark eyes. She offered him coffee or tea. He declined both—they both upset his stomach—and waited with a current

7

Newsweek.

At five after one, a fellow in a light gray suit came in, extending his hand, "Mr. George Walker, pleased to meet you. My name is Minton, Harvey Minton, Head of Data Processing."

He nodded his head and accepted the smooth hand, which stopped just short of a firm, full handshake.

"We are pleased that you are interested in First Federal. If you come this way, we can discuss your qualifications as we tour the facility."

Walker followed him to the elevator; data processing was on the top floor. Minton didn't speak in the elevator. He wondered if there was a taboo against speaking in the elevator; he would have to know things like that if he worked here.

As they stepped out, Walker noticed that the walls were gray, the floor was gray, the cabinets were gray.

"So, tell me a little bit about yourself. Were you stationed here?"

Walker tried to answer as they threaded their way through a maze of cubicles. He had expected some question like that. "I got out of the service here, then found a good position at the observatory. Similar to what I was doing in the Air Force." He noticed that the computer frame was a dark gray, that the windows made the sky seem gray. He was introduced to every employee on the way, the interview suspended for introductions. He forgot each name promptly as it was offered, not wanting to clutter his own memory with names he might not need to know.

"And this is Mark McNally, the night supervisor. You will be working for him directly."

McNally queried, "You worked for Morton, on his IBM 1130? What languages do you know?" dispensing with the amenities.

"Yes, Dr. Morton is very capable. FORTRAN, a little BASIC, a little COBOL," he replied.

"Well, you won't be needing any languages here," Minton smiled grimly. "No operators are allowed to interface with the programs. If you think there's a program error, the proper procedure is to call a programmer. Perhaps, someday you will want to work your way into programming."

"Well, it's good to know that I can move up, if I work hard," Walker replied, thinking that it was not likely—he didn't want brain damage from programming; he'd seen too many green-screen zombies before.

"Good, good, that's the kind of attitude we like here." Minton said as he steered them to the coffee room.

He felt he had to have coffee with them, although he didn't swallow much, on an empty stomach. He described some of the research projects he had worked on at the Observatory, careful to mention that the funding had been cut. He was amazed at the polite interest that covered a broad-spectrum ignorance in these commercial breeds, not even knowing what a red giant star was.

Then, they described the operation of the bank in minute and unnecessary detail. His smile started to crumble; if only he could stick it to his gums until someone said something interesting or until they were finished. They were finished, and he injected new enthusiasm into his lip curl. He was respectfully led back to the reception area, where he also thanked the receptionist, asking with his eyes how available she was. Her eyes were as neutral as mirrors.

He was sure that they would hire him. They had spoken as if they were sure, also. But he checked with the receptionist at the Clancy agency, who told him that his counselor, Betty Tolley, was with another client, he had no messages, and she would call him if he did. He wondered if prostitutes called their johns clients in the same way. Anyway, he was free until tomorrow. He raced back to his apartment to get his swimsuit.

Along the tree-lined streets, he recounted the interview with satisfaction. He was familiar with the IBM hardware; he was willing to work a night shift, he seemed to get along with the bank people. Minton had promised to call him tomorrow, after the decision was made. It was quiet along the canal. He thought that it might be interesting to try to swim in it, but it was oily. He never had much time to swim when he was working. Maybe with the bank job he could swim every day.

He cut back toward the boulevard, noticing the people on the streets; busy, busy, busy. The only ones not busy were the panhandlers, who eyed him back. People only seemed to make eye contact when they wanted something. He passed a gas station lush with weeds. Concrete couldn't conquer the weeds on the islands. Some of the houses were Victorian. Even they looked more in place that the new glass boxes. He would like to buy one of those old houses. His apartment was in one, surrounded by the new boxes, with a pitifully narrow view of the sea—none from his windows.

The house was a lone hold-out with four porches and four entrances. His faced south. He shared a sidewalk with a young Japanese woman living next door. She had never spoken to him, but they had progressed to nods of acknowledgment; that was encouraging. Always, on opening the door, he was overwhelmed with the musty smell of mildewed rugs and walls that he associated with the tropics. Now, they were his rotting rugs. He took his trunks off a hook in the shower, stripped to his socks and put them on. He looked at his face in the mirror, the bags under the eyes, the permanent frown. He felt the fat on his stomach as he bent over to put on his sneakers. His spare tire was indicative of comfort and complacency, but it was being deflated by the bad stress of not eating and by the good stress of biking, walking, or swimming everywhere. He finished tying the sneakers and locked the door.

He checked his 10-speed bicycle, a white Raleigh, the most expensive thing he owned. The beach was just a mile off, so he jogged, eager to be in the sun. He thought of his dream. Dreams are not single, separate, or simple. Certainly the logic of Aristotle did not hold; what is true may also be not true. His eyes itched.

He had not been sorry to leave the observatory, although he was sorry to leave his job. The observatory was over 9,000 feet elevation.

Living there was a strain. His trailer was drafty. When the observatory dome was open, he was always cold. There were ice storms, and snow. There was less oxygen, so it was harder to breath. Still, he would miss it. On Mount Haleakala, on Maui, almost half of the air and 90% of the humidity was below the observatory. The bare peak cooled rapidly after sunset; winds brought cold dry air from higher layers, breaking up any clouds. Most nights were very clear. The dryness and purity of the air caused less scattering of light. The observatory was particularly suitable for researching low intensity light phenomena, such as the light of the night sky and zodiacal corona, which is what he had worked on, after his funding for stellar modeling was cut.

He meditated on the light of the sun reflected. So much light, so little of it intercepted by the earth. Several times he had worked day shifts on prominences. Prominences. He had been born on the morning of one of the largest prominences ever photographed—so large it had been visible with the naked eye as a dark filament. It had been blown out from the sun, a graceful arch growing almost as large as the sun itself. He had seen pictures of "Grandpa," as the prominence was called, taken from the observatory in Boulder, Colorado. He had been born at 4:00 p.m. Greenwich Mean Time; the prominence had started then and lasted until 5:30. It had been photographed through an H-alpha filter on the coronograph, which created an artificial eclipse. By 5:30, its height had reached almost 800,000 miles above the surface of the sun; the sun, whose own diameter was 864,000 miles.

From the earth, the surface of the sun seemed smooth, except for an occasional spot. As the telescope brought it closer, it blazed. It was a boiling cauldron, a burning honeycomb with rising and falling cells. Near the surface, energy was carried by convection, like a pan of boiling water. Prominences hung over the surface like dark veils for days or even months. They did not rise, but just materialized out of the corona and fell back to the photosphere, the surface of the sun. Sometimes, they erupted and billions of tons of gas were expelled from the surface.

Glowing gases flared far out into space. Torches rose, then flowed back to the surface, bound in lines of force. Dark, cooler regions marked the surface, where the magnetic fields of layers had become tangled.

From the center of the sun, crushed by the mass of gas, the inner shell of nuclear explosions generating temperatures of 14 billion degrees, light radiation fought its way to the surface, taking years, years to travel just 300,000 miles. Then, with less pressure, the flight was easier. The surface temperature was only 5,600 degrees, bright yellow. In the confusion of escape, the packets of light collided and generated more heat. The temperature rose to 20,000 degrees. Sound waves were generated and traveled out to the corona to be dissipated. Supersonic shock waves drove the temperature of the corona to one or two million degrees. The sun did not have a sharp boundary exactly; the gas simply became less dense through the solar system.

He looked up as he jogged. The sun was so bright that all other stars paled. Yet, at night, those stars became as real as trees; Mira, the red star noticed by Fabricius, the German clergyman, in 1596, fourteen years before the telescope was invented, was one. So massive and strange that it increases its brightness by 100 times every 300 days before dimming. Algol, the demon star, winking every other day as its light is blocked by a faint companion. The Orion nebulae, a gas cloud, perhaps a birth place heated by some unimaginable source so that it changes from red to orange, to green and yellow, with bright lines and dark patches. Cassiopeia, destroyed in an explosion, so its shell of destruction radiates more brightly than the cinder left in the center.

Astronomy was such a mystical science. He studied charts of things he could not see, that could not be seen by any eye, but had to be followed across the sky and built-up for hours on chemical plates. Things filtered by unimaginable distances, so old and remote, whose histories were so long that there had been no change from the dinosaurs until now. Stars that might be cooling cinders when the first flush of their light reached his observatory. Things that could not be explained, reached or fixed, experimented on or mixed, or touched. What of the dark in between? Even more mysterious.

He stopped up short to the sound of honking. Better watch the traffic, he thought as he ran across the road, against the light. There didn't seem to be many people out; that was good. He staked a claim on the beach with his shirt and sneakers and rushed into the water.

He struggled to get out past the waves. The ocean was warm, like a warm bath, but unlike his last bath drawn from rusty pipes, clear; the bottom looked only several feet away, although he knew better from experience. He could still hear splashing noises from the beach. He turned on his back and kicked out toward sea, thinking about his interview, unwillingly. He hoped that he got it, because he was going to run out of money next week. Just two weeks ago, everything had seemed so secure. He still had a year and a half to go on his contract; the grant had been for three years. If he had had more notice, he could have saved more. But the government had canceled the grant retroactively, to the month before he had even heard about it. It wasn't fair. The job market in Hawaii was shit. He hadn't thought about as long as he was working. Being a veteran wasn't any help; everyone else looking for work seemed to be a veteran.

Astronomy was all he knew; he didn't know anything about banks, although he had his account in one; all $97.47 in it. Then there was his emergency $100.00 under the lining of his suitcase and a set of air coupons from his last grant. Too bad he didn't know accounting or nursing; those seemed to be in demand. Well, he would know tomorrow. He turned over and began a slow crawl; silly name, the crawl, so Australian, but butterfly was too tiring, breaststroke was too slow. After a few minutes of relaxed crawling, he started swimming below the surface to look at the bottom and enjoy the cooler water. Then, he heard something rushing through the water toward him.

"Shark!" he thought, diving slightly, trying to see it before it struck.

"Jerks!" he screamed silently, recognizing the form of a catamaran.

13

They were twenty yards from him by the time he surfaced and looked back at them. Must have their heads up their asses. He turned around, making sure that nothing was coming towards him. The shore must be a mile away, he guessed. As he dropped back into the rhythm of motion, the bitterness and anger dropped away, as he knew it would in the water.

This time the dark shape in the corner of his vision was silent. He stopped, trying fearfully to identify it. It had to be a dolphin, probably following the boat, or looking for one to follow. The silhouette had a fin and tail, but the tail was wrong, not vertical.

"Dolphin," he breathed, losing air. He grabbed air and dived under, keeping his arms straight ahead and legs together, whipping from the waist. He hoped that it would appreciate a dolphin kick. A second shadow spiraled closer. He recognized the long nose like a collie's, but the forehead was higher. Bottlenose? he wasn't sure. Flipping his feet and rolling, he caught the dolphin regarding him; after it rolled, too, he flipped forward and rolled again. Much further ahead, he saw the dolphin roll again and then seem to wait for the next trick. It wants me to do the trick first, he realized. Angling slightly toward the surface, his movement started with his neck and rippled along the body to his feet and pushed against the water with straight toes. He swept his left arm around and performed a barrel roll, still angling toward the surface. The dolphin counterpoised flippers and barrel-rolled ten feet from him. Then he kicked full speed for the surface to gasp for breath. The dolphin apparently thought that was good fun and added a tail-slap when it surfaced.

"Oh sure, you can hold your breath longer, anyway," he reproved it.

It squeaked an answer of some kind. He took several quiet breaths, then a deep one, and returned ten feet underwater. He straightened to a forward glide, arched his back and swam gracefully in a loop. The dolphin repeated it three times as fast. Oh, sure, he thought, you weigh twice as much and have big flippers and a tail. After surfacing for a quick breath, he corkscrewed down as fast as he could. When he stopped and looked right, he saw two dolphins repeating the trick in unison. He laughed, losing most of his air in bubbles, and had to surface again.

He went down again and again, losing track of time. His hands and feet were pathetically small by comparison, and could not match their fins and tails. Whatever he did, they duplicated faster and better. He noticed that the first one was a pale gray; the second one, still acting shy, had a pucker mark in back of a dorsal fin. They were clicking and whistling, now, but nothing was communicated to him, except possibly enthusiasm for the game. His surfacing became more frequent. He realized that he was becoming exhausted. He began breast-stroking toward shore. The dolphins leaped about as a pair, and then took off in different directions. He decided to call the first one 'Gray' and the second 'Shy.' He wondered if they had names that they called each other.

He remembered a quote that he had read in virtually every book on wild animals. From Beston. "We need another and wiser and perhaps a more mystical concept of animals ..." it began. He thought that we see animals from the other side of the glass of our knowledge, not from playing with them. We condescend to them, as below us and less complete, then remembering another phrase from Beston— "but their world is older and more complete than ours; they have senses we lost or never had. They are not pets or brothers, but other beings, other nations caught in the same web of time and space." And we have never learned how to exchange ambassadors or respect their territory. He would visit again tomorrow.

Going back to shore, he knew that he had miscalculated his energy. He had to float and rest several times. His right calf was tightening. When he got to the beach, he was too tired to go to the library. He had to stop and rest several times walking home, laying on the sidewalk for a few minutes, praying that he did not look homeless; he wished that he had wheels.

That night, listening to the rat-patter on the ceiling of his apartment, he thought of his contact with the dolphins, the aliens. They were aliens, with shiny, rubber suits, and a funny fast-click language. He wondered what they thought of him; the spindly limbs and hairy head—not much in the water, his slow "duh-duh" speech not fit for new-borns. Games, they were playing games, trying to communicate? Was it because he could not do their tricks—swimming fast and leaping, diving deeper—that they took such pleasure in his? Well, it was the intent that mattered; they couldn't handspring or roll across a beach. Lying back, with his hands under his head and eyes open, in the dark, he thought of a trick they couldn't do: curl up in a tight ball and tumble forward. He knew that they couldn't bend in the middle or at the knees—what knees? Tomorrow, he'd try it.

He rested for a while, not thinking, just glad to be resting. He was still too tired to sleep. He'd only had a part of a pineapple for dinner; it cost a little less than on the mainland, and there was so much of it, even in vending machines, with luau punch and orange juice. The apartment was more important than a full stomach; weekly rent was ridiculous, but that's the way it was. He imagined all the foods he would have when he was hired. He wondered if he should write to his congressman and suggest regular random layoffs as part of national diet program. Mass, two month-long layoffs, with each person being given $100.00 to live on until they were rehired. Necessity was the mother of discipline, not the mother of invention, who was actually the child of leisure.

Gradually his thoughts drifted back to the dolphins. Swimming was natural to him, even if he wasn't as fast. Maybe that odd theory was correct: humans were aquatic apes, hairless, fatty, and streamlined—but he not too fatty, anymore, thanks to Uncle Sam's federal budget and warfare diet center, funneling more money into Vietnam. When he remembered that, he forcibly turned his thoughts to the bank, hoping they would come through. Then, he would treat the dolphins with more courtesy than he received from his fellow man. A small movement shifted his attention to the wall. A fly perhaps. Stray light through the shades gave character to the old plaster. He drifted into the net of sleep.

***

"We have snared our fly and taken him indoors, buzzing vainly, to glue to a plate, alas, one less in the ensemble of life. By the help of the microscope there is nothing so small as to escape our inquiry. There is a new visible world discovered to our understanding. The earth, which lyes so neer us, shows in every particle of its matter almost as great a variety of creatures as we were able to reckon in the whole universe. The subtleties of nature may be more fully discovered, from whence many advantages admirable towards the increase of mechanic knowledge, of gears and optical glasses to which this age seems so much inclined, because we may be enabled to discern the secret workings of nature, as we do those that are productions of art, and are managed by wheels and springs devised by human wit," he wrote into his notebook.

He leaned down and tightened his stocking. Then turned to the lens, his doorway to adventure among the strange apparitions in light. The fly was in place, buzzing less, now. He took up a pen to record his observations.

"Its curious feet: The foot of a fly is a most admirable contrivance, for by this the fly is enabled to walk against the sides of glass, and to suspend itself from the ceiling; it is able to do this with the help of two talons and two palms on each foot; the talons are large ...

"Its admirable wings: ... variegated with all the range of vivid colours imaginable, the whole is delicately rang'd in the fine flourishings and ornamented paintings on Persian carpets.

"Its impressive eyes: The greatest part of the head is nothing else but two large prominent bunches of eyes; the surface of each is shaped into small hemispheres in triagonal order, rang'd over the surface in rows, with long and regular trenches between. The hemispheres are divided into two sizes, the bygger and higher ones looking up, and the smaller lower ones pointing down; there is an eye pointing in almost every direction. In each, I discern parts of the landscape before my window, from a hundred slight perspectives."

He stopped taking notes; took off his glasses and rubbed his nose. Their eyes must have originated in air, in the bright chamber where everything moves, not in the sea. The dry crystal mosaic with sharp, flickering patterns. They see so clearly, but what do they see? Mountains of plaster, but not the wall. The mounds of paint on Rubens' painting of Venus, but not the Goddess beneath his feet. His own wings, but not constellations at night, nor the buds blossom twice. And what do we not see? he wondered. The natural philosophy of a fly—how strange? Never fall to earth, a real angel, pummeled by particles of smoke; every rain drop a torrent. Even should a Bacon among the flies reach us with a tract, we could not understand it. He moves so fast, the human world must be dull and slow; our interests and needs as distant as the sun and moon.

He turned back to the lens. Then fell through it. He looked back and saw his body as a hideous monster, each breath a shrieking wind. Did he look thus to all animals? He covered his mouth. He watched it, his senses doubled. Truth is the face of the Medusa; we would be petrified if we looked at it directly. Like Perseus, we must find a mirror to look at her. Mayhap the mirror of the microscope will let us look at our selves?

He pulled the fly off the plate and set it on the windowsill.

"Mrs. Hogarth! Dinner!" he announced.

"Yes, Master Mellin," came the faint reply.

He gazed out the window, at people going to church, under misty Dutch skies. He thought. The church is a chamber of forest-filtered mists, where the radiance of light is stained and dimmed to fit our minds. Our eyes are the eyes of the seas and forests, and need they shade.

Colors hide in white. The sun is stretched to red. When it sets, its last ray is green. Green comes from burning. Sun fire drives the world. The sun is the heart of the planets as the heart is the sun of the body. The sun quickens the heart of flesh; it becomes a heart of fire, blood its light. Grass and forests burn at night. We live in a green night. He looked towards the sun.

***

The sun played over his eyelids. How wonderful to be wakened that way—much more smoothly than an alarm; alarms should be saved for fires and emergencies. He got up and fixed toast with his water. The toast was better than just plain bread; it tasted better. Artificially made stale, but warm. The trouble with rationing—or dieting—is that you're always hungry—no remedy for that.

He went by the library before hitting the personnel agency, spending an hour reading about dolphins and whales. To the dolphin, Plutarch had written, "Nature has given what the best philosophers seek, friendship for no advantage;"—simply put, the dolphins were always friends to humans. Humans, on the other hand, did not seem to reciprocate the friendship, killing dolphins for sport, for competing with them for the fish, or hurting them by accident. The Greeks regarded dolphins highly. There was the myth of Dionysus turning pirates into dolphins to be reformed from their ways. He read dozens of stories of dolphins helping humans, keeping them afloat, driving off sharks.

He read an article that suggested that dolphins were neotonous, like humans, having characteristics of the young throughout their entire lifetime. Maybe it was a characteristic of mammals that returned to the sea. That must be why they devoted so much energy to play. He looked through the pictures, trying to identify which of the many kinds of dolphins were the ones he met yesterday. They must have been 'spinners.' He got lost in the welter of information.

He glanced up and saw that it was almost 11:00 a.m. He hurried by the agency, hoping to find out about the bank job. Since there were no messages for him, he went right back and changed for swimming. On the beach, he spied a pair of flippers. Thinking that was just what he needed, he borrowed them, leaving a message in the sand that he would return them later in the afternoon. He was eager to swim out again, but he enjoyed the rhythm of the strokes so much that he didn't hurry; the flippers made movement much easier. After twenty minutes, and a mile out, he heard a whistle. Stopping and looking up, expecting to see a boat, he saw only two fins approaching. He was still afraid that it was sharks, although he knew better. He kicked under in a smooth glide. The two sleek mammals immediately closed in formation with exaggerated movements. As he surfaced and took a deeper breath, he saw a third fin coming toward them. Since his escorts didn't seem to get excited, neither did he. He decided to swim in a large circle, much easier with the fins on. When he went for his next breath, two of them swam in a circle around him; just like Indians, he thought—no, not hostile or threatened, or human.

He dove again, reaching one arm out to try to touch the single one, which came within a foot from him. He remembered the tumble roll and tried it, holding his shins in his hands. His shadow tried it but could not tuck as tightly; but it was a good try; it had a flexible tail. Laughing underwater used up the remainder of his oxygen; he followed the last bubbles up for more air.

Gray surfaced and began whistling his pleasure. The excited whistles combined into a scream, then slowed again to a whistle. He had to surface to 'talk,' since it used too much air, unlike the sonar clicks. As he dove and swam toward the awkward one, he emitted a constant string of clicks. For the best reflection, he had to swim slightly above his target. He picked up the reflected sounds through the bones of his jaw and head. When he was excited by a new game, his clicks ran together into a high pitched creaking, as if a rusty locker door were opening. When he came close enough to Walker, he stopped and remained motionless. As Walker struggled to the surface, Gray tilted his head to follow with his eyes.

The single dolphin, Gray, followed and wagged his head, then dove deeper. He seemed to want Walker to follow and follow his antics. Walker tried, but could not get as deep; he guessed he was maybe thirty feet. He could see two or three shapes faintly below him, white undersides flashing as they turned. As he exhaled and kicked for the surface, all three dolphins hurtled past him, their wakes pulling him up faster. As they reached the surface, they peeled off in different directions. He gasped for air, seeing more fins; six, he counted. He lay on the surface, paddling weakly on his back. He felt a rubbery nose push against his back, so he rolled over and made a shallow dive. Dolphins raced all around him. Two swam close and let out a trail of feces, a faint cloud. Waited for him to copy that movement. Can't, he thought, still have the suit on. Tomorrow, I'll swim naked and try that, too. Every time he descended in the next hour, two or more would frolic vertically around him. The lone male, or female—he couldn't tell—always came the closest, as though assigned to him or expecting to be a playmate. The understanding and playful look communicated well.

He was slightly nauseous with effort. All he wanted to do was swim away with the dolphins and copy them, be a dolphin. As he turned back to shore, he saw their fins circling at a distance. He left the flippers on the beach. Back at the apartment, he ached from the sunburn on his back; his feet ached from the rubber flippers—wrong size; his head ached from the water; his stomach ached from swallowing water. He opened the loaf of bread and fixed a peanut butter sandwich. After two more sandwiches, he remembered to check the pay phone on the porch for any messages; there were none, but that only meant that no one had answered the phone. He got a rust-stained glass of water from the tap. The rats were quiet; probably too early for them.

***

He swam out and met the nine dolphins. He could travel as fast as they and as deep; he went anywhere with this new strength. They traveled far and heard tales of many tribes. After days of swimming, they came to a bay where the waters had turned red with the blood of relatives. He knew that the same tragedy had happened the year before. He was amazed that they would continue to try to feed peacefully there. He tried to ask why.

Gray answered him, projecting images. He could understand. He saw that the levels of salt and water were always changing; which streams led to fish; which volcanoes and canyons to avoid; where temperatures rise and food is scarce; where cascading rivulets excite the skin and tumble the body until the cold awakens the need to surface. He understood the roles of songs, songs for saving the thoughts of wiser, farther-traveled individuals, or for tasting great adventures,

the beauty of speaking them again; songs for entertaining, mating, the giving of
air and sperm, for expressing the intricacy of balance, for creating fluid ideas that
crest and evaporate in spume.

He tried to indicate his nonunderstanding of the slaughter. The images
changed. Stories were invented to explain the working of waves and the purpose
of breathing, the indeterminacy of water, the strangeness of air and its relation to
life and death, the substance of other intelligent beings, the role of reason to mold
the universe and increase it; finally, the role of tribes to help others.

He swam, leading them, to a distant tuna fleet. Approaching the nearest
boat, he pulled a net into the prop. It fouled. When a diver came over the side,
he rammed the suited figure. He felt the organs burst. The diver stopped moving.
Then, he searched for a weakness in the hull.

***

He woke, lunging against the headboard. His head ached as he got up.
He left for the bay before dawn, on the bicycle. From a hill, he watched
the spinner dolphins enter Maalaea Bay quietly after sunrise. He counted
thirty or thirty-one. They socialized for several hours, playing with
leaps and slaps. He watched as they rubbed and rolled over each other,
pushing reluctant individuals in the middle with their beaks, chasing
each other and copulating. When the sun was overhead, they started
feeding, diving and surfacing in groups.

Later in the afternoon, he decided to join them. He left his suit on
the beach. He didn't get very far out when he noticed an escort coming
in. He recognized the pale gray of Gray; there was Puck, with the mark
behind the dorsal fin. There were five. The other three he named for
idiosyncrasies or lack of them. Notch had a notch in the fin; Flipper's fin
was slightly bent over; Purity was perfect, and seemed to act it, although
she—he guessed a female—was slightly smaller than the others. As he
changed to a dolphin stroke of his own, keeping his hands in front, Gray
threw his tail up and head down in an exaggerated mimic of motion.

When they reached a larger group, he whistled. Whistles answered.

Some of them were still feeding, through a small sphere of fish they had rounded up; anchovies? Gannets or some birds were diving into the melee for fish, too. Gray brought a six-inch fish to him and held it in front of him. Walker tried to take it in his mouth, but it flipped away. Gray swallowed it before it got very far.

Dolphins were everywhere. He saw a mother with a young one. He, in turn, was scrutinized by many wonderful eyes. Several rolled by and defecated as they passed. He wasn't offended, although he still didn't know exactly what it meant. He tried to defecate but couldn't. He leaked a little urine. One of the dolphins swam by, but that was the extent of the response.

Shafts of sunlight angled into the depths, reflected and deflected to exhaustion. He saw air bubbles rising in a screen from beneath; the air bubbles expanded as they rose.

Most of the dolphins seemed to be in pairs or small groups. Gray was diving every time Walker dived. Somehow, they had paired up. Perhaps he was just a special guard or an escort for the slow, skinny breather, which is how he thought they regarded him. He waited until Gray was close to him, then he extended his hand, fingers spread. They were ten feet under, facing each other vertically. Gray examined it in detail, even turning on his side. He gave the hand a nudge. Walker closed in and nudged Gray's back. After some minutes of bumping and nudging, he held on to Gray, at the base of the fin, and flipped his feet. Gray took off immediately, taking him for a submarine ride; he had to close his eyes immediately from the water, which was pushing its way into his mouth and ears. He let go and surfaced for air. Gray sported around him, so he watched how the dolphin swam. The tail was flat in the water; when it moved downward, the flukes bent slightly; when Gray pushed upward, the flukes locked flat; the whole rear end of the dolphin moved up and down with tremendous energy.

The image of a dolphin eating a fish entered his mind. Gray was looking at him, making some high-pitched sounds. Could Gray tell that he was hungry, that he hadn't eaten? He was offered a fish again. He waved his hand, and thought of Gray eating the fish. Gray ate the fish. But it didn't mean anything necessarily, he knew. He felt for a moment that he was possessed by the dolphin, but he knew the feeling was silly. Still, it was a strange feeling.

Like a good ambassador, Gray initiated more play.

"Too bad I didn't bring a beach ball," Walker mused aloud, after surfacing for air.

Gray bobbed up and down chattering regularly. Two others came for him and the three sported around Walker, who observed them again. They always swam in groups. He got used to their blowing breath around him; a constant "pphhuuuhhhh!" He was treading water; they were taking turns waggling their heads and rolling on their sides nearby. They seemed to be reading his mind. When he thought of them coming back to pick up his slow motion, they were there. He felt as if he were in a field of signals, the water was alive with questions and answers.

Play and eat, play and eat. He wondered if there was anything more for them. Here was a play ethic to match any human work ethic. He couldn't help feeling that both ethics were overkill; each species could benefit from exposure to the other. Play in humans was considered the hallmark of intelligence, indispensable for learning and creativity. Some of the dolphins play turned into a complex courting, far more sophisticated than anything he had done in high school, or since.

He took a deep breath and dove down ten feet, then he flipped his way through the surface and almost completely out of the water, grabbing a breath and diving again. When he came up the second time, the surface was being churned with falling dolphins. He laughed with enjoyment.

Everyone seemed to be talking at the same time. He received images of dolphins leaping far out of water. The noises he could hear were so complex he wondered if they sent complete pictures to each other, like he had received, instead of serial words. Pictures in the brain; not words, novels, pens, paper, computers—just pictures in the brain.

He received images of the immense reaches of water; a whole planet Ocean, spacious beyond experience, his experience. Then he was overwhelmed with images and questions. How many cubic miles of ocean? Up room, down room, living room, above and under room. Did they map it? All of the ocean, or just where they went? Why did they go where they went? Climate, instinct, food? What did they think of the increasing numbers of ships that killed more of their food, sometimes even them? He felt the weight of a beached companion, the inexorable falling of a mate back to the water. But in water, weightlessness; no force, no limits; perfect for movement. He felt the sea breaking over his beak, streamlining down the skin and breaking over the tail, leaving a vortex as it passed. Freedom of movement. All their art was dance, imitation and movement. The sea was their buildings, ships, and clothing. Only food needed effort. Mating and play were not efforts, but enjoyments. He saw the metallic surface of the sea from underneath, the blackness of colder waters, yellow rays probing. They had mountains and forests and deserts, too. With a leap out of water, they could sea the mountains and clouds of the overworld, the human thinworld. There were no secrets in the thickworld. Everything speaks to ears and eyes that collect. Everything is touch, even sounds.

Walker shook himself. This was no paradise. Men were hunting the dolphins. He thought of death, thinking of images of fishermen killing ones caught in the bay, caught in nets.

"You are predators, killers already. You kill sharks. Men are killing you; do you know how easy it is to kill men? You must retaliate—hurt back!" he harangued above the water.

The dolphins swam away. He wasn't sure what had happened. Gray returned and rolled in front of him. He had an image of Gray catching fish for food. He had an image of Gray attacking a shark, for protection. Then he saw Gray helping a man in the water. He understood that Gray would kill for food or protection, but not from fear or revenge, and never kill an intelligent being.

In return he formed his own images of the dolphin deaths at Iki and Hano, in tuna nets in the Pacific, by sportsmen in Hawaii, who shot them for removing live bait from their hooks. He formed images of captive dolphins for shows, for research, for—then Gray gently mouthed his arm. He was afraid to take it away, though it didn't hurt. He realized that Gray was crooning with his eyes closed; he also realized that Gray had an erection. So, he thought, you are a male. Too bad I'm straight. He refused to be put off, surfacing and slapping the water, forming images of the entire pod dead. He went limp, exhaled, and sank without moving. He felt someone come below him and nose him to the surface. Gray was agitated; he cracked his tail on the water surface. Then he started pushing Walker toward shore. Walker tried to form an image of himself sabotaging a tuna ship, so that it sank. Gray dove, only bubbles rising where he had been.

The others were zig zagging slowly toward the mouth of the bay, obviously leaving for the day. Walker turned back depressed. He would act on his own. As he stroked slowly back, he wondered if they were even intelligent. Maybe he had been creating the images all himself. Maybe, they didn't mean the same thing, the dolphins wanting only to eat and play. He knew that it was foolish to doubt. There may have been ambiguity in the messages, but not about their intelligence. Dolphins changed their behavior to adjust to new situations; that was the most comprehensive definition of intelligence he knew.

He knew from his reading that, as dolphins developed in the sea, their brains grew to a larger size than that needed to explain the simple control of their bodies. That state had been reached 20 million years ago. The complex brain created a complex world in a complex and incredibly large ocean. Probably a world with a longer past and a longer future, with complex rituals and complex cultures. Aristotle did not know dolphins well, when he distinguished between man and beast. The bible knew less, when it taught only human ethics. He could respect dolphins.

Suddenly, he realized that he was sinking. He could see the light on the surface, just beyond his outstretched fingers. He pulled—no retention, no cup. No breath. Solution present, no key. Dissolved in noise. He was very heavy and tired. He closed his eyes. Suspended, he saw a pitted column on the ocean floor. Fish scattered as it moved. Bubbles rose. He saw a form break from it, leaving a disturbance in the dust. It was human. The eyes were looking at him. The mouth formed words.

Chapter 2. Traveling To The East

He sat up, confused. What was he? Who was he? There were clues, but he could not remember enough, could not piece it together. Should he undertake a quest? Was that it? A quest? Who am I? What is my purpose on earth? A quest. He was in bed; he had made it back finally.

He cursed the suddenly remembered bank. The bank had never called. He went outside and called the agency. The agency said that someone at the bank had called them, telling them never to send someone as unfit or unclean for an interview again. He rubbed the stubble on his cheek, not knowing what to think or do. He walked down to see his counselor, but she was not in. He left a message.

Three days later he had to leave his apartment. He sold everything that didn't fit into his suitcase. Some of it he had to give to Goodwill, because he couldn't sell it. Suddenly, he was homeless. His first two nights he had spent in the park and by the beach, not comfortable in either place. He gave up shaving entirely. He wasn't eating properly; that he knew. He wasn't sleeping properly, either. He was tired.

He remembered his air coupons; dollar poor, coupon rich. For a moment he considered selling them, but decided to use them. So, he caught a flight to Maui. He walked from the airport. He walked through the town and up the mountain, thinking he should apply somewhere as a laborer. The only job he felt up to applying for was as a pineapple picker. He wasn't sure he would get it—he had seen only women in the bulky clothes and masks. But, it might be worth trying. Upper Paia Mill was a cute place; cute, but not postcard cute. He decided to walk into Kahului, to kill half the day. In the new shopping center, Toyota station wagons were being displayed; most of them were white or a light pastel color. He daydreamed about being given one to make his walking a little easier. He didn't want to spend any of his money, so he left.

Before dusk, he made his way over to the Maui Community College, a two-story brick building. Finding the men's room on the second floor, he made himself comfortable on the toilet, and started reading from a science fiction, Slan. He looked at his wrist to see if it was nine p.m. He rubbed his wrist where his watch had worn away the hairs; his father had given him that watch. Later, on leave, he had sent his father a $900.00 watch from Tokyo. His had been worth $22.00 at the pawn shop; Swiss. When he thought it was after nine, he locked the door from the inside. Unfortunately, he had finished the book before becoming tired.

He tried to meditate for a while. Events seemed to be moving him. After several hours, he pulled thirty or more paper towels from the dispenser and spread them four deep in front of the urinals, the only place where there was more than six unoccupied feet of space. He turned out the light and lay down on them, praying that no one was going to want to come in. He awoke; something was crawling on his hand. He flicked it off and rushed to turn on the lights. Roaches. He spotted three more headed toward a corner shadowed by a toilet seat.

"Shit! All I need is get eaten alive in here," he cursed, shivering. It had gotten colder. Rain was blowing through a vent. He peeked through it; there was no way to close it. "The rain must travel sideways," he said out loud, listening to the echo for company, "sideways." He moved the paper towels. Under the flat fluorescent light, they appeared a very dead brown. He decided to leave the light on to discourage the little pests. He put his head on the suitcase again and closed his eyes.

***

He was on a cloud, sailing smoothly. The cloud was his bed. A running wind the horses. But he was not a passenger. Then he fell, floated, to the sea. And lay in a trough. The waves were the oars of his barge. But he was not a passenger. Not a passenger—

***

He woke, crawling. He tried to sleep again. Several times more he got up again, from discomfort or to check on the roaches; his skin still crawled. When it got lighter it was harder to sleep; he knew it was false dawn, but he wanted to be awake.

"There is no ache like concrete ache," he vocalized. Profound, profound. He must have slept longer, because there was sunlight. He got up in a hurry, eager to avoid any cleaning crew or students.

The sky was beautiful. A rainbow. He had heard that the native Hawaiians saw rainbows as giant nets to capture souls. "Walking the rainbow" was dying. Maybe he was dying; he felt the part. No, it was an atmospheric phenomenon; that was his bag, the atmosphere. Unconsciously, he traced the rain drops through a wave cloud, bending light into a rain blanket of white, yellow, and red.

He made it back to the main road and was intent on walking to Kahului. He had put on a less rumpled shirt and was feeling all of one percent better. He had to buy something good to eat in a grocery store. He hunted for a store. He had only been on the highway for five minutes when a maroon Malibu with mag wheels stopped to pick him up. He saw the brown uniform of a soldier, as he hustled up to the door.

He opened it and sat down, leading off with a grateful "Thanks."

"Get out!" was the surprised response.

Confused, he backed out, case still in hand.

The man in brown turned off the engine and got out. He came around the front of the car, and spoke, "May I see identification, please?"

Walker looked at him with a puzzled expression, not moving.

"Police officer, I would like to see identification," the man in brown explained.

Walker understood his behavior, now, but the car was still a mystery. "Are you going to give me a ride?" he asked, still more concerned with getting to a store.

"ID, please," repeated the officer, gritting his teeth patiently.

"Hitch-hiking is legal, isn't it?" asked Walker, putting down his bag and reaching for his wallet. He handed over his wallet, with his University of Hawaii ID.

"Please take it out of the plastic," continued the officer, intent on form. "Don't you have a driver's license?" he asked, patience failing.

Walker replied, carefully, "No, sir, I don't drive."

The officer asked automatically, "Is this current?"

Walker replied automatically that it was, realizing first that he no longer worked for the university and second that the card was still valid; at last he was grateful for a retroactive budget cut.

"So, you work for the university, huh. What are you doing here?"

"I, uhhm, vacation. Wanted to see the island."

"Why are you walking?"

"I'm on a budget sort of. I don't drive."

"Please open you bag."

"Why?"

"Please just do as I say." As Walker opened the bag, an old leather bag with two straps and metal guards on the corners, the officer knelt down to rummage through the shirts and socks. The question wasn't answered.

The officer dropped Walker's other pair of trousers on top and concluded, "You may close it now."

As Walker was flipping the clasps and tying the straps, irritated that everything had been messed up even more, the officer asked, "Where did you spend the night?"

Walker hesitated for just a moment, "On the porch of a friend, in Upper Paia Mill, a Japanese woman."

Officer Wilson, Walker could see his name plate now, consulted his clip board. As if relenting his mystery, he added, "We had a report of someone walking off a beach early this morning. Did you spend the night on the beach?"

"Good grief, no," he responded, relieved at the facility of the lie, hoping that no one saw him leave the rest room.

Officer Wilson looked at him, "All right."

Walker had picked up his bag, when he heard, "Please get into the car—back seat."

Officer Wilson went around to the front without waiting. Walker shrugged and opened the back passenger door, hoping that he did not look as worried as he felt. A squeal and a jerk later they accelerating to one ten-millionth the speed of light.

He wondered if this was a regulation car and asked, "Is this a regulation car?"

"They're our own cars," came the terse reply.

"Nice car," he muttered, not wanting to antagonize this guy. There wasn't much to talk about; he didn't want to try the weather, too transparent. Still, why was he being taken somewhere unless they suspected that he had been sleeping on the beach and meant to stick him with it.

A short ride down the highway and there it was, in all its marble glory, the standard courthouse of America, two stories, federal, new, and on a grassy rise. He was driven around back. They parked at the end of a row of four customized cars; he assumed they were police cars.

"Please get out; be careful of your head," came another automatic sentence. He was getting used to them. He was escorted into a reception area; through a glass window, he could see the dispatcher in a matronly dress, He was asked if he wanted to make any calls, but he couldn't imagine what for, or to whom. Then he was asked to wait, while officer Wilson went to report somewhere. He regarded a six-month-old Sports Illustrated with little interest, thumbing the pages backwards.

After half an hour, Wilson reappeared with a decision, "You're free to go," was the unexpected verdict, "Don't sleep on any of the beaches."

He wondered what had happened. Had someone called Morton?

He muttered "Thank you," and walked out into the sun. At least he was closer to the store. Now, he was hungry from being nervous.

He walked into town and called the pineapple farm. They hadn't chosen any new workers, yet. He looked half-heartedly for jobs, but didn't expect anything. One more day. He decided to try to sleep around the shopping center that night.

There was a guard; no good. All the doors had been locked. He ran into the trees.

The next night he spent on the beach; fortunately it did not rain. The sand bed was better than the concrete bed, but he was much colder.

The next day, he walked back up the road, thinking to get a good view of the island. He passed several small houses, found a small school. Finally, he worked up enough nerve to stop at one of the houses and ask for work.

He knocked at the door and waited. The door opened slowly, revealing an elderly woman in the shadows, her white clothes dimmed by the shadows.

"Good morning. My name is George Walker. I'm looking for work," he paused, "I'd be willing to work for food, that is, if you have anything you need done."

She looked sympathetic, but said, "No, thank you. My son comes up every other day."

He thanked her and walked down the sidewalk.

She called after him, "If you need a place to stay, you could sleep on the outer porch,"

He glanced back, then nodded in thanks, but he was too confused and embarrassed to accept. He just kept walking down the road.

He walked until it was dark. The airport, he thought, 'I'll go there and ask about a plane. No one's going to fly at midnight. Then I'll wait until morning. They should have a bench or sofa.' They didn't; a plastic chair. He was too dirty and tired to sleep in a plastic chair. He slept.

***

He was seated in a cell. Cross-legged on the dirt. Moisture condensed on the dark stones. The cell became brighter.

***

He shifted in the chair. New day, new luck. He was able to hitch a ride to Oahu, with a veteran who had his own plane. He hoped the guy would offer him a job, but he didn't ask. At the Honolulu airport, he checked the survival kit in the bottom of his suitcase: An Air Force voucher, which he could use to get to LA on a military plane. And $100.00 in traveler's checks. He checked his left pocket; he had $3.66 cash. He was able to arrange a deadhead immediately—maybe his luck was changing.

Since he had six hours to go, he put his suitcase in a locker and went to the lavatory for a sailor's bath. He took off his shirt and washed his armpits, not caring if anyone was offended. He rinsed his hair in the sink and dried it under the hand dryer. He had just finished when a suspicious porter came in, eyeballed him, and went out again. He took a wet paper towel and went into a toilet to wash between his legs. Not too bad, not much in, not much out. His piss smelled almost sweet, from pineapple.

33

He policed the area, found part of a newspaper and an old paperback, Flounder, by G. Grass, and waited. The plane was relaxing, once he got on board. He filled the long hours with dreams. He dreamed of flying, only not as a passenger. In the clouds, the earth didn't matter. Nothing mattered.

Chapter 3. Heaven And Hell (Supermarket Version)

Los Angeles was something else, yellow and hot. The plane had landed after five in the afternoon. The terminal was crowded. And he had to walk over a mile just to get to the road to hitchhike downtown, if there was one.

He got a ride. An old man in a cream-colored Karmann Ghia (he had carefully lowered his thumb for custom chevys). The old man was a retired police officer. He didn't care; part way into the old man's life story, he related a recent death in his family to the old guy, who was, after all, kind enough to pick him up. The Captain, he had been a captain, respected that and asked no more questions. He was dropped off near the center of town.

The first night he stayed awake because he couldn't figure out where to sleep; he would walk for ten minutes then sit on a bench or a lawn for an hour. He did all right until 3 or 4, when everyone else finally went somewhere and the street was his. At dawn he started looking for a good bench. He waited until the rush hour was over before finding a bench to sleep on.

He woke about noon, and decided he needed a regular place. He searched parks. He wanted one with at least one other homeless person, but not more than 2 or 3. He found a little park on Billwert Street. It became home for several days.

It was time to use the last $100.00. The next day he deposited 94.52 to open a checking account, keeping the difference. He found a cheap studio apartment, on Fourth. The apartment. His apartment. It was the first one that he looked at; in an old house, on the second floor. The ratty carpet looked like it was disintegrating into gouges in the floorboards. The door looked solid. There was a mattress located on the floor in the studio part. Then there was a bathroom with a small metal shower. Under the radiator the wall was missing, as if whoever built it had gotten too tired to finish it. There was no kitchen exactly, just a hot plate and a refrigerator rounded with age. The owner, who, he found out, taught at a university as well as operated several buildings, happily told him that the bathroom sink could double as a kitchen sink. Since the stove didn't work, the toaster oven on top could be used. If he wanted a frame for the bed, his son would bring it tomorrow.

"Yes, thank you. I would like that. Would it be possible to get a cover for the chair?"

"I don't think there is one. I will need the first two weeks rent, now, if you don't mind, that is. $50.00." the owner fidgeted.

Ichabod Crane, Walker thought, that's who he looks like. He wrote out the check to 'Irving Crane' and the studio was his.

He was confident that he could find a job here. Dr. Morton had assured him that he was highly trained; he believed it. That day he bought a paper and just walked around. After dark, he realized that the bed had no sheets. He was also cool, but couldn't figure out how the heater worked. He put on an extra shirt, lay down, and pulled his empty suitcase over his body. But he couldn't sleep. Latin music was flooding through two walls, punctuated with shouts and laughter. The words were barely intelligible to him. He fell asleep trying to decipher them.

The orange rolled off the table. It rolled under as he reached for it. It receded just beyond his grasp. As if a charm he could not possess. Stars and particles of strangeness. Trees lifted fruit beyond his reach, water lowered beneath his thirst. No effort could capture what he desired. It was his desire that offended. He learned to love the distance between. Tantalus smiled and reached.

The next morning he decided to splurge and buy sheets. The sunlight was coming through the bathroom window, which was cracked and had been stuffed with cellophane. He thought the light on old cracked plaster walls to be very sculpted; interesting, not dreary. Pigeons cooed from under the eaves. He remembered the dolphins—Gray. But he didn't know what to do, much less how to do it. He had to be ready first. He washed, then turned off the refrigerator to defrost.

The Goodwill store was a long walk. Better take the bus next time, he realized. He found some sheets for a dollar. They felt like cotton. He verified that they had been cleaned, even if there were some yellow stains in the middle. He bought a thermal weave blanket for a dollar. The walk back was exhausting. He stopped off for a $0.35 hamburger and a $.025 milk.

When he got back, he went across the hall to ask his neighbors if they knew how to turn on the heat. Zavala, the door read.

A pretty, black-haired girl of fourteen or so answered the door, "¿Como te Ilamas?" she asked. He shrugged.

"¿Y tu de donde eres?" she asked. He shrugged again.

"Momma, it's the new one," her English surprised him.

"I'm sorry to bother you, but I can't seem to figure out my heater. Could you help me?" he asked to the room behind her. He saw children in a bed under sheets giggling.

"My younger sisters, Blanquita and Paquita," she said, "My name is Ada. That's Antonio," she added, nodding.

An arrogant boy/man of seventeen sauntered out and across the hall and into his open door.

"Mannn," he started, drawing out every vowel, " this is stilll filthy." Snapping his gum, he went to the radiator in the bathroom, the only heat in the studio, and turned the knob all the way to the left; nothing happened.

"Steam only come on after nine," he explained, sauntering back out.

"Thanks," was all Walker could think to say, cursing himself for not asking the owner.

"Lrii" came the answer from across the hall. He smiled at the girl and went back in to plan his attack of the metropolitan job market for the next day.

He slept better on the sheets, although there was no evidence of heat.

He found another placement agency the next morning and filled out the familiar forms. They recommended that he apply for unemployment right away. Later, he visited the center, but couldn't bring himself to wait with thirty other people, just then. He had $37.18 left and 12 days before the next rent was due. He had to have a job before then. He stopped by for another hamburger and milk. They were cheap enough that he wouldn't run out of money eating. But, he wanted more. He decided to go to the grocery store for dinner.

He had always loved grocery stores. The small, wooden ones when he was growing up. The new chain stores, A&P, with fruits from all over the country, when he was a teenager. And now, the ultramodern sanitariums, where food was too unripe and cold to smell, and the aisles stretched on, brand after brand, drygoods, nylons and silverware, across America. It was heaven. Mutated harp music in the background, the helping angelic clerks, the clouds of mist from frozen foods, stacked vertically for easy identification and access. Hundreds of fluorescent lights imparted a white glow to the ceiling, from which hung giant pictures of perfect foods, Platonic forms to the foods of everyday below them. The floors were clean; no spill visited their surface for more than minutes before a fresh, smiling crew in white swept away the traces of any organic mess. He drifted down the aisles, starting with the canned vegetables; the ones in glass were much more attractive, each piece could be seen to be perfect, and expensive. The glass containers were easier to open than cans; no special opener was needed. He opened a jar of pickled asparagus and took three stalks. Putting the stalks in his mouth at once, he placed the jar behind another.

Chewing very slowly, he went by canned fruits. The fruits were heavily sugared, not so much to preserve them better, as to tempt the people by their sweetness, as if the whole, fresh fruits were not sweet enough or attractive. The whole human lust for sweetness betrayed a heritage of fruits and berries, that became sweeter and sweeter until they ripened; later, they became fermented and alcoholic on the vine. The cans were invincible, but he found a plastic-covered tray of Turkish apricots, slit the plastic, put two in his mouth, and rotated the stock. He went over to the cake and bakery product aisle to be tempted. The covers always looked so inviting. Chocolate, chocolate, chocolate. He loved chocolate. General Mills even had chocolate chip cookie cereals now. Too bad he couldn't try them here. He meditated on chocolate; the word was his mantra. How could a technology that was responsible for the delight of a chocolate chip cookie, probably the foremost innovation of the millennium, invent the nuclear warhead with the same aplomb? How? It was if humanity was of two minds, torn between extremes, and destined to be torn by one of them. Did aborigines eat chocolate chip cookies? Never. Technology had conferred unparalleled wealth on civilization. Chocolate was worth the crowding and pollution, almost.

But those packages were not available to him, now. He proceeded on through pet food and canned and bottled soda. There didn't seem to be any new brands. The meats occupied the back of the store, wrapped in sanitary cellophane. The cuts were so thin and bloodless that they bore little resemblance to living animals. Perhaps that was how they were meant to be presented, for consumer consumption. How many people could eat their hamburger after seeing the cow stunned by an air hammer and dragged to the abattoir floor for butchering? Once he was sure the butcher was occupied with a customer, he inserted two fingers in a package of hamburger and drew out a mouthful. It tasted better than he thought, raw, so he lingered long enough for another mouthful. The seafood looked fresh and appetizing, especially the flounder. He regretted not being able to pick out a filet mignon and lobster tail. He decided to skip the frozen foods, since they were of little use to him.

The dairy section was against one wall. He liked cows and was sorry that they had to be pushed so hard so that farmers could hysterically oversell their products for profits that only the federal government could guarantee by fixing the price and buying half the milk produced and stockpiling it. Two kinds of chocolate milk. He started up the produce aisle; the most amazing assortments of fruits and vegetables, it was also the most dangerous. He ogled six different kinds of apples. He touched the oranges, grapes, tangerines, and ugly-fruit; pears, cherries, strawberries, avocados, potatoes, lettuce. These foods were like gifts from the gods, sweet, firm, tasty— he broke off, amused at himself for sounding like an ad. Except for blueberries, probably nothing in the store was blue. We eat the colors we trust, the white, red, brown, yellow, green of nuts, meats, roots, fruits, and leaves.

He waved pleasantly to the produce clerk, who nodded back and said, "How are you today?" Later, at the bulk foods, he was able to fill up on peanuts.

He pulled out a large cart and began working his way through the store again, starting in produce. Never shop when you are hungry, he had once heard. Since they were having a special on pineapple, he bought half; reminded him of Hawaii, long ago—last week. He didn't take anything else; produce people had the eyes of eagles. He had heard of people being arrested for popping a grape in their mouth without paying for it. Best to avoid that kind of trouble.

He made rounds again, stopping for a few more asparagus and apricots, careful to be looking for mayonnaise or pickles. The meats were being guarded again so he passed them. In the cereals, he opened a box of breakfast tarts. Extracting one, he put the box in the back, satisfied with his customer stock rotation. He ate the date tart from the palm of his hand while he selected a small can of orange juice for the cart. Drinking in the store would be too risky; he would have had to buy a quart bottle. After a risky Hershey's chocolate bar in the peanut/snack/ ice cream aisle, he headed for check-out.

"Not hungry today?" asked the smiling girl at the register.

"Oh, you know," he replied seriously, "I read that you should never shop before you eat, so I always eat first. Trouble is, then I don't buy enough food." She rang up the charge: $1.96, including tax. He silently bid farewell to the dollar bills; he never really got to know any of them well.

"Thank you for shopping Safeway," she parroted, as she handed him his bag. There was a waste of trees, but he needed the paper.

"Yes, thank you," he remembered to be polite. As he left, he realized that there were not very many grocery stores in this area. Tomorrow, he would dine on raw hamburger and a cupcake in the paper towel aisle at the A&P. If he started repeating stores, it might be risky. He could try other tactics, but what? He had tried the Rescue Mission, once; boiled glue. And the company was pickled; he didn't think he could stand another life story.

"Let me tell ya" was all he ever remembered before turning off into daydreams of wealth, power, comfort, sex, in various orders. Garbage cans were the mark of real desperation, and he wasn't that desperate, yet. He had followed the last bum he saw eating out of a can, curious about what else could follow it. After several blocks, the skinny black in a raincoat leaned against a building and vomited casually. Then he straightened up and walked on. Walker looked up and saw the sign "Pacific Bank." He wasn't ready for the cans.

He made a ritual out of eating that evening. Unless something happened fast, he was going to be in real trouble; no job, no money, no place to stay. Maybe it would be a good idea to apply for unemployment. Damned government, giving and taking with different hands. There is a time when poverty isn't romantic, when hunger isn't an exercise in will. All he could think about was food, good, warm food, in endless quantity. He couldn't remember his parent's poverty. He was grateful that they had shielded him from the problems of debt when he was growing up. Now, he could appreciate his own. Like them, he would try to bear it with dignity. Unlike them, he would fight it differently.

He went up on the roof to see the sunset. He looked out across the street. Tall square buildings, each identical, but each with a different shade of sunlight from slightly different angles or changes in texture or paint wear. It was an abstract beauty. He felt Citrona, the mother of his neighbors, come up behind him. She looked for a while before speaking.

"Look at this project there. Seventy, eighty apartments. Full of every kind of criminal, queer, pervert. An every one of 'em uses the washing machine before I do," she said.

Before, Walker could say anything, Mateo came up behind them, looked at his mother, "She's got a cause to dream."

Citrona looked at her son, "That a tattoo?"

"It's a tattoo. Tac-Mateo, that's me!"

"Ya lo veo. Why?" she asked. "Now you want to be branded?"

"Cause it's cool."

"It'll last until you die," she pointed out.

"What? It's a problem? I'm a warrior! I'll be one all my life."

"Jus don' fall."

"I won't."

Wolf pointed to plants on the fire escape, "medicinals?"

"She's always planting medicine on the stairs and stuff," Mateo answered.

"She makes medicines?"

"Yea, from her mother's sisters."

"¿Y tu de donde eres?" Walker asked, remembering when he was asked that question.

"South," Citrona answered. "In the city were soldiers. But we were careful and respectful. We sold cigarettes. My sisters sold fruits and beans. At the end of the day we bought a little table from a vendor from Honduras, who made tables. Then we had to leave."

She examined her fingernails for flaws.

Walker nodded at the short biography, stayed respectfully silent, and then went back downstairs. Mateo went looking for a chicken.

The next day he applied for unemployment. The waiting was boring; the interview was boring. When he heard about the six weeks wait, he panicked.

"What will I do?"

"I'm sorry, sir. This office cannot provide any advance on your compensation check," replied the comely black girl.

He didn't say anything. As he was walking away, she called him back.

"Some of the local soup kitchens have beds for the night. I know that doesn't help much..." She shrugged.

He waved to her and walked out onto the sidewalk.

"Shit." He kicked the building. He would get his $59.55 a week, beginning in six weeks. In the meantime, he had to keep looking for work. How did anyone live for the six weeks? Did they save for it? He would talk to his landlord and see if he could earn the money for rent for a month or two.

To satisfy the unemployment office, he had to apply for five jobs a week. Due to the lack of openings in astronomy, he soon started applying for any professional position. Later, any position at all.

Chapter 4. Getting By

Most of the applications disappeared into a black hole of paper. So, he was surprised when he was told at the office that he was going to be interviewed for a position as a social worker at the Home of Merciful Rest.

The Home was located in a brick building facing a tree-lined boulevard, an old parkway, he learned. Dr. Bernard Grotius was poised behind his walnut desk as Walker was led in. Grotius was an elegant-looking man who dressed and posed for effect. As he spoke, he absently fingered his white goatee. He resembled nineteenth-century caricatures of the devil; Walker wondered if he knew that and cultivated the look. He spoke mostly about himself; Walker was willing to let him do the speaking. He described how he was the resident physician, who had enlarged his private practice to include the state prison, two other rest homes, and the California State Governor's Drug Abuse Council. Understandably, he could only spend one hour a week on the premises. He hired Walker as Coordinator after a one-hour interview. Walker forgot to ask how much it paid.

Grotius showed Walker around the premises. The main building looked like a traditional apartment complex, so it blended in with the neighborhood. In fact, Grotius explained, that is what it was before being remodeled. There were forty private rooms, for patients with terminal illnesses. Usually, they were women, ranging in age from 19 to 70, with cancer, diabetes, cerebral palsy, and Alzheimer's disease. Half a million people had Alzheimer's; it was responsible for most of the beds in nursing homes. Mostly it affected people in their seventies and eighties. It started with the loss of learned skills and progressed to total shutdown. Sadly, it was not fatal. Its victims could live to advanced ages, as vegetables. What was it caused by? Who knew? He didn't remember any virus name associated with it; just that it was related to kuru.

There were two full-time nurses, four part-time, and four lay volunteers, who helped with the shopping. An emergency room was on the third floor; it was not necessary to be fully equipped, since the state hospital was six blocks down-hill. The first floor had a large meeting room, for relatives. He would have an overnight room, with two beds and a color television, for sleeping over. He immediately moved his suitcase there, since he would not be paid in time to keep up his rent.

His first night, he came down and spent in the Doctor's room and watched a science-fiction movie about a man-eating plant. The color emphasized the green; he wondered if he should fix it—he would try, later. For now he was content, happy and clean. He decided that his stubble wasn't bad-looking when it was clean so he decided to grow a beard.

After the first paycheck, he rented a small room six-blocks up the hill. The home was depressing to work in. There were no rewards, as in a hospital. The patients were there to die. It was a warehouse for the terminally ill. It was bleak and badly managed, but the nurses were compassionate. And it was better, he supposed, than having the families destroyed by the costs of dying. It was a state supported home, that received donations from those who could afford it. From relatives of the patients, that is.

He got used to the schedule. After a while, he altered it so that he wouldn't be there when the families were. Sometimes it was more important to be there at night, or during the early morning. He understood his job was just to be a listener, basically. He started reading the medical books and journals in the offices. He started listening to political television programs.

Sometimes he wondered if some of the patients would make better presidents and governors, senators, than the current crop. Many of them had more compassion and a better perspective. He was interrupted by one of the volunteers.

"Mrs. Denison refuses to take the chewing gum I bought her," was the complaint.

Walker took the offered package of gum. Doublemint. "What kind did she ask for?"

"Spearmint." Becky answered contritely.

"This is spearmint." Walker observed.

"She says it's the wrong kind!"

"Umm, could be," Walker shrugged. "What kind did she ask for?"

"Wrigley's."

"Tell her we're getting the right kind, immediately, okay. I'll talk to her, later."

"Yes, sir, thank you."

"Oh, Becky, be sure to ask explicitly what brand, when you go shopping. Most people here have little enough to look forward to."

"Yes, sir, I know," Becky replied. She was a sensitive high school girl, who had volunteered to do some of the shopping for the residents.

Each resident had an 'allowance' of five dollars a week for personal expenditures. Volunteers from high schools and ladies aid societies actually did the shopping for them. Most of the residents had little necessities that made their time easier; a special deodorant or hair spray, a candy or magazine. Mrs. Denison needed gum.

He poked his head in, "Claire, keep this gum for now. I'll bring the right kind in tonight." He tossed the gum on the bed.

She nodded.

The next week he killed Mrs. Denison. He could not stand to see her loss and pain progress. An hour after she had received her medicine, he stood by her bed in the dark. He placed his hands gently on her temples and pressed softly while whispering to her about her family and wonderful life. Fifteen minutes later, she was dead. He kissed her forehead. Then left. He watched a green talk show for a while. When his vision had become too blurry, he turned it off.

***

They had torn his wings off. The silken, ten-ribbed, perfect wings. And left him under the bridge, on a cinder path. He cried, but could not move. He looked up through the cavern.

A form blocked light from perfect, golden eyes.

"His eyes can make us move or burn ours out. Tear them out!"

They left him by the river of oblivion.

He spoke, "Mother, father, crippled judges, can you take away my perfect heart?"

***

After several weeks, Grotius took time out to talk to him.

"That's a handsome beard you're starting," he observed self-consciously, stroking his gray hairs.

"Thank you, yours is quite, uh, Dutch," Walker replied politically, terrified that he had been found out. .

"Yes, uuhhhmm, Have you had any experience with drugs, in your studies, uuhh," he spoke haltingly.

What is he leading to? Walker screamed silently. "No, haven't had time," he replied. "Health is more interesting and more mysterious," he added thoughtfully. "I want to know how my own mind works."

"Well, You're young, with long hair and a beard. You would be trusted by other young people, of similar constitution. You would understand their problems; you could learn about them fast enough," he observed.

Walker was gripping the chair arms.

"You see, Dr. Weinstein at Hoag Memorial Hospital has just been incapacitated by bleeding ulcers. He is in charge of drug abuse problems at the hospital. I have been asked by the Governor's committee to find someone who can replace him on short notice. The summer season is approaching. Most of the problems increase in the summer. Are you familiar with Huntington Beach, California?" Grotius concluded.

"Yes, well, aren't I needed here?" Walker asked, flooded with relief. He had not been discovered.

"You would have a raise, a room at the hospital, and a new title."

Walker was suddenly depressed. He needed something brighter, but this didn't sound much brighter. Its main attraction was that it was something new.

"Of course, you needn't work hard. I will arrange for medical doctors to be visiting a week at a time. These are specialists from the Los Angeles area who want to help, and who will be provided with accommodations at the shore. You will not prescribe drugs or offer treatment. You would be mostly responsible for preliminary diagnosis and conveying them to the clinic." Grotius smiled grimly, his pointed beard dipping.

"Well, the offer is tempting, but I do not feel qualified," Walker offered, "I no nothing of drugs or problems."

"Yes, I understand that," Grotius replied, "but we need someone whom with, uh, with whom, ah, the young people can identify and trust. Besides," he added, "I know that you have taken an interest in medicine and read widely."

"It's, well, a very attractive offer. Let me think about it tonight and call you tomorrow," Walker said. He was in conflict because he was planning Mrs. Martini's escape from a world of pain. He wasn't ready, yet. What should he do?

"—take too long or the offer might be filled," Grotius concluded.

"Of course, thank you. I am grateful,: Walker acknowledged.

His opening day at the hospital was a shock. He was early and had found the second floor clinic with no difficulty. The hospital was gigantic, with a new addition every decade. At seven, the junkies came shuffling in like damned souls approaching the River Styx. Walker watched them congregate around the orange juice for the measured sip and reprieve from hell.

It was his responsibility to interview the souls regularly. He called the name of Marga Roland. No one answered. Confused, he asked the nearest nurse, who smiled tiredly, and pointed out a girl in dirty jeans and peasant blouse. Walker escorted her into the glass cubicle.

"Are you satisfied with your program?" he asked.

"Yes, it's wonderful," she replied. But her eyes said 'soon you will be like us—you are damned.'

Walker laughed uneasily.

What Grotius hadn't told him in the interview was that he had to undergo this three-month training program at Los Angeles General, at the methadone clinic there. He worked at the hospital from six to ten in the morning, when dosages were available.

Grotius visited very other day. He and Grotius had long arguments about the virtues of methadone maintenance, which kept addicts addicted for an indefinite period of time on an artificial narcotic. After reading up on it, Walker wondered why a negative reinforcement on heroin wouldn't be just as effective. Then a program of heroin reduction. Or even just cold turkey with tranquilizers, under supervision—perhaps he was naive or ignorant.

Chapter 5. Mysteries Of The Mind

When Walker related his latest interview to Grotius, Grotius just shrugged it off.

"It's a double-bind. They need support and a positive social role, but we can't trust them, because they don't have a positive social role. So they are cunning children who cannot delay gratification; they challenge us with their cunning—it's a game." Grotius dismissed the problem.

Walker depended on his reading to keep him a step ahead of the disaster of ignorance. He found out that methadone was first made in Germany in 1944. After the war, it was marketed in America as a synthetic pain-killer named dolophine—named after Adolf Hitler. "Dolly" never became a popular street narcotic because of the difficulty of manufacture.

After it was discovered to facilitate the detoxification of heroin addicts, it was dispensed at hospitals in baby bottles. Most of the nurses regarded addicts as children, also. At General Hospital, now, it was offered in paper cups, mixed with equal parts of Tang. The program currently treated fifty three out-patients. Sometimes a few more, or less.

Walker's responsibilities included helping the nurses monitor daily urine samples, which always created tension and an attendant bodily humor. He learned that heroin, cocaine mixed with quinine, and amphetamines showed with the test, but snorted cocaine did not show. He was also expected to conduct therapy groups for the addicts, but, with the exception of three or four older ones, most considered the groups a form of brain-washing, and avoided them. And, of course, the interviews.

His next interview went more smoothly for both. He asked Harper Went if he was being helped by the program.

"This is godsent, godsent," Went answered. "I been messing around with drugs for fifteen years more or less and for once I can go straight ahead. I can go to bed and I don't have to worry about being arrested; I can get up and not worry about breaking into no house and stealing teevee sets. I feel good. And with meth I can still get tore with a beer with some pills behind it. I can do my thing, man, and I don't look no different'n you, now, do I? Do I?"

"No, you look fine," Walker answered.

"Shittin straight," Went emphasized.

"How's the job search going?" Walker asked. He even felt slightly guilty that he himself had this job. And he knew how frustrating it was to be without.

"Not good. People afraid of me. Like I'm a freak. They don't understand meth—it makes me normal. I'm no threat. Sure I'm a freak, but I feel good about myself. I'm out there trying to find me a place. I applied for many jobs. You think I could get a job here?" Went asked.

"No, sorry, rules say you have to be off the program for a year. You could try, though."

"Shit! You want'em all for yourselves."

"The hospital could not employ everyone that came here," Walker countered weakly.

Went drummed his fingers on the chair, waiting for the interview to conclude. Walker felt dissatisfied, but couldn't think of anything else to offer.

The three months carried that same theme, repeated endlessly. Then, Walker was declared ready to set up the Beach clinic. He was in Huntington Beach for Memorial Day. He stopped and had a milkshake at a little dairy stand. He checked into the room that had been rented in his name in a private home. Mrs. E. M.. Malley, a widow. She rented the top floor of her house; three rooms. Walker got his key and carried his bag upstairs. She followed him wheezing. He backed down a stair and offered her his arm.

She waved it off, "I'm all right." She followed him into the room. "I have rules, here. No drinking. No smoking. No sinning."

Each commandment could have been carved in rock for the time it took her to list them.

"All right?" she asked.

"Absolutely," he swore.

The Hoag Memorial Hospital was four blocks away. It was four stories and painted yellow. Possibly so people would see it coming. It was on a residential road, but had entrances on three sides. The building was situated on a slight rise. His office was next to the morgue, in the basement. Room 6. It had a desk, single bed, color television.

"Used to be a patient's room, but we don't put anyone down here anymore," the hospital administrator, Nick Thurmond, explained. "We can have someone move the bed out for you." .

"Oh, no, I'll move it later. Show me the emergency room."
Thurmond introduced him to the resident staff and the nursing staff.

"Watch out," he confided, "the nurses really run this place."
Thurmond acted like a weasel.

Later in Thurmond's office, Thurmond was explaining the set-up, as he understood it.

"As you know, Dr. Grotus, a fine doctor, fine man, was asked by the Governor, Peterson, a fine governor, just so progressive, to coordinate drug abuse counseling in the state. He made arrangements with this hospital to have its services available to the community. A social worker, that's you, will be in charge—"

"Excuse me," Walker interrupted, "I was hired as a psychologist."

"No, I'm sorry, I'm looking at the contract here. It says 'social worker.'"

Walker grunted. He wondered how alert Grotius was with his diagnoses. Probably not very. 'Growtus' Thurmond had called him.

"Now, where was I?" Thurmond was deciding. "The social worker will be in charge of counseling, therapy, and recommending admissions. He will work with the special program doctors, who will—"

"Excuse me, what special doctors?"

"Ah, uhhm, the ones listed here."

"May I see the list?"

"Certainly. These doctors will each be here for one week, on call. Most of them are bringing their families—"

"On vacation?"

"Yes, that was part of the attraction. They are only receiving a stipend of $300.00 for the week."

"Where are they staying?"

"Someone will have to rent a house on the beach for them."

"Have they been contacted, yet? Have dates been arranged?"

Thurmond shrugged, so Walker continued, "May I have a copy of this list?"

Thurmond nodded. Walker could tell this was a royal fuck-up.

When he got back to his room, a telephone message was pinned to the door, to call Mrs. Carson. Under the note was scrawled, 'I don't take messages. Don't leave this number.' Mrs. Carson was a friend of Grotius's. She and her husband were also more comfortable than most duPonts.

He went down the street to a pay phone and called. She wanted him to come to a party tomorrow night, given for him. He agreed to go.

The Carson summer house was located inside a walled estate, with other summer homes. It was one story, gray stone. He was greeted at the door by Mrs. Carson, a heavy-set blonde woman charging through her twenties and into her forties.

"Hello, George, we're so happy to have you working on this terrible problem. Bern can't be here tonight. Let's get you a drink and introduce you."

Bern was Grotius, of course. George shook hands politely. Some of the accents were from San Diego. He recognized one from Mill Valley, one from Los Angeles. Judging from the number of husbands who were vice-presidents of movie companies, banks, silicon valley companies, this neighborhood had to be the vice-presidential ghetto. He was surprised to see one of the doctors from the hospital, until he learned that it was his wife who was from Mill Valley.

Some of the women who came and spoke to him later had sons or daughters with drug problems. Walker was treated to hearing about their problems. Dinner was chicken with stuffed tomatoes. Walker traded his for two more tomatoes. Prepared by the Carson's cook from the Virgin Islands, Raphael.

Walker was sitting in a rocking chair on the porch when Mrs. Carson came out to talk to him.

"You know," she began, "I am on the steering committee for the

Newport Beach Drug Abuse Council. Jim Trip is the head of that. Are you familiar with it?"

"No, I didn't know there was already a Council in place here. What does the Council do, exactly?" he expressed curiosity.

"Well," she wound up, "we intend to have an information center. Downtown. We would like to provide drug—ahh—education materials to the public. There's a lot we could offer ..." She put her hand on his thigh and continued for some time. Walker found out that the Council had weekly meetings on Friday in the Conference room of the Hoag Memorial Hospital. Tomorrow was Wednesday. He left Mrs. Carson frustrated.

When he left at 2:30 a.m., he was already working out his plans for the county. The people on the councils and boards and committees meant well, but had trouble acting. There were three groups that had intentions and plans. Very well, he would unite them.

Wednesday, he arranged for a meeting in city hall. He called the local papers in each city, Seal Beach, Huntington Beach, Newport Beach, and had an announcement entered for Wednesday evening. He called the county sheriff's office, the city police offices, the state police, the hospital board, the council and invited them personally to the meeting. That night he went home and laid out his plans. He knew the talk would work—he cobbled it from everything he had read. What he didn't know was if he knew enough or if people would see through him. He was at heart and by training an astronomer, not a social worker or psychologist.

"Good afternoon, officers and citizens, ladies and gentlemen. My name is George Walker. Last month I was appointed a psychologist with the state of California and empowered to set up a drug abuse treatment program in the city of Huntington Beach, for LA County. This program is sponsored by the Governor's Office, the Governor's Committee on the Treatment of Drug Problems, The Department of Mental Health, and the LA County Medical Society. According to Dr. Grotius, who has coordinated this effort, the program is geared to first offenders. It is an attempt for rehabilitation and education, in place of punishment and prison.

"Here is how a typical case would work. Any person caught with drugs by the state or city police would be taken to a magistrate, who would determine the seriousness of the offense. Sellers, or pushers, would be handled in the standard way. First offenders, would be taken to the Drug Abuse Clinic at Hoag Memorial Hospital, which I am setting up, now, to be interviewed and counseled, and, if necessary, treated by a Clinic Doctor. The Clinic doctors are in the process of being selected from a pool of applicants. Dr. Hotzman of the hospital has generously put two of the twelve psychiatric beds at our disposal. Let me emphasize that the program has been formed to provide a better alternative for young people just learning the legal restrictions on drug use. We are going to offer them information and a medical facility.

"I am aware that there are already many fine groups making plans to combat the drug problem. That is why I have asked for this meeting, to find out what your plans are, and to see if I can be of any assistance. Before you tell me of the particulars, I would like to outline my own plan for a comprehensive approach to the problem. Then, perhaps you can help me with it. First of all ..."

Walker outlined his general ideas. First, he discussed 'What is.' The habituations of society, and the associated behaviors. Illegal habituations and criminal behavior. Then he broadly outlined 'What is wanted.' Health, without addictions to nicotine, alcohol, and drugs. Meaningful work and recreation. Vital lives in a loving community and clean environment. Then he proceeded to 'The Means.' Individual and community responsibility—the Hippocratic oath for everyone. The physical and social resources. Time to change.

"A three-pronged approach should be tried. Education, Counseling, and Treatment. There should be some public unit dedicated to making information available; perhaps in a storefront in Huntington Beach, with another in Newport Beach. HELP telephone lines."

Everyone knew that Newport Beach was the critical city. It had the beaches and the motels for summer visitors. And there were plenty of those. LA and San Diego, as well as all the towns inland let out during the summers. And people flocked to the coast on weekends. North were other beaches. South were more beaches. Newport Beach was in the center of vacation land. It was also in the center of drug traffic from Mexico to points north, San Francisco and Oregon and Washington.

"I think that we should present an honest case against drug use, by admitting the good things about drugs, and then—"

"What good things?" a voice demanded.

Walker recognized Corporal Hall from the state police. "All right. Let's consider the good things. Physically, drugs relieve pain, kill infections, correct maladjustments, other things, too. Socially, drugs, like alcohol, release inhibitions. Mentally, drugs can alter awareness—"

"A fever can do that." Walker looked up at a comely woman in white, who later introduced herself as Jean Moyer.

"Please, people, contain yourselves, you'll get a chance. Mr. Walker," Vince Harcourt, the mayor, indicated for Walker to continue. Walker looked down at his notes, searching for a point of continuation.

"In any case, we can't fool ourselves that drugs don't have good effects. That is why people use them. What we have to do is complete their education, by telling them of the bad effects: physical dependency, imbalance of the brain's own natural drugs, risks from impurities; social insensitivity, paranoia, financial cost, illegality; mentally, habit, delusion, mental imbalance—" He was going too fast. He forced himself to slow down.

"—and the multitudes of unknowns. We don't know all the effects of most drugs, or even many of the ingredients. So, after putting drugs in perspective, we also need to show them alternate ways to have the same benefits: physical exercise, artistic creation, meditation et cetera."

Walker paused and looked around at the faces expecting something from him. He wasn't sure how his next sentences would go over.

"I would like to propose as part of the program that we consider having weekly concerts on the bandstand, that we have races or frisbee contests, and perhaps painting sessions, to raise money, as well as consciousness." The murmuring had been swelling after the first mention of the word 'Concert.' Now it crested.

"You can't mean rock concerts. That would be terrible. We can't have that—" Chief Alfred Purdy's voice broke.

"Why not?" asked a younger man with large eyes and limp hair; the Reverend Melvin Bull would be a valuable ally.

"Please," Vince's voice rose like a break before the wave.

Walker waited a moment, and then continued, "We can leave that for later consideration. The counseling, which was the second prong, will be coordinated by me. It will include drug counseling, personal, family, and community counseling as well. I am hoping to arrange for a separate place for counseling. I also hope to arrange work opportunities for those who want them. Three or four other, part-time counselors will probably be hired or accepted as volunteers." He didn't think that now was a good time to mention that most of the other counselors would be reformed users, rejects from other programs, or released prisoners.

"Last, treatment will take place at the hospital Clinic. The physicians in charge will be responsible for emergency and voluntary treatment. A Methadone program will be established for those people trying to conquer a heroin habit. Methadone will be dispensed—"

"We don't have hard drugs here! We don't—"

The angry father was interrupted by Thurmond, who calmed him down with, "Then, we won't need that part of the program."

Walker could see that Corporal Hall and another state police officer were chuckling over something. "That's basically all I have to say right now. I am still looking for a summer residence for the physicians to use. I would be grateful for any help. Mayor Harcourt, if you will take over the microphone." Walker stepped back on the little stage and sat down on his folding chair, between Lt. Gibson of the state police and Jim Trip, the chairman of the Newport Beach Council on Drug Abuse.

The mayor was saying, "—a few words on another effort, by Jim Trip. Jim?"

Trip outlined the founding of his council four weeks earlier, in May, by a number of concerned parents. Since then, they had had weekly meetings concerned with area drug problems.

"We have decided that the best way to combat drug problems," Trip began, "is to provide as much information as possible. We have written to the American Medical Association in Chicago, requesting a number of their pamphlets, including one titled, 'The Crutch that Cripples: Drug Dependence.' We are negotiating with the city, now," he nodded at Walker and at the mayor, "for the vacant lot next to the Newport Beach Hotel for an information center. We would be very pleased to join forces with the state effort, directed by Mr. Walker. It is our understanding that his abilities were to be concentrated on the counseling and treatment end." Walker suspected the old fox had been a lawyer; he knew something about separating territories.

After Trip concluded his presentation, Lt. Gibson gave a few sentences, indicating that the police would certainly work to cooperate with the Governor's wishes. Thurmond gave a short testimonial for the willingness of the hospital to offer its facilities. Mayor Harcourt closed the talks, expressing the city's desire to be clean and drug-free, to avoid all the horrendous troubles experienced by other cities with their wild youth. He turned the microphone over to the public for questions.

"Who's going to pay for it?" Harcourt leaned over and whispered something to the speaker, who spoke again, "My name is Jean Moyer, over at Hoag Memorial. So, who pays?"

Harcourt gestured to Walker, who stood up, but didn't use the microphone, "The state has allocated $200,000, after July first. Our share—LA County's share—is about $29,000."

"Who gets it?" she asked.

"The hospital will administrate it," Thurmond answered.

A heavy-set, balding man approached the microphone, "I'd like to know where Mr. Walker got his information that hard drugs were in—"

"Ed!" Harcourt warned.

Walker confessed, "From your children. They wouldn't tell you."

After ten more questions had been answered, the panel broke up and circulated in the audience. Walker met most of the rest of the state police, including Corporal. Moyer, head of the Drug Disposal Unit of the state police; and husband to the nurse.

Mayor Harcourt said to Walker, "Say, I'm sorry Representative Wynn couldn't be here on such short notice." Then he went over and talked with the group from the V-P ghetto, Carson, Hollinsworth, Theiss, Tonemaker, and two others he didn't recognize or remember.

Trip invited him to the Council meeting on Friday. He agreed to come.

That afternoon, he made notes in a journal. He set up a bank account for the LA County Drug Abuse Clinics. He wrote letters to the editors of local papers and to the county radio stations, asking for coverage. He wrote another letter to the city council, asking for permission to have jam sessions on Whiskey Beach and Wednesday evening concerts on the Bandstand. Before he finished that letter, he was interrupted by a knock on the door. He hoped it wasn't the old woman with another rule. Instead it was the Reverend Bull from the meeting. With him was a freshly scrubbed young woman with an innocent expression and a sophisticated beehive hairdo—altogether a masterpiece in contrasts.

"Hello, I'm the Reverend Melvin Bull, with the Baptist Mission. This is my wife lovely wife Pamela," he stood aside so they could shake hands. Walker kissed her hand, instead.

She blushed. "Oh, a southerner, I see," Bull observed.

"Well, southern Maui, anyway."

"Are you an African? I didn't think you were that dark," Bull started.

"No, honey, that's in Hawaii," she corrected.

"Really! I don't think we've ever met a native. And we were there on our honeymoon. Are you a native?" Bull asked, hanging on the answer.

"No, unknown composition on both sides."

"You're so brown," she touched his arm. "And your profile—it's so Greek. I love it," she reached to touch his nose, but he stepped back, secretly pleased now deprivation and exercise had chiseled his frame, and addressed the reverend.

"I had hoped to talk to you more at the meeting."

"Yes, I wanted to talk to you, too," the reverend became serious. "I think that we can help you. Pamie and I run the Anchor House for the church. We would like you to stop by tomorrow, and see it."

"I've got a meeting at five. Would three be all right?" Walker asked, looking at Pamela, who had fastened on to her husband's arm, possessively, and was smiling back at him.

"Oh, yes, fine. We'll expect you then." Melvin started to leave the room, but Pamela anchored him there.

"You'll have to come swimming with us. Saturday. We love to swim."

"Oh, yes," Melvin added. "We're like little children in the water."

Walker started to answer, but was pre-empted by the widow, who was standing in the doorway. "I hope your not doing any—oh, I'm sorry Reverend. I didn't know it was you. Well, I didn't know what to think when two people went up the stairs. And then it was so quiet. Well, you just can't be too careful."

"That's all right, Mrs. Malley, Pamie and I were just leaving. Thank you, Mr. Walker. See you tomorrow." .

After everyone left, Walker packed his bag, and moved into the hospital, room 6. Some aggravations were too costly. He celebrated the move by masturbating over the memory of Pamie's breasts.

Friday, he made final arrangements with Beach Real Estate to rent a four-bedroom house on Bay Avenue, overlooking the water. It was $250 a week. He left a $100 of his own money for deposit. In the afternoon, he was given a tour of the Anchor House. The Bulls had two young women living with them, Angie and Lisa, who were as freshly scrubbed as Pamela, but not quite old enough to wear beehives.

The reverend was saying, "Call me Mel, that's no bull." And he cackled at his own joke.

Walker smiled and said, "George."

"Well, George, we—the church—want to do something to stop this pernicious plague. What can we do for you?"

"What did you have in mind?"

"Well, sing-alongs, picnics, things like that."

"That's very nice of you. I'm sure that that would be a help. But that would come later, you realize, as part of fitting back into the community, after rehabilitation or detoxification."

"Hey!" Mel remembered. "We have two extra beds that you—well, you could send people here if they needed someplace to stay. Kind of like an accident pad."

"Ah, a crash pad," Walker identified. "We could keep that in mind. Aren't you worried about the two girls?"

"No, they have their own room. Oh," Mel realized. "Jesus would protect them."

They had some iced tea in the kitchen together, the five of them. The girls were cute; walker thought they were too sweet to be flirting with him, but Pamela seemed to always flirt and then look back immediately at her husband. They invited him to services on Sunday. He declined saying that he had not decided what services to go to here, as there was no Royal Hawaiian Polynesian church in California. They looked uncertain, but invited him to sing with them Sunday evening. He promised to try to come.

The Newport Beach Drug Abuse Council held its meetings in the conference room at the hospital. They were all there before him.

Trip introduced him to the steering committee. "Mr. Walker, this is the reverend Hardy Cane, our treasurer. Reverend Cane is with the Huntington Beach Presbyterian Church. Rebecca Pope, our secretary. Becky used to teach school."

"Substitute." Becky said.

"Ed Evans, the Principal of Nixon Junior high school, is a member of the steering committee. Dave Bosenkrantz is vice chairman. Dave couldn't come today; he's bank manager of California First, in Newport Beach. Oh, this is Roger Sims," Trip indicated a thin young man, hopped up on something, adrenaline possibly. "Roger is a student at the university, in Stanford."

"Hey, man," Roger acknowledged.

"As we all know, Mr. Walker was hired to head the state's program here."

Everyone murmured cordially. But Roger hungered for his job, for power—Walker could sense it.

"Now, this meeting will come to order. Mrs. Pope will read the minutes of last week's meeting. Mrs. Pope, you have the floor." Trip sat.

As Becky read the minutes Walker looked at Trip again. Maybe not a lawyer, maybe military. He certainly ran a tight meeting. Walker enjoyed watching. Why lead where others were competent?

Trip took the lead again. "We have a number of things on the agenda. First is funding. Hardy, what have you got for us?"

The reverend stood, with several sheets of paper. He was short and chubby, with pleasing features. "As you know we are entirely dependent on donations," he nodded at Walker, "being entirely separate from the state program. This week I received $300 from the Kiwanis, thanks to Mayor Harcourt's recommendation. We have not heard from the Eagles, Elk, Moose, or Odd Fellows. I think we should ask the Masons, also, but we haven't, yet. Uuhhm, we have received a total of $104 from private businesses; Good Medicine was the latest store to donate."

"Should we even be accepting money from stores like that?" Evans asked.

"What's wrong with them?" Roger flashed.

"They sell drug paraphernalia," Evans replied evenly.

"But, not drugs—" Roger emphasized.

"Let's let the report finish, before any discussion. Hardy?" Trip suggested convincingly.

"Uhhm, where was I?"

"Businesses."

"Businesses. And we have $92 from individuals. Our total operating capital, after expenses, is $418."

"What were the expenses?" Trip asked.

"I'm passing around a report. The first page lists current expenses and cash income. Note the expenses were mostly paper, letters, postage, and printing. On page two are estimated expenses and income, through September 15th. Notice—"

"What is this bake sale listed here?" Becky asked.

Hardy and Jim looked at each other. Jim answered, "Becky, we would like you to coordinate a bake sale for Huntington Beach and Newport Beach. The proceeds would go to—"

"I'm not good at baking, Jim. Let's ask Mrs. Carson. Her servants are good cooks."

"All right, Becky, we'll ask," Jim sighed.

"Are there any corrections or suggestions?" Jim recovered. Walker raised his hand slightly, "Yes, what about banks and large businesses, TransAmerica, Yellow Cab, Carson Communications?"

"We're working on them." Jim answered.

"What about concerts? Or cash donations, like, for the United Fund. You know, cans on counters?" Sims offered.

"We should consider everything," Jim admitted reluctantly.

"Well, are we in agreement that the treasurer's report be accepted as distributed?" he paused. "Good! Now, next on the agenda, we have the problem of deciding on a program director." Trip glanced at Roger, and announced, "I'd like to recommend Mr. Walker as program director—"

Both Sims and Walker were surprised. Sims looked at Mrs. Pope, who averted her eyes. Walker looked questioningly at Trip, sure that Sims was going to be a real problem, now.

"There are a number of advantages to us," Trip justified. "First, he is the choice of the state; he is educated." But not for this, Walker breathed. "He is being paid by the state, so we shouldn't need to pay him. And he is our contact with the state; this assures us a close working relationship. And finally, he will unify the two largest county programs." Trip sat, satisfied with his promotion. Mrs. Pope rose awkwardly.

"Shouldn't we consider someone local, who knows everyone, who can give a different outlook?" She still would not look at Roger.

"I think we need someone professional," Hardy added.

Walker was nominated and confirmed as director. By 3 to 1. He asked if he could appoint his own assistant. No one saw any problem with that, so he appointed Roger Sims as Assistant Director. Becky Pope was smiling. Jim Trip was frowning. Roger was trying to do both. Walker thought that his Brutus had a lean look about him.

Trip took over again. "The next item on the agenda is the information center. That is my bailiwick. Bosenkrantz is sure that the bank will let us use the empty lot between the bank building and the hotel in Newport Beach. But we have to insure it first. He mentioned a minimum of $100,000 liability. According to Harve Mason, that's only $15.00 for the premium. We need to put a stand there. Any ideas?"

"I could build one," Roger offered.

"The state has trailers, used for emergencies—firestorms—that they move around. We might ask to borrow one." Walker suggested.

"Good idea, you ask. Next item on the agenda. What? Oh—"

"Can we have a resolution on that? An official resolution?" Becky asked.

Trip pronounced, "Let it be resolved that the Chairman and Secretary of the Council are authorized to sign a lease for the lot at 15 Newport Beach Avenue in the name of the Council. Furthermore, to insure the property for Public Liability at $100,000 with the Farmers Bank being the beneficiary. That do? Now, has anyone had a chance to think about the drop cards, a design, how many? Roger?"

"I have a design." He passed around a sketch of a thick, three-colored triangle.

"What does it stand for?" Evans asked.

"Ultimate reality, the earth, and man." Roger replied, anxious to clarify it.

"Could be man, God, and earth," Hardy suggested.

"Three is a mystical number. Could be sky, sea, and land, too. Let's use it," Walker agreed.

"All right, let it be resolved that we will adapt this symbol for our logo. What else should we have on it? How many copies should we have printed?"

"I think a 1,000." Roger recommended.

"Let's wait until we get a telephone, before we go with it."

"What about the letter?" Becky reminded Jim.

"Oh, yes, thank you." He passed around a sample letter asking for donations. "4,000 of these ought to do. Look okay?" Jim asked.

"You need a comma, before the 'and' here," Walker corrected.

Becky marked her copy.

"These will be distributed, along with yellow information sheets—you haven't seen those, yet, George—to every household in the Huntington Beach-Newport Beach area. Oh, Hardy, I have some bills for postage and envelopes." Jim handed over the paper to Hardy, who added it to his folder. "Let it be resolved then, that the letters and cards be prepared for distribution." Jim pronounced.

"Wouldn't it be wise to wait for a phone number for those, also?" Walker questioned.

"Not necessary," Jim responded. "We have a post office box, and Hardy's number."

"Is there any further business? No? The next meeting will be Friday June 12, at 5:00 p.m. Meeting adjourned." Walker was properly impressed. The council had gone through more business in an hour than the Governor's committee did in a month.

Trip came up to him, "I guess we don't need the phones until you know about the trailer."

Walker shook hands with him, "No, not before."

"You mentioned that you wanted a place to conduct counseling. It turns out that the Boy Scout House in Newport Beach is empty for the summer. Jed Walker, head of the Kiwanis, is in charge of it. He's a friend of mine. Want me to put a bid on it for you?" Trip offered.

"Yes, I'd be grateful if you would," Walker responded.

"No relation, are you?" Trip smiled.

"I doubt it."

Things fell together fast. Walker confirmed most of the doctors by phone on Monday. He had eleven doctors for twelve weeks: Paulson, Pool, Baker, Gill, Brown, Montgomery, Martin, McCall, blank, Proctor, LaBine, and Wiklander. Grotius agreed to fill in the blank, himself. The state had two trailers in the county. He got them both by Tuesday. Jim Trip found a truck driver to haul them for the cost of gas. They had the phones installed Wednesday in the trailers and in the Scout House. Two bake sales were set up, one each in Huntington Beach and Newport Beach. For Saturday, at the Huntington Center and the Newport Safeway. The Chamber of Commerce gave $100.00 to the Council, and agreed to try out Wednesday evening concerts at the Bandstand; no Whiskey beach sessions, however. He interviewed twenty-six applicants for volunteer positions.

Chapter 6. Generators

He asked Mrs. Carson if she could find volunteers to help him clean up the Scout House to prepare for counseling. The House was a single-story, single-room log cabin about twenty-four by forty-four feet. Off the front door were a single bath and closet. He took an inventory of furnishings. He set up four areas with chairs and tables. Then swept the floor. He found a hand mower and decided to mow the grass, which had escaped attention since the Scouts left in April. He had been pushing for twenty minutes when someone came around the side.

"I'm Patty Theiss," she introduced herself. "Phyllis said you needed help."

"Pleased to meet you. Who is Phyllis?"

"Mrs. Carson."

"Ohhhh," he rounded his lips.

"You must be Dr. Walker," she licked her lips.

"Oh, yes, George Walker, not doctor, though," he corrected.

"Ohh," she rounded her lips.

"Please come in, and we can talk," he licked his lips. And dropped the lawn mower in its path. He followed her up the three wooden stairs, letting his eyes follow her round buttocks as they announced her successful negotiation of the stairs. She turned and smiled at him.

They sat in one of the neat counseling areas talking. She had two children and was divorced. Her parents lived here. So she was renting, just to put her life together, in a familiar place. He was curious to know what life in Newport Beach was like. She told him about high school and marriage, and moving out to Pittsburgh. She offered him a drink at her house.

"There's water here," he commented.

"Don't you want anything stronger?" she asked.

"Are you trying to tempt me with drugs?" he asked, mock-seriously.

"Well, alcohol, then," she qualified.

"Okay," he agreed quickly. He showed her to the door, then turned out the lights. As he groped toward the door in the dark, the tops of his thighs collided with her buttocks. As she turned around, he leaned over slightly and kissed her. He felt an electric discharge between their lips. She messed up his hair and ground against him. They melted down to the floor.

When he was conscious of anything outside of them, he noticed that the door was still open. He pointed his toe and nudged it shut. Enough light was coming in from the street for him to see the outline of her face; her head was crooked in his arm. Her face was attractive, her hair was attractive. He looked down at her small breasts and exquisite thighs. Her generating equipment didn't seem much different than anyone else's, but she sure managed to make more sparks. Neither of them had made a noise. He kissed her tenderly, then started to get up. But, it was too late. He was taken by the current, again.

He met with Dr. Paulson, who had just arrived five days late for his week of vacation on call. Paulson was a pediatrician from Los Angeles. He stopped long enough to get the keys to the beach house, check in, and promise to be back. As Walker saw shiny his rump disappear into the station wagon, he suspected that was the last he would see of Paulson. He was right.

He still had two hours before the staff meeting in the conference room. He was tempted to apply to Ms. Theiss for more electric shock therapy. But two hours wasn't enough time. He walked up to the wards, looking for Mrs. Moyer. She wasn't there. He went back to the cafeteria and procured a pre-made, pre-heated cheese sandwich in a plastic wrapper. Hospital food may be bad, but at least it tried to be warm. As he was sitting at an overly large table, looking through a handbook on thoracic surgery, one of the doctors approached him.

"You must be Walker." He held out a freckled hand. Walker looked up to see freckled arms and a freckled face, under a shock of red hair.

"My name is Mark Sullivan. My wife is colored like this, also," he added, tracking Walker's eyes.

"Erin Go Bragh, Dr. Sullivan."

"And may the road rise up to greet thee, Mr. Walker," Sullivan waved. "I thought I might be able to offer my services."

"I would be grateful. Especially since it seems that you might not be so easily lured to the beach. What is your specialty?"

"Psychiatry."

"Oh, you're the one."

"No, that was Weinstein—with the ulcers."

"So sorry."

"No problem. Anyway, I noticed from the list that Thurmond passed around that all you specialists are pediatricians, IMs, or EENTs—Ear, eye, nose, throat." he explained.

"Oh, I had hoped that Paulson was an exception."

"No, the rule. Anyway, If I can be of help, please ask me."

"I will," Walker intended. "Sit down for a minute. Can I get you an artificial sandwich?"

"No, thanks, but I will sit. I'd rather not eat that." Sullivan waved at the yellow and brown cardboard sandwich.

"Tell me how you got here?" Walker asked.

Thurmond started talking before everyone was seated, but after the second hand had left the 12.

"Dr. Grotius has asked me to describe to you the hospitals involvement with the Governor's Drug Abuse program. Dr. Grotius is the physician in charge of the program, and he has arranged for a number of physicians-on-call for the Drug Abuse Clinic." Walker sighed with the realization that Grotius was getting the credit for everything in absentia. He went on listening to the weasel.

"—are to work closely with the Clinic physicians and utilize them to the maximum with any drug problem you encounter. The program began June first and is intended to run through September seventh.

"Mr. Walker is a social worker from the Los Angeles Medical Center who is to be used specifically for any people with drug problems. He is working closely with the Kiwanis organization in Newport Beach beach, where they have a special trailer on Newport Beach Avenue. The phones there are manned twenty-four hours a day by lay volunteers. Furthermore, the police have agreed to take obvious drug cases to the emergency room, where they will be screened by Mr. Walker. Are there any questions?"

"Yes, Nurse Sanderson?" Thurmond acknowledged.

"What do we do if the Clinic doctor is not available?" she asked. Everyone, especially the nurses, knew the level of expertise to be expected from the 'specialists.'

"Wait until doctor can be contacted. Mr. Walker is not authorized to prescribe any medicine or treatment for patients. He is expected to refer patients to the Clinic physician, who will eventually prescribe the appropriate treatment."

"May Mr. Walker make informed recommendations?" Nurse Moyer asked.

"Of course. You are to use his expertise whenever possible. But it has limits."

Walker fooled with his beard for a moment. "I would like some write-up sheets, please; some stationery. Also, is it possible to avail myself of the secretarial pool?" Walker inquired.

"Of course, see me afterwards," Thurmond admitted.

"If that's all the questions, the meeting is over. Thank you."

"Do we have to keep any special hours for the Clinic?" Mrs. Moyer asked quickly.

Thurmond glowered. The form of the meeting was ruined. "Ask Walker, he will have the schedule." And he left.

"I'll type one up for you and the staff," Walker said. "In general,

Methadone will be available from eight to ten in the morning only. The Clinic hours will officially be from 4:00 p.m. to 4:00 a.m. and I will be in residence during that time, or at the phone in Newport Beach, on demand. That sound reasonable?"

"Why those times?" she asked.

"Those are the exact times people experience drug overdoses. Just kidding, sorry. Probably ninety percent of our problems will be during those hours, with peaks around 11:00 p.m. and 2:00 a.m."

He went back to the hospital room and spent the night composing rules and procedures. Roughing it out first in the journal.

Compromising Conditions for Contacts

> A. Keep within sound of phone and sight of trailer at all times. This is your primary responsibility—be there
>
> B. Be able to give attention or help to anyone who asks or needs   it.
>
> C. Limit friends to one in Trailer One, the display trailer. Trailer two is set up for counseling and crashing.
>
> D. Use discretion with volume of music; yield gracefully to complaints. Use the area behind the trailers for games (horseshoes, ringolevio, dice)
>
> E. You may eat, read, or sleep on duty. Just be ready to help.
>
> F. Operators have priority on parking and phones, and the authority to enforce the priority.

Physical Contact

I. Opening

> A. Extend greetings and invitation to enter
>
> B. Offer information or help

II. Next

> A. Information
>
> > 1. What: just facts no judgments care understand
> >
> > 2. How: verbally, nonverbally

B. Help

    1. Referrals: advice, crash pads, lawyers

    2. Medical counseling, hospital

III. Then

  A. Observe signs and symptoms

    1. Straight

      a. curious

      b. sincere concern

      c. other—bureaucratic, emotional

    2. Crooked

      a. loss of control

      b. feeling of rejuvenation

      c. alterations—in image, expression, perception

      d. indescribable

  B. Observe your own reactions

    1. inform

    2. determine if you can help

      a. take it slow, get facts

      b. use intuition, be positive

    3. get help if necessary (refer to phone numbers)

IV. Specific drug groups; blanket action patterns

  A. Alcohol depression

  B. Narcotics: heroin, morphine, codeine

    1. effects

    2. treatment

  C. Sedatives and hypnotics

  D. Tranquilizers

  E. CNS (central nervous system) Stimulants

  F. Hallucinogens

Phone Contacts

I. Opening

A. Identify yourself 'Hello, my name is Feelgood, may I ...'

B. React to caller

    1. If he/she is talking, make sounds 'uh-huh'

    2. If he/she is listening

        a. Be definite in offering 'May I help you'

        'Do you want to talk about ...'

        b. Be aware of background noises, comment on them

    Is that the radio?' 'You sound out of breath'

    c. Allow silence to continue for minutes if nec.

    but comment 'I'm still here if you want to ...'

    d. If no response, make a final offer

    'Can you speak or make a signal?'

    e. Offer the possibility of calling later

    'I have to hang up, now, but you can call ...'

    3. If he/she becomes aggressive or obscene

    a. Listen and reply with unflustered language

    b. Try to move conversation to positive exchange

    c. Close gracefully

    4. If caller is speaking dialect or foreign language

    be patient let them know you can't understand

    5. If caller threatens suicide

Walker put away the journal and lay down. The wake up call was coming at 5:00 a.m. He had to open the information center at 6:00 a.m. He wondered, how could he be so naive to get involved in this? This shallow hell of misery. Some people do anything for food and a dry place to sleep. He would have gone out and looked at the stars, but between light pollution and smog, he wouldn't be able to see any.

At the clinic, Walker started, "Okay, here are the general procedures to follow when you're on duty. Nothing is strict or firm. Follow your nose and fly by your seat. Everyone else will be," Walker smiled. "The first sheet lists general suggestions for working in the information center. All the telephones, displays, and handouts are in Trailer One. This is the one closest to the sidewalk. The one with the open door; people are more likely to approach it anyway. Trailer Two is set up with two beds in one half, for crashing. If they are available and you need them, feel free. The other half is set up for counseling; there are four chairs and a table.

"The most important thing for you to remember on duty is that you are here to inform and help people. And the people who come in here for both may not be easy to inform or to help. Sincere concern is going to be cleverly disguised as bigotry or anger. As long as you know that, you won't need to be angry or prejudiced in response.

"Each of you has been selected because of important characteristics; you are warm, under the age of eighty, and can talk. Some of you have experienced the pain and pleasure of drugs, in various doses—wake up Roger." Walker prodded playfully with his foot. "Let's go over these sheets briefly."

As he read over the handouts on contacts, he evaluated the volunteers as they sat in various stages of consciousness. Molly Hoody was a slim blonde, an army brat. She looked like she was fifteen; she was twenty three. She was also one of the more successful pushers in town. Mary Hostetler was a tall, slim brunette. He didn't know much about her history; she was interested in counseling, and seemed intelligent and knowledgeable. Kevin Murphy was a college student from Claremont; sophomore? His family doctor was one of the visiting specialists. He was short, bowl-legged, and enthusiastic. Jodi Friend was Mrs. Theiss's half-sister; she was a senior in high-school, a large-boned girl of good humor. She was sitting on her boyfriend's lap. Mike Camp had graduated from high school the year before and worked in a Getty gas station this summer. Walker remembered him with his Mustang. Andrea Marinetti was a heavy-eyed, heavy-bodied Italian girl in gypsy clothes. He recognized her from the methadone program in Los Angeles. He also knew that she could never be allowed to work alone. Mike Koestler he recognized. The remaining boy must be Bill Mariner, who had talked to him over the phone, to ask to work. He hoped they all worked out, but knew that the odds were against it.

"—with suicides, don't argue, don't give platitudes. Don't say 'it's wrong,' or 'don't do it,' or 'it can't be that bad.' Get them to talk about it. Be positive about helping. Invite them down. Offer help. Or, offer coffee and a donut. If you can get name and address, do it, but don't try too hard.

"On the general guidelines: remain calm, don't talk too fast. Remain neutral; accept obscenity, pedantry, idiocy without replying in kind; use your own language. Remain objective; don't expect miracles; admit your limitations, give away calls you cannot handle. Remain task oriented; try to get the caller to the appropriate facility. Don't ask more than is necessary.

"For special cases, be sympathetic, but avoid judgments. Understand the situation as soon as possible. Is he drunk, is she on acid? Let them talk about the pain or fright, but don't over-react. Follow up on everything: How did your foot swell up and fill the room? What did the chair say next? Be positive if you can. Give the caller all the information you can.

"For referral, we have the phone numbers of two lawyers, Jones Gordon and V. Milo Sanders. There is a psychiatrist at the hospital. We have a Clinic doctor on call—if you can't get the clinic doctor, try the emergency room. The Clinic doctor is supposed to take his beeper to the beach, but—" he shrugged his shoulders, and everyone laughed knowingly. "

"Just a few more things. First, drug testing or disposal. For testing. If you think it's bad, and it's on the street, call Corporal Moyer of the state police. The number is on the board. He has agreed to respect our confidence. All we are worried about is warning people about bad dope.

If you don't want to do it, I'll do it. Moyer will also dispose of dope we give him, I mean, that others give us—stop smiling, you know what I mean. Chief Purdy of our beloved local police has also—"

"Can we smoke it to get rid of it?" Mary Hostetler asked. Everyone laughed.

"Use your discretion. Purdy will dispose of it, if you ask him. If you dispose of it yourself, or intend to, call him first and leave a message telling him of the intention. If you're busted with someone else's dope, tough luck.

"Now, the facilities. We have a doctor's residence on Bay Avenue. The Clinic has two psychiatric beds for emergencies. For counseling we have Trailer Two and the Scout House on Kent Street and Columbia Avenue. Crash pads: two female beds at the—"

"What's a female bed?" Bill asked unnecessarily.

"If you don't know by now, it's too late for you," Jodi chided.

"It has a hole in the middle," Andrea whispered to him.

"—Anchor house. Two neutral beds in Trailer Two. Later this week, we will have five beds in a house on the King's Highway. This is the official Half-way House. And I need volunteers for tomorrow, to help clean it up. Volunteers?" He waited a moment, then continued, "Sign up later. We have designated the following businesses as outposts: Rexall Drugs, Owl Boutique, Hotel Newport Beach, Fantasia, Good Medicine, and Something Else. Most of the people there are willing to help and have experience with drug problems—"

"Especially Josh," Molly giggled.

"The Scout House will also be the planning center for the art poster contests and the Wednesday night concerts. Lastly, and leastly, the Duty Log. That's it next to the phones. Use it. Sign on and off duty—the duty schedule is posted on the wall, there; log all calls; add anything else that might be useful, later; and use 24-hour notation. Any questions? About anything?" he paused.

Bill looked sheepish for a moment, "Can we trade hours?"

"As long as the phones are covered, I don't care."

"Should we record every visitor?"

"Is there a dress code?"

Both questions came at once. Walker answered them both. "Use your discretion, on both. Roger, did you want to say something about dress code?"

"Pepperland. It's cool."

"Thanks. The schedule's posted. I'll open every morning at 6:00 and stay until 2:00. Then I'll be at Hoag Memorial from four to four. Some of you are scheduled with others. Those are the times we think will be heaviest. Everyone ODs at the same time, I hear."

"Do you do drugs?" Molly wondered.

"No, too expensive," Walker shrugged.

"Did you ever?"

"No, never." He decided to offer them a pure image, a shining example from the fount of purity. Why not? He thought of himself as pure reason.

"What are you doin' here then—get your kicks from telling people what to do?" she demanded.

But, before he could answer, Roger woke up, "You can't know how to help if you haven't done it."

"Why not?" Walker reasoned. "Lawyers don't have to kill before they defend or prosecute for murder—"

"Boo, boo!"

"Bad example? Okay. Doctors don't have to have appendicitis before they operate. Friends don't have to commit suicide before they talk to someone who wants to."

"But how do you know?" Molly repeated.

"Like Plato's philosopher-king—by listening to others, and learning. By acquiring the experience second-hand, without making the mistakes."

"We could turn you on without a mistake," Roger offered.

"I'll pass. Besides, there are better ways to get high—"

"What?" came a chorus, "Yea, what? What?"

"Going without food, spinning around until you're too dizzy to stand, then lying on the ground watching the world spin, swimming with—"

"Hiss, hiss." Someone laughed.

Walker shrugged. "Let's move on to whatever we're moving on to."

Later, he watched the people walking toward the beach. Some of them looked interested as they passed by, but didn't come in. It looked kind of bare in the trailer. The display hadn't been finished. He and Roger had compromised on the design. Instead of resembling a series of triangles that Roger favored, or the circle and square he wanted, it looked like nothing except a giant eye, with writing on it. They decided to emphasize the likeness with a pupil.

He was adding lines to it, when a nine-year old boy came running in, "Are you a doctor?" he asked and went on without noticing Walker shake his head no automatically.

"My brother's, he's under the pier, acting funny. I think he needs someone to—help, I think."

Walker left the door open and went out with the kid, asking how old his brother was, and if he was doing something funny. Under the pier, they found the ten-year old giggling by himself. Walker looked at his eyes and sniffed his breath. He found a container of glue under his leg.

"What's wrong with him?" the younger brother asked. "Is he going to—will he be all right?"

"Sure he will. What's your name?"

"I'm not supposed to tell."

Walker sighed and pocketed the glue.

"What shall I do, now?" not-supposed-to-tell asked.

"Splash water on him. He'll be all right." Walker reassured not-tell. As long as he never has to add more than two digits, he added under his breath.

Two men, one middle-aged with brown shoes and brown socks and one younger with black shoes and a crew-cut, were sitting in the trailer when he got back. He saw their shoes first, as he came up the wooden stairs. They were both sitting, looking at the 'Drugs: Threat or Menace' type of pamphlets the reverend had ordered.

The older man spoke, "I wanted someone to talk to."

"My name is Walker, can I help you?" Walker offered, trying to remember his own rules.

Before the man could respond, a young woman ran up the stairs, shouting, "Help, someone fell down on the sidewalk!" Walker noticed her red and white striped uniform, but didn't recognize it.

"Excuse me," he called back as he followed her down the street. He immediately saw the form on the sidewalk, plaid shirt and jeans. Now he recognized her uniform. She was from the Chicken Delight fast-food place, looming over the still form. He registered the brown hair and pale skin of a late-teenaged face, as he moved the body onto the grass strip off the sidewalk and checked for a pulse. The girl was still standing by.

"Call for an ambulance, please," he asked her. As she ran inside, he checked for food blockage and started giving mouth-to-mouth, holding the tongue flat. The girl reappeared. The pulse was stronger and breathing regular.

He stopped, and asked the girl, "What's your name?"

"Mary-Anne. Did I do the right thing?"

"Yes, thanks. Mary-Anne, did you see this guy take anything?"

"Yes, that's why I came up to get you. He had a bottle of pills on his table." Walker felt the hip pockets—nothing.

"Would you check inside, please." She ran back into the restaurant. And came back a moment later, with a vitamin container with one red pill. It was probably a red devil, but he had never seen one before. What else was red? He tried to remember all of the pictures in the Physician's Handbook.

"Did you see him taking pills like these?" About four people were standing around them. Walker was still kneeling over the boy.

"Yellow."

"I think they were yellow," someone else added. Yellow jackets. Seconal and Nembutal. He tasted the slight alcohol on his own lips. This dude must have been drinking, too. As he looked up, a black squad car, state insignia, pulled up.

"I called them," a portly man announced.

The girl glared at him. Walker assumed he worked in the restaurant, too.

He addressed the officers, "I'll help you get him in the car. We need to get him to the hospital." One of the officers opened the rear door. The other helped Walker load the limp body.

He bent over the face and sniffed, "Hey, this man's drunk!"

"We have witnesses saw him taking pills. Let's let the doctor decide," Walker urged. The two officers huddled in conference.

"We're going to take him to the drunk tank."

Walker got angry. "I want you to take him to the hospital. My name is George Walker. I'm in charge of the Drug Abuse Clinics, that the Governor—"

The second officer interrupted him. "He's ours. And we're taking him in, where he belongs."

"If you're wrong, Officers Bailey and—" he checked the other name plate, "Kolley, then I'll have your hides stretched on the fence," he promised.

"Back off, buddy, or we'll take you in," Bailey pointed. They drove off, lights flashing, and Walker ran back to the information trailer.

No one was there. He called Grotius, Lt. Gibson, and the Governor. Gibson called back and promised to call the hospital immediately. Finally, he reached Roger and begged a ride to Hoag Memorial. The police car had just gotten there, with its unidentified male passenger. He helped Bailey carry the man in.

Bailey apologized, "Hey, We're sorry, we didn't know about the program."

"I'm sorry, too. No harm done."

In the emergency room, he asked the duty nurse to call the Clinic doctor. She held on to the phone for a minute and then informed him that there was no answer.   "Damn," Walker pronounced, watching the emergency room doctor check blood pressure. "Dr. Gianelli, my name is Walker. I'm the Clinic psychologist. I think we should hold this man over for observation in one of the psychiatric beds assigned to the clinic." Gianelli nodded. Walker escorted the police out, apologizing for any misunderstanding. When he got back in, Gianelli had finished the examination, and was ordering the patient to be taken to room 218.

"Alcohol and pills?" he asked Walker.

"Barbiturates, we think" Walker nodded.

"He's down pretty deep—comatose." Walker nodded.

"Shall we check for ID?" Gianelli asked.

"Good idea." They went through the shirt and jeans, but found only $6.85 and no identification.

"I've got to get back to the center," Walker resigned. "Thanks."

Huntington Beach to Newport Beach was a fifteen minute drive. Both he and Roger were did not speak on the way back. Jodi was on duty when he came in.

"Heard you had an emergency."

"Thanks for covering. You're not on for over an hour."

"Yea, I was rapping, over at Good Medicine. Bad news travels fast. What happened?"

He told her.

They only had two visitors in the next two hours. Parents who wanted to know how to tell if their children were using drugs. The night clerk at the hotel called up at 10:30, saying that there was some strange behavior on the top floor. Since the fire escape overlooked the lot with the trailers, Walker went up that way.

In the hall, seated on the gray carpet, was a twenty-year old Caucasian male, staring at his hands, which were resting awkwardly on the floor. "They're getting larger," he shrilled.

Walker whispered to the young man and woman standing on either side of the tripper, "Please go back to your room. I'll handle it." He pointed to the information center, "I'm from down there. Or you could stay, if you wanted," he added.

They nodded and left. Walker sat down in a lotus position opposite. He stared at the young man.

"Oh, look, I can see through them—God, the bones!"

"Look!" Walker commanded.

As the eyes raised slowly to meet his, he locked into them, spoke and dreamed for both of them, 'running down a spit of rock, and leaping off the low cliff into the ocean, surfacing in a spray of air and water, then weaving in and out of the surface ...'

"They're beautiful," the young man whispered.

After two hours, Walker was tired. He knew that the terror of hallucinations was the lack of control, so he was the control. The night-tripper was dozing off. Walker planted a subliminal message, 'the tripper cannot surface, the water gets darker, lungs labor, and as the last air leaks away, water floods the mind.' His eyes rolled wildly, then he collapsed into an exhausted sleep. Walker knocked on the door of the couple, but there was no answer. He rolled the young man into a comfortable position and left.

Jodi was ready to leave when he got back. Mike had been due half-an hour ago. Walker decided to stay in his place. For a while. At 1:00, two visitors showed up and wanted to know what the eye meant. Walker suspected that they were drunk and curious. While he was talking, the tall one fell asleep in the chair, dropping one shoe on the floor. The other, who finally identified himself as John Tilson, wanted to know why people took drugs. Walker was getting blurred by fatigue. "Same reason as alcohol, to feel good."

"But alcohol's legal."

"Yes, it is," Walker replied, "but not necessarily harmless or nonaddictive."

At 3:30 he woke both of them and closed up. They were irritated at having to leave. Walker got Mike to drive him back to the hospital.

June was an unreal month. Walker spent most of it in a haze of exhaustion. He set up HELP telephone lines in Newport and Seal Beach, using volunteers attracted by ads in the local papers. The Half-way House opened without flourish. He failed to get one single prisoner released early, to work on the program. One who was released after a maximum sentence, stayed at the house only two days before he got fed up with the 'dips,' who were also staying there.

The July fourth weekend was relatively uneventful. Two Thorazine ODs were taken to Hoag Memorial. One man sped for several hours in Trailer Two. The Chicken Delight people called with a D&D. Walker took him home. Where San Diego had 186 drug-related arrests, and Los Angeles went over 200, Newport Beach and Huntington Beach had 0—goose egg. Luck? Coincidence? Fate? Good Work? Who knew? On the 10th, he copied the duty logs, and bound copies for the Governor's Committee and the Newport Beach Council. He scanned over them, picking out typical entries. .

> 06/08 0020 Terry Row OD to Hoag Memorial
> 0150 Susan visited; Terry okay. Sam Bakeman juiced.
> 0230 trespasser   out by RBPD (no contact)
> 0345 shift over Murphy out
> 06/11 1604 Mr. B. visited, wanted to see some dope
> 1800 city inspector for electrical
> 1839 Jack came over   Jack left
> 2153 Alan called going to BB

0630 shift off no activity MD out

06/13 1200 shift on Mary here

1438 Samantha your mother called

1500 Jim Tripp came work for a couple hours see what it was

1620 friendly visitors 'can't believe it's so progressive!'

1810 Gary brought guitar and played.

1844 Judy taking darvon for her teeth, wanted to know if okay
was perscription

2025 J.A and C.G. here – not too together

2310 Mike came with burgers

2350 Roger "on"

06/22 1030 open for public

1110 visiting nurse from Los Angeles, just looking

1343 man in suit visited

1630 shift change   french fries

1700 Alan to kent st. for counseling

2030 bad acid trip   took to 2 for talk

2245 strange visitors   bikers

0330 useless to keep up Walker off

06/27 1100 day shift on Mariner

1150 Tina Williams looking for Walker bad news

1230 Jim Trip to pick up tools from display

1320 9311 caput telephone people called on other line coming

1700 hmmm hummmmmm

1420 drove Davis to hosp. for check.

1500 Social worker from Cleveland

1555 Rev. Bull called for George

2100 Ron bad?

2310 Mrs. Lovatos referred to Walker for couns.

06/30 1015 Koestler in

1100 McCarthy asks questions

2100 no comment

2140 Ralph Gore admitted to hosp.

2230 Walker back   call about methadone

2310 Guy with Mary to see what time it was told him

2317 visit from obvious narc, ex-narc, and cop

2356 stereo too loud—complaint from hotel agree to turn down

0015 Mary says Ted offered $50 for a fuck, could we use the
money NO!

0100 Jack wants to appeal case   who is lawyer?

0130 Darvon + wine = nausea

07/01 0940 open with Walker   garbage man cometh

1010 Belle from the east with Librium on vacation   walk by
shore, swim to relax

1030 Bill here two people want to join clinic live   in Newcastle

1220 Walker back Rep. Wynn waiting   VIP tour

1615 Trip here with Johnson from newspaper   want case studies
for art.

1900 Old man came in wanted to smell heroin didn't have any
son was busted for possess.

1930 Middle-aged couple with kids fro Penn, wanted info   and
good rap

1950 Girl with cut hand driven to hospital by Mike.

2230 Joy Kurney and her scag want test for powder called Cprl.
Moyer

0400 Walker out

July promised to be a busier month, and August, worse yet. That
morning, two people from the HELP telephones in San Diego came in
to see what was what. The Chamber of Commerce had wanted papers
signed for insurance. One of the counselors landed in jail and had
to be bailed. More state officials were interested and coming by. Two
Correctional Institute personnel had been given the tour.

It was 2:20 in the afternoon, and he had to get ready for the meeting at the hospital. As he left the trailer, his peripheral vision located a gloved hand descending toward his temple. He bent at the knees to a crouch. The hand missed and dragged an unbalanced body over him. Walker grabbed an arm and leg and lifted from his knees. He tossed a large body over the stairs onto the sandy dirt in front of the trailers. He jumped down the stairs, locked the free arms behind a dusty black jacket and asked reasonably into a lumpy ear, "Pardon me, did you want to talk to me?"

"Let me up and I'll break you," the man threatened.

"Common sense is an alien concept to you, isn't it?" Walker pressed the arms toward the neck so they creaked. "I already have you down. Now what is it?"

"My girl, don't mess with her," he groaned, straining to keep his arms down further on his back.

"Now, I have to guess? Did she have a tattoo on her chest, with your name on it?"

"Bastard! Theiss, Patty Theiss," he grunted, feeling dirt on his tongue. Walker stepped on the man's buttocks so he could stand up without any surprises.

"You ought to work that out with her," Walker suggested.

The black jacket came at his ankles in a hurry. Walker jumped back then up on the back again, smashing it into the dirt.

"Oahh, I'm hurt," the jacket complained.

Walker got in the staff car and drove to the meeting at Hoag Memorial. His heart beat wildly for the entire ride. Either the fight or thinking about Patty, whose social schedule rarely meshed with his.

The meeting was as tightly run as ever. Mrs. Pope read the minutes. Hardy Cane handed out the latest budget sheets. Everyone was thrilled at the $406.40 from the bake sales. The state coughed up $500.00. The American Legion and Rotary Club punched in $50.00 each. Over thirty individuals had donated amounts ranging from two dollars to fifty. The treasury stood at $6152.00.

Walker was glad, since he submitted expenditures for the Council totaling over $879.00. For the Half-way House rent telephone and cleaning supplies; for telephone and janitorial for the Bay Avenue doctor's house; for telephones, paint and art supplies for the Scout House Counseling Center.

During his report, Walker notified them of Roger's arrest and release. And of his decision to remove him as assistant. The Council affirmed his authority. The Council felt that anyone caught with drugs be discharged. Walker was relieved, since Roger was making deals left and right, while trying to consolidate authority for himself. The funds were approved, and resolved. The musical programs for Wednesdays were voted to be continued; no one dared call them rock concerts. The Council set its next meeting for the following Friday.

That night, staring at the phones, once called instruments of the devil he remembered, he and Mike were surprised by a HaHa visit from the Chicken sisters and Niki. Every week or so, after the 1:00 a.m. closing time, three of the girls from the Chicken Delight would come by with buckets of chicken and cheeseburgers—all ostensibly left over and unsold. Walker could not think of any more generous reward for working at the devil's instruments than spontaneous gifts. They sat around eating and talking of high school, which Walker barely remembered, having flunked out, and which Mike still thought of from college, and which the girls were just enjoying. Grease had become popular with fast food chains, but cold grease had a punishment all of its own. Walker ate his french fries ceremoniously, knowing that his time on the toilet would come shortly.

There were five regulars on methadone at the clinic. There was a sixth almost regular, Benny Raider, who hated hospitals and cops, but couldn't afford the scag or the jail sentences. Him Walker was trying on a heroin reduction program. They both knew where the 'shit was hid' as Benny laughed. The agreement was that Walker would always parcel it out and Walker would be responsible for the consequences if they were caught; that commitment let Benny be committed, too. The five regulars had to take their methadone in orange juice between seven and nine in the morning. Walker had to supervise them. They all tended to come in together. Walker found out why the second week when he caught them hoarding the juice. Each one would take the dose under supervision of the nurse, but only pretend to swallow it. Then they would spit it all into a thermos, and sell it to Molly for resale. It was a nice profit for everyone. Walker never would have guessed if one of them, Peggy Coles, hadn't been angry at being cheated by Molly, and ratted.

That afternoon, he met Patty Theiss in an apartment on Oregon Avenue. It was a two-story redwood; the apartment was on the second floor. When Walker came in he saw a pile of vegetation on the counter that resembled parsley.

"Oh, shit," he said.

"What's the matter," Patty poked her head around the corner.

"That," he pointed.

"That is parsley. I was dicing it for your lasagna. The grass is in my purse, but you can search me if you want, officer," she flirted.

Walker sighed deeply and went in and laid down on the bed. It was a studio apartment so he watched her as she sautéed onions and mushrooms.

"It won't be as good as yours," she said.

"Sure it will, I watched you," he grabbed her hips and buried his face in her stomach; then levered her onto the bed.

"Forty-five minutes," she managed to say.

That night was busy. Two more overdoses and a couple freaked by the eye display, which had become more psychedelic; someone had outlined it with different colors of phosphorescent paint. When it was quiet, he went out and looked at the sky. Bill had put a spotlight in the branches of the tree, so it was lighted up dramatically. Then he noticed someone slumped in the phone booth on the sidewalk. He ran over and opened it. The figure straightened out as it thrust a knife into his ribs. Walker turned sideways, feeling the blade skid through muscle. He rammed himself backwards, grabbing the collar of his assailant. He pulled the knife and flung it aside, kicking the figure in the back, pushing it into the street. An engine roared, and headlights glared. The car stopped, the figure dived in the open window, rubber squealed as the shape leapt forward. Walker watched, holding his side, feeling the blood leak between his fingers and the sharp pain of each breath.

Then he ran down the street paralleling the car. He knew it had to turn right in two blocks to get to the highway. When he realized that he could not get to it, he grabbed a garbage can lid as he ran. As the car turned, he threw the lid. He saw the white face in the open window open its mouth before it was eclipsed by the metal lid, which missed. The car kept going. Walker slowed down and turned back toward the staff car.

Mary Sanders was on duty at the emergency room. He took off his shirt. She probed the wound.

"Are you going to report it?" she asked skeptically.

"Report what?" Walker responded. "He missed."

"Doper?" she asked.

Walker shrugged. "Could you just tape it? I heal fast."

"You might scar, though," she considered, then noticed the other scars. "Tape it is."

Walker was back at work that evening. Someone had been working on the eye display. The blue of the iris was identified as consciousness. Green rays in the iris as perception. There were yellow, orange, and red lines radiating out, making it look slightly bloodshot; the lines were identified as physical needs (eat, sleep), emotion, and sex. The whole image from a distance did look like an eye. Close-up it had the aspect of a flow chart diagrammed by a mad computer programmer. Classes of drugs were superimposed on categories of reaction (fear, aggression, nervousness, curiosity). A young couple came in and traced some of the connections. Walker fell asleep before they left, helped by the Darvon from Mary. He did not think he was dreaming anynore.

Grotius was holding a special meeting on the third Friday in August. Kirby Frazier, the new state coordinator for drug abuse programs would be there. And Representative Wynn and Senator Marshak. Mrs. Carson, Jim Trip, Hardy Cane, Vince Harcourt. Grotius was scheduled to take over as Clinic doctor on call the following week. It was the eleventh. The preliminaries of the meeting were short. Introductions and then a talk by Grotius.

"I have been considerably annoyed by what I have heard about the LA County Program," Grotius complained, looking at Walker. "I have been most patient with Mr. Walker during his assignment to Hoag Memorial Hospital. He has called and written me dozens of times about his paycheck and about the Methadone clinic. I have been patient and helpful. Well, he will have to shape up or resign, now," He pulled his nose, then smoothed his van dyke.

"Our carefully paid plan has deteriorated under his direction. Let us examine what has gone wrong. First, he became involved with the Newport Beach Drug Program under Mr. Trip. I'm sure that this was an interesting area. After all the boardwalk is more exciting than the hospital at Hoag Memorial. But this was not his primary effort, which should have been the Clinic. Instead of it being voluntary, he has taken to signing his name as director of the Huntington Beach-Newport Beach Drug Abuse Facilities," He pulled at his trousers. "We told him," Grotius reverted to the 'royal' we, "that it was all right to work with the Huntington Beach group to advertise the Clinic, but we would expect them to finance their part of it. Much of the use of the car was for their program, not ours. The same with paint and signs, and other supplies; their program, not ours.

"Then, the Huntington Beach group has been collecting money for their program, perhaps as much as $22,000. What happened to that money? Can Mr. Walker, as director, account for those funds? I have heard from a reliable source—" and Walker smelled that source in the person of Roger Sims "—that he has been very arbitrary with those funds, going to Sacramento, on an all expenses paid junket, to 'check on the drug scene.' Can he deny that?

"And again, he has become involved with the drug patients more as a doctor than as a counselor. He told the hospital which patients to give Methadone. His actions were so disruptive to the staff, that Mr. Thurmond had to telephone me six times to straighten out the program. We found that he had prescribed medicine that no doctor had okayed, for example. Kirby may want to look into possible criminal charges.

"We have lived up to our part of the contract for the Clinic. But we feel that you have not. Your present attitude is bizarre, and we resent it. Perhaps counseling is needed. I have always enjoyed working with you in the past, and had planned to involve you in our drug programs in Los Angeles or San Diego. Now that will be impossible. Kirby will have his hands full salvaging this program."

Grotius sat down, folding his papers. Walker stood up, slowly, glaring at Grotius.

"I would have preferred to discuss your—hallucinations—before the—"

"Please," Kirby asked, standing also. "I would like to speak about the program, first. Thank you."

Walker sat down, concentrating on shriveling Grotius's heart.

"I do not intend to take anything said at face value. If you wish to respond to me in writing, as Dr. Grotius has, then I would weigh your opinions, too. There are many people here who feel the overall program is successful. There are those who do not.

"As the newly appointed State Director of Drug Abuse Programs, I want to hear from as many people as possible."

Walker tuned him out. The limp-wristed twit was another political hack who had made up his mind, but wanted desperately to preserve the image of fairness and blind justice. He looked around the table. State Senator Marshak was nodding his head like a jack-in-the-box with a weak spring. Wynn was preening his white hair. Grotius was looking arrogantly attentive. Roger was smiling in satisfaction. Thurmond looked serious and sour. The Reverend Cane was contemplative. Only Jim Trip seemed angry at the dirty-trick power play. Walker wasn't sure whose it was, even. Roger's? No, too stupid. Grotius's? No, what would he gain? Kirby's? Maybe he wanted his own man in?

Kirby was looking expectantly at him, "I said, you may speak in turn, now, Mr. Walker."

Walker stood up, playing with his pencil. "I am perplexed. By Mr. Grotius's arg—"

"Doctor Grotius," Grotius interrupted.

"—attitude and beliefs. Because my paycheck was nine weeks late, I had to borrow money for bills. Because the Governor's committee was slow with their bills, I had to borrow money to make the down payment and rent on the physician's home at Bay Avenue. I am still waiting to be paid back. I confess I don't know what's happened to the money raised by the Huntington Beach program—"

"Aha!" Grotius grunted in triumph.

"—program, because the Reverend Cane, the treasurer, handled all of it. I'm sure that he can—and will—tell where it's gone. I went to Sacramento for a day, to pick up the pamphlets Mrs. Pope ordered. But I didn't stop to eat. I paid for the gas out of my pocket.

"As for my aspirations for doctorhood, I recommended medication for as many people as who came to me for help, that I thought needed it. In most cases, the Clinic doctors thought red devils was a nick-name for peppermint candy, and were only too happy to take my recommendation and get back to their beach house. I never wrote any prescriptions. In fact, I don't know of any nurses stupid enough to fill illegal prescriptions. If Grotius knows of any, perhaps he would tell the head nurse, Jean Moyer, and let her deal with it.

"As for my titles, I was appointed director by the Newport Beach Council. I was also head of the HELP lines in LA County. We all thought it would be a good idea to unify the local programs to minimize waste and conflict. Apparently, Grotius brought his own conflicts with him. And I agree that counseling is needed for Grotius, but I will not be able to fit him in my schedule. I suggest, Kirby, that you do investigate these charges, not to mention my expense requests." Walker concluded.

Roger shouted, "What about the personal calls, huh!?"

Walker looked at the Reverend Cane. The reverend sighed and volunteered, "Last week, Mr. Walker paid $42.00 toward the phone bill, for his personal calls, mostly to Hawaii."

Jim Trip stood to talk. The arguments intensified, between the failures and the successes.

"About that interview you wanted?" Walker initiated. He had called Dan McCormick at WSEA-FM, when he returned to the information center. McCormick agreed, and came over that evening, with a recorder.

"I'm speaking with George Walker, Director of the LA County Drug Abuse Programs. Could you tell me, George, just how big a drug problem is there in this county?"

"I don't think there is a problem."

"Ahh, what do you mean? You were hired because of it. The state has told us there is one. Hasn't it?"

"Yes, it has told us. But, remember that is the same state that told its eighteen-year olds to be drafted to fight in an undeclared war in Vietnam. The state defines problems; it makes problems."

"Please explain." Dan was getting really interested. Something unexpected was happening. Well, he'd hoped for the unexpected.

"Ask yourself, what is bad about drugs, that make them a problem?"

"They're addictive."

"So, what's wrong with addiction?"

"It's ... it dulls the mind, causes violence."

"Not necessarily. Consider. An addiction is a habit that revolves around a material object. Television is an addiction. Driving fast is; food, certainly. Alcohol, cigarettes, music, sports—all habits, all addictions of different kinds. How many of them are problems?"

"Well, none of them—but all of them can be. But drugs are different."

"How?"

"They are dangerous and illegal."

"They are illegal because the state makes them illegal, the way alcohol used to be illegal. Prohibition made alcohol illegal. Those laws resulted in contempt for the law, a division of society, and rampant gangsterism. The law did not succeed in banning alcohol, just in making it more difficult to get."

"But alcohol—I mean drugs—are still dangerous, to the user and to the public."

"Why are they dangerous to the public?"

"Because they—people—steal and kill to get them."

"Isn't that because they are illegal? Wouldn't the violence stop, if everyone could get cheap pure drugs, any drugs, without a prescription?"

"No! It wouldn't. And I'll tell you why. Because some drugs make people insane and out of control."

"You're right. Like alcohol. Like any addiction, even cigarettes—a man with two cigarettes in his mouth driving a car can be almost as dangerous as his son at the wheel after a hash brownie in his mouth. Furthermore, any emotional imbalance makes people insane. The young boy who's girl rejects him, or the girl rejected by someone else. The man fired from his job, as a result of poor economic indicators or falloff in demand for steel. The woman who catches her husband sleeping with her best friend. These people are dangerous. They may threaten our lives in the haze of their anger or despair. Should we ban marriage, sex, jobs, cigarettes, and alcohol, as well?"

"No, but I—"

"Some people will always ruin their lives. Those who do so with drugs will do so anyway. Besides, most of the damage I see comes from the uncertainty of the purity and the dosage. When those are known, taking drugs becomes much safer."

"What would you recommend then? Medical supervision?"

"No, simply the legalization of all drugs. And federal controls on uniformity and price. Generic heroin, generic marijuana, generic tranquilizers."

"That's ..."

"Insane? No, good common sense. That way the government can get more taxes—taxes that they cannot collect from an illegal market."

"But what about the health of the people?"

"What about it? Illegal drugs don't help it. The government lies to them about the hazards of drugs. Ever see 'Reefer Madness?' Funny isn't it? The government ignores the good side of drugs, the side the kids find out about from their friends. Why not tell them the good and the bad? And let them decide? How much of the urge to try drugs comes from the romantic aura of the lone pusher? The glamour of hiding and trying the forbidden? How glamorous is aspirin? Or penicillin?"

"Why not try to ban alcohol, again. That would be consistent?"

"True, but people want it, and we do listen to the voice of the people, eventually. Think of the effort that goes into the police, narcs, social workers, hospitals, that could go to making a healthier society? Why don't we admit the human weaknesses we see, and strive to make a healthier place for everyone? A whole society on a whole earth? We could start by stopping the pretense about a drug problem that can be legislated and police-forced and counseled out of existence. Can we start, now?"

"I ... don't know what to say. Are you going to campaign to put your views across?"

"No, I don't think so. If they are good views, other people will have them; maybe speak them."

"What do you intend to do, now? Will you stay with this program?"

"No, I have been invited to leave. I think I'll work on a smaller, more personal scale."

"Who asked you to leave?"

"I'd rather not say. What is important is that this program serves the public within the limits of the law, as they stand. This program is an information center for people who need or want to know about drugs. It is to help those who get in trouble with drugs, which are still very illegal. Hundreds of people have worked together to provide a service for others. That service cannot be denied or demeaned. I am grateful to have worked with all of these people, and proud to have helped them." Walker nodded at Dan's lipped question.

"Thank you. We have been talking to George Walker, the director of the LA County Drug Abuse Programs. Tomorrow, we have Randy Jade, a singer who set his band on fire to—"

Walker wrote out his resignation, giving three weeks notice, and went for a swim on the night beach. There was a bonfire on the sand about a mile down, so he turned north and ran. He turned into the water after a mile, and ran between the waves. He went out further, so that a larger wave would knock him off his feet. For that moment, he would be lifted and carried to shore, and tossed, out of control. He lay on the sand, panting, licking salt from his lips. Then, he undressed and swam toward Hawaii. Until he got tired, anyway.

For the next three weeks, he supervised the schedules for the information center and the Clinic. He took some counseling himself, and followed up on cases from June and July, to see how the people were doing. Some had gone home; others had jobs. Over half had given bogus addresses and couldn't be contacted. Benny had been arrested for running a red light on his Harley; he had two bags of scag at the time. Walker called him in jail, but couldn't get him out.

He evaluated the different parts of the program. He had found volunteer positions for some of them at Zero Population Growth and the Humane Society. A few of those had led into paying positions. Many of the formerly disenfranchised were helpful with the poster campaigns to 'Care for Pets' and 'Save the Seals.' And some were helped by the therapy of artistic expression. In two weeks, thirteen people consumed $143.53 worth of paints and poster paper. Walker remembered the seals sunning on the rocks north of Huntington Beach, when he first drove down in May. Just as their ancestors had done under the watch of condors. The gulls waited for scraps. He hoped that they had been helped. Mrs. Theiss left for Pittsburgh with her children. She had been bothered by reporters once too often to say good-bye.

Andrea Marinetti came in one day and dragged everybody out to see the new windshield on her Rambler.

"Where'd you get the money? You have a job?" Molly enthused.

"No, I did a job," Andrea stated proudly. "A blow job!"

She laughed uproariously, Molly and Walker joining in a little. Walker went back to the hospital to pack.

Molly and Andrea were on duty for Labor Day. Walker smiled again at Andrea, who didn't seem to have any equipment beyond that required for basic life. No brains, no morals, no heart. She had already stolen two weeks worth of collections from the outpost stores. Until Walker put Mary in charge of donations. Andrea had added worse publicity a week earlier, when she had the indiscretion to buy a large, plastic play hypodermic, that the dime store had the indiscretion to stock. And Roger had the indiscretion to fill it with a quart of orange kool-aid and chase Andrea down the main street, screaming, 'Fix! Fix! Time for Dope!' He had to write letters of apology to the Chamber of Commerce and City Council for that one. Walker should have had them do it in a play.

He had nothing again, no job offers, little money. Unless the state paid back some of his expenses, he would even be in debt. Mrs. Moyer came down to his room, as he was packing.

"George, I have some strange news for you. I don't know where to start," she hesitated.

"At the beginning?" he suggested.

"Well, remember that knife attack?"

He felt his side unconsciously. It had healed in a few weeks. He showed it to her after four. He nodded.

She continued, "Well, the Mafia put out a contract on anyone who tried to hurt you."

"Why?"

"Because you had once said that the Mafia was the best place to get drugs—for quality control—you remember, in the interview in June."

Walker did remember. He advised people not to buy drugs from their friends, because of several poisonings. Talcum powder or draino substituted for sugar in cut heroin. When he had been asked where to get safe drugs, he had said the Mafia, they had standards, minimum, but standards.

"That's not all," she was looking at him. "After you dropped the bon-mot-shell about legalizing everything, they dropped the contract."

He looked at her, "You mean anyone can kill me, now?"

They both started laughing.

After a moment, he asked, "Who told you?"

"My husband." He knew her husband, Corporal Moyer, was reliable.

"Thanks. I appreciate it. Gotta pack," he gestured at the half-filled bag, with a hospital white sleeve sticking out.

She kissed him on the cheek and left.

The bus back to LA didn't go through Newport Beach. Things were shutting down, now, slowly. He wondered what the state was going to do, but found that he didn't really care. The reverend Cane had called him last night, telling him how Jim Trip had defended their program, and wangled some expense money out of the state. With that Walker's total earnings that summer came to just over three hundred dollars. He paid the $157.00 back to the bank. He thanked Hardy and said that they were good men and good friends. During the bus ride, he read the paper he had bought in Huntington Beach. In it was one letter of praise, from a Mrs. Dobbs, who related that the summer program had been a valiant gesture. It had helped her family. She knew it had helped others and hoped that they were as grateful. Walker couldn't remember anyone named Dobbs. On the record page was a notice of a Los Angeles physician admitted to a psychiatric bed at Hoag Memorial for treatment.

Chapter 7. In the Realm of Books

Back to the beginning of the cycle, one cycle anyway. He went back to Zavala's to rent a room. He went back every day to the unemployment to look for openings, conscious of his stronger smell and whiskers. He made sure to check in with the counselor, Betty, who one day asked him if he was a veteran. When he admitted he was, she said they had an opening in a college library that was covered by the veteran's retraining program. She would refer him if he agreed. He did, but with one request: If she could lend him a razor and soap. She looked questioningly, as if the investment might be risky, but agreed to bring the things the next morning. He asked if the interview could be made late the next day.

Washing and shaving wasn't as much a problem as drying his best set of clothes. He hoped it was good enough, but then he didn't realize that it was fashionable for students to wear ripped and worn jeans and shirts.

The clothes were still a little damp when he arrived at the California Pacific library—some of that was probably sweat from walking the 3 miles. He stopped at a drinking fountain and swished water in his mouth. He looked at his reflection in a window. Was he that skinny now? He tightened his belt.

The secretary's office was right where the map said it would be. The library was an older building, Mission Style, large yet nondescript; the offices were in a refurbished wing. He introduced himself.

"Good afternoon, my name is Walker. I have an appointment with the Associate Director," he smiled and beamed at the secretary.

She nodded and spoke into a depressed button, announcing him. She was very attractive in a non-California standard way—conservatively dressed, shy, and reserved, as if hiding a threatening depth.

A short, dense man bounded out of the adjoining office, extending his hand and sending his voice at the same time, "Hi, I'm Bill Heck! Associate Director. Good to meet you Mr. Walker. Let's go sit in the conference room." They shook hands as he led the way.

"Yes, sir. George Walker."

"How do you like our library, George? We're planning a new addition right now, to double the floor space—of, course, we won't get any furniture for decades, but at least the books will have shelves. Sorry, I do go on. Do you have any library experience?" Heck was wearing a black shirt with black trousers, white belt and white shoes.

"Well, yes, sir, I've done a lot of research in libraries. I'm familiar with the classification systems and literature searches."

"You know the LC system?" Heck asked.

"Yes, Library of Congress," he felt compelled to expand the abbreviation if it was a test. "I spent most of my time in the QAs, though."

"Yes, astronomy," Heck replied, expanding Walker's test. "I noticed that on your application. Our director is interested in astronomy. He indicated an interest in speaking with you after me. We usually hire students, although most of them think of their work-study as a free ride to socialize and relax between classes. We wouldn't be hiring you unless you were a student except for this federal program, which will pay 80 percent of your wages. Do you think you might become a student? Do you have the employment response card?"

"Yes," Walker said, replying only to the last sentence. He handed the card over. Heck examined it, then put it in a manila folder.

"Well, have you had shelving experience?" Heck asked. "Have you reshelved books in proper order?"

Walker looked at him for a moment before he spoke, "I've located books before. I'm sure I could reverse the process."

Heck continued, "You'd have to be checked for several days if you start work. That means you will have to shelve the books on their spines until someone can go around and make sure they're in their proper place. Then you might have to be trained to work behind the circulation desk. That would—well, I'm getting ahead of myself. Do you have any questions?"

Walker's stomach growled—he hoped Heck hadn't heard. "Yes, I wondered if you were responsible for the brochures and help-sheets on display in the lobby?"

Heck glowed. Obviously a good guess. "Yes, they are nice aren't they? Useful, too. Carol, Ms. Nueman, the secretary, did the layouts. I wrote the text. Yes, well, let's get you to see Faron before he leaves for the day." Heck looked at his watch in disapproval.

Walker remembered that he hadn't asked how much it paid or when it started.

Heck left the conference room and came back a moment later, with a tall slim man with white hair and a trim beard, who came in and sat down, ignoring Heck's overture at introduction. Heck backed out.

"Faron Vane," he held out his hand, "I noticed that you worked at the observatory on Maui. I'm sort of an amateur observer myself. I've never been there, but I'd like to go some time. What did you study?"

"Seyfert galaxies. We were just starting to perform infrared observations," Walker paused, realizing he couldn't remember when he last worked on his project—seemed like years had passed—Vane was talking.

"—special about them? I haven't read about them, I don't think."

"The energy is not related to size in any way that we can account—" Walker trailed off. Vane was looking at the application.

"I see you were in Vietnam. My son served with, what was it now?" Vane paused.

Walker continued, "Infrared gives a better reading of what is happening. Umm"

The silence was awkward. Vane didn't know if Walker wanted to talk about galaxies and not about Vietnam—he remembered his son's pain at talking about it; it was the only time his son had ever written poetry to him and his mother.

"Do you write poetry, Mr. Walker?"

"I, I'll admit it if it won't prejudice your treatment of my application," Walker smiled.

Vane smiled, "No, you're hired, if you want it. It will be good to have someone intelligent to talk with from time to time. Well, I have a meeting. Talk to Carol about the details." Vane got up and shook hands again, before leaving the room and going right out of the library.

Walker sat for a moment, visions of food and a soft bed materializing above the table. Vane looked like the vain Dutchman he had left behind; he wondered if it was a California style for middle-aged men to try to resemble the devil. He suppressed the thoughts and went out to see the secretary, aware that he still had not gotten any details.

"Yes," Carol asked.

"I think I'm hired," Walker said, "but I don't know any of the details. Could you tell me?"

"What do you need to know?" she smiled fleetingly.

"How much does it pay? When does it start? When would I get paid?

Do I have to go through training of some kind?"

"You can start as soon as you like. It's near the end of the quarter and the stacks are a mess, students are cramming, administrators are panicking," she replied, looking in a staff manual embossed with the trademark of the school, a torch and a book circled with Latin mentioning light and learning. "I'm afraid the pay starts at $1.65 an hour; after a couple of months it should go up 10 cents—if you're lucky. What else?" The smile was back for a moment.

"When paid?"

"The school pays every two weeks. You need to fill out these forms, W-2 and whatever. Oh, yes, don't worry about training. If you're not sure if the book is in its proper place, just tilt it out and another shelver can check it. You should be up to speed in 40 or 50 seconds."

"I'll start tomorrow morning, then?" Walker wondered if he should start now, but didn't want to seem desperate.

"Start at 8:00. That would be good," she offered her hand.

He bowed a little, thinking he would kiss it, but feeling like an out of place monster from a vampire movie, just shook it lightly.

He found himself in line at the Post Office, having passed miles in a daze of fantasy. And, when he asked for general delivery, he found that his first unemployment check had come. Luck in one thing, luck it all, it appeared.

So, it turned out that the night before he started work, he had a room, and in it, a few clothes and some soap. He didn't even mind that there were no sheets again. He had dried fruit and water. He went for a walk, came back, and went to sleep.

"Hi, my name is Charles, but you can call me Chuck or Charlie," said the speaker, without modulating his voice in any way.

"Yes, good morning, I'm George," Walker said, suppressing the temptation to call 'Chuck or Charlie' Chuckie as a compromise, eager to make a good impression, to keep his room, with its very own bed and mattress.

"Let's get started. Have you had a tour of the stack plan?"

Walker shook his head.

"No. I'll arrange one later. Let's start here at the circulation desk. These shelves here against the wall are for storing books temporarily if there's overflow. Your job is to off-load books from those shelves onto these little green carts. You can place them in here so that the call numbers are facing up. The books will more or less be in order on the shelves; try to put them in order on the cart. Normally you will have enough for a section of one floor—that will minimize your movements and maximize your efficiency. Let's take this loaded cart here, since it's unattended," he smiled as he wheeled the cart through the swinging waist door toward the elevator.

"This is the staff elevator; the public isn't allowed to use it. These books are mostly 'B's. You know what subject area that is, I presume?" Charles asked, while pressing the 2 button.

"Philosophy," Walker answered.

"Yea, and do you know what the order is within the subject?"

"Chronological?" Walker guessed.

"No, and yes. It starts with essays and introductory texts, then subjects like metaphysics, which are arranged by schools, then by major philosophers in chronological order by era and alphabetical order within eras, so you see, every kind of order has its place in the Library of Congress classification. This book, B829.515, is phenomenology, so we just go down the shelves to the 800s—"

"Excuse me, you know this awfully well. Are you a graduate student, librarian or philosopher?"

"Yes, very perspicacious. Actually, I'm a graduate in philosophy. I worked in the library as a student. It turns out that there was an opening just as I graduated—been here ever since," Charles rolled his eyes up to try to glimpse some memory of promise. "Could have been worse. I could have been a history major," he laughed at some private joke.

Walker smiled. He took the next book down a few shelves and fitted it between two other books. Charles checked it and rotated it 90 degrees.

"Just right, but you should turn them down for the first day, just to be sure. You should be up to speed in a couple of hours," Charles watched as Walker shelved a couple more books.

"Are you a student around here?"

"No, a graduate—astronomy," they both snorted little nasal laughs.

"Not here, I hope. There's no sky," Charles commented.

"Hawaii, got laid off."

"Swim much?"

"Not 'til I got laid off," Walker smiled, wondering if his eyes had rolled up involuntarily.

"Swimming—surfing, too—not too bad around here if you can find room," Charles indicated that they go around the next stack. "The books go round the corner—good for a browser, but you have to go down each aisle twice."

"Why not shelve backwards for the second side?"

"Whatever works, just so the books are in the right place," Charles brought his lips together and stuck his chin out from thinking. "Listen, you've caught on fast. I have to go back down to the newspaper room. Finish this cart and load another. You mastered the skill, just repeat it 800 times this morning. I'll check back in an hour or so," Charles started walking off, then stopped, "You ever sort newspapers? Never mind."

Walker kept shelving books. It was repetitive, like exercising or meditating. After an hour, he was in architecture. He had just opened a book on Barcelona when the director came strolling around the stack. He closed the book and put it on the shelf sideways.

Vane smiled and said, "Good morning. I'm just taking a tour of the place, see what's needing to be done." Vane checked the book's location. "Ever been to Barcelona? Great architecture. My wife went over to study. You study it?"

"In my field, domes were popular. We even had a geodesic for staying at the site."

"Was it lush and green there?"

"No, surprisingly, it was more like a moonscape, beautiful and exotic in a different way."

"Oh," Vane emitted, perhaps a little disappointed at his guess. "Well, maybe we can talk about architecture. Well, carry on. I'm sure you'll be up to speed in a couple of weeks."

Walker watched Vane retreat toward the stairs. He sighed and continued shelving.

Charles came up after 1:00. "You can take lunch, half an hour. I'll show you the employee lunch room. Oh, you can leave the cart here."

As he was punching out Heck came and stood next to him. "I love libraries myself. If I'd been an Egyptian, I'd have worked in the Library at Alexandria. Do well?"

"I felt good about my work today," Walker answered.

"Good," Heck slammed an open palm on Walker's arm. "You'll be up to speed in a couple months and you can enjoy more of the books."

The first day he kept count of the books he shelved. The second day he made sure to shelve more. The third day more. By the fourth day, he figured he could shelve for four hours and read for four.

He started reading in the 'B's with a book on the Pre-Socratic philosophers, Thales, Pythagorus, Heraclitus.

***

"So, what do you think it is Leukippus? Water, like Thales, or Fire, after Heraclitus?" asked Hippolytus, reclining in the dust on his side, beads of sweat each stopping as they gathered dust, then making light brown trails on the skin.

Leukippus looked up before answering. He was standing with his hands on his knees breathing deeply and thinking 'too much wine.'

The younger Hippolytus smiled and said, "Ready to run again? We should bath in the pool, but to get there we must run again."

"I'm sure if I ran I would burst into flames and my essence would flee to the sun."

"So, you admit, it is Heraclitus."

"Just metaphorically. Everything seems to burn in a way. Wood, dung, bodies."

"Even water?" despite his preference to continue exercising, Hippolytus wondered how Leukippus could argue his way out of this dead end.

"Even water," Leukippus nodded. "You are made of water, are you not? You will be drinking more of it in a short time. When you are dead we will burn you."

"Not you,"

"Someone," Leukippus had been reminded of his mortality earlier, when he could not get enough air to keep up with the younger man.

"I am sorry, I did not mean—let's go on. Even water must be made of fire then. Is that what you are saying?"

"No, I think there is another substance that makes up water and fire, which are just states of these things at different rates of motion. Water seems to burn when its motion is speeded up—"

"No!"

"Yes, think, when you run very fast, you become warmer. If you could run fast enough you might burst into flame. That is what happens with the sun. It moves fast enough—it has to, it is so far away and covers so much land in a day."

"And these are those mysterious atoms you have referred to?"

"Yes, particles. And they are the same everywhere. In the universe. For every world and every sun."

Hippolytus laughed. He knew there was only one place; the stars were lights, the wanderers were lights.

Leukippus looked over the landscape. Fewer trees this year than last. More sheep and more people. Each day fewer trees. Soon there would be no shade at all and new ships would be made of sheepskin.

"Not fire," he started, "but light. Particles are made of light. The light slows as it enters us. After we die it all escapes to the sky, slowly but completely. Light.

Light."

Hippolytus put his hand around Leukippus's calf, "Why don't you wrestle with that thought for a while. I will be the thought," he laughed and pulled Leukippus's legs out from under him.

Leukippus landed on his back but kicked Hippolytus away with both feet before Hippolytus could jump on him. He got up first and started running toward the distant pool. He could hear Hippolytus start after him. It couldn't be light—it had to be particles. Then what?

***

He woke up in his room. It didn't seem as plain now that it was his room. The imprint of a few fabrics chosen from Good Will shelves. Sheets and a bed cover. A few books. He felt like he was back in an acquisition mode. Pretty soon a stereo, then who knew what.

He got to the library early that day and just sat and watched the staff and students. The staff members each seemed to be developing a widow's hump from bending over books. The student help was still young and had not been molded by the work. Maya was the most attractive he thought, but she went through boyfriends rapidly. Deni was as attractive, but married; she and her husband had fled from Iran with much of their money in tact. Josh had bad pimples and bad teeth, but a keen intelligence. Then, he had to start.

"Hey, you're sweating!" Charles exclaimed.

Walker smiled, "I know. My body just operates at a higher temperature when I work—even when I eat. It's nothing."

"Just don't burn up. These books and all."

"It's just hot out, too. Is there air conditioning?"

"Just for the offices, since they don't need it," Charles reflected. "It might attract more patrons, who might use more of the books. The librarians wouldn't like that. Some of these books are museum pieces.

Here look at this one: Animal Magnetism," he opened the book. "I think it means that if you increase your magnetism scientifically, you can attract female animals. 1890, huh. Seemed to have worked. The population has increased."

Walker was looking out the window at central LA. The increase here was dramatic. He continued shelving in the BFs, psychology. He was halfway through reading that section. Not every book, just one from each shelf or each section. Time passed as quickly as the ruffling of pages.

He was called into Heck's office, again. The first time, six months ago, it was to get a raise. He hoped that was the purpose today.

Heck motioned him to a seat, but did not get up or even look up.

"Have you used the cash register recently?" Heck asked without preamble.

"No," Walker hesitated. "Not for a while. Not since I subbed for the xerox operator. I think, I'm sure, I used it then to get change for patrons."

Heck paused for a moment and then concluded, "I'm sorry but we're going to have to let you go. Maybe you didn't take the money, but two others said that they saw you around the register before the shortages."

"What shortages? I didn't take any money," Walker couldn't think of any thing else to say. In fact he did take a quarter once to get a peanut butter cup in the vending machine. "How much is missing?"

"Forty two dollars and five cents," Heck answered exactly, "in the past two months."

"Then you've got a problem, because if you fire me you're still have the person who took the money," Walker answered harshly.

Heck backed his chair against the wall, "We'll see. You're not being fired. You're being let go. You've worked hard for us. You'll have good recommendations if you need them."

"And will you give me my job back, when money continues to disappear?"

"I honestly don't see how we could do that."

"Then why let me go if you're not sure. You haven't even asked me. Who was it who thought it might be me."

"Obviously, Mr. Walker, I can't tell you that. It would violate our rules?"

"And firing an innocent worker doesn't violate them?" Walker wanted to defend his habits, his small paycheck, his easy job, his small room, but the decision seemed to have been made without his knowledge or participation.

"You'll have to leave now. The secretary will give you a check that has a full day of pay for today."

"And if I don't leave?" Walker wondered if he could test the situation, his rights, the libraries.

"You have to leave my office now."

"I don't think I can do that. I'll need more information, names, dates. That sort of thing."

"Leave now!" Heck urged. "I can have the police called."

"That could only be to my benefit," Walker replied, stuck to his seat with some irrational desire to cause trouble or find answers or be treated fairly or something.

Heck stormed out the office. Walker could hear him muttering down the hall. He picked a library journal off Heck's desk and started reading it. Although he could hear voices in other offices, no one came into Heck's office to bother him. He wondered who his accusers were; were they the thieves? Or did everyone in the library take a quarter out once a month for vending machines? He calculated the size of the staff at $0.25 a month. No, it would have to be every week. Probably just one person. What could be keeping Heck or the police? What could Heck be doing? What the Heck? Probably standing in someone's office waiting.

After half an hour of doodling and reading, he leaned over Heck's desk and opened the center drawer. There were several quarters and dimes and pennies. He took a quarter and left.

Chapter 8. Direct Action

So he went back to his cheap room, already retreating to the familiar. And he found that he could not collect unemployment because he had been fired. His landlord would not accept work in place of rent.

Thursday morning, he pawned the toaster oven for a gun. That would teach the fucking landlord. Maybe he should go practice with it at the library. After dragging it home in his coat pocket, through legions of plain clothes detectives, he went directly to the bathroom mirror and practiced "whipping it out." The barrel was truly magnificent. Perhaps the closest in life that anyone on the other end of it would get to infinity, that hole, without actually watching the bullet spin down the tube through the air and between the eyes. It should have the desired effect.

He broke it down and cleaned it on the broken stove. Tomorrow: bullets. Then a trip to some likely prospects, to "case" them well. Chance favored the prepared crook, he was sure. He put the gun in the refrigerator, wondering if he could pawn that.

That night he was invited to eat at the Zavala's apartment. The father, Jesus, the name sounded like "Hey, Zeus," was home. The children were surprisingly well-behaved for dinner. He sat between the two young girls, Blanquita and Paquita, with black hair; everyone had black hair.

He complimented Jesus on his family.

"Them hellions, the devil's own, come down on me laughin, carryin on, pokin my eyes and ears. No peace at all here," he laughed good-naturedly."

"¿Hay que comer, no?" Antonio asked.

"Everyone has to eat," Jesus answered, "but only after the prayer."

Walker bowed his head with the others.

Papaya, corn, tomatoes, avocados, chiles. The food was hot and hot. He ate it anyway, thinking. Eating dominates our lives, as it does every animal's. Food occasions are social occasions. Food sharing marks the completion of the successful hunt or successful season. Even for the unsuccessful. He watched everyone eat: the greatest concentration went into eating; the stare that greets an arriving plate is as intense as any received by a mouse from a cat. The dining room was small. Everyone sat so their backs were to a wall. The food was delivered from the front. He wondered if they expected an attack. He talked about astronomy. They all spoke of cars and marriages.

He complimented Citrona on her cooking, and offered to help wash the dishes.

"No, I aint no proper cook," she said modestly, adding, "No you cannot help with dishes. They are assigned it."

Antonio said, "I'm finished," and got up.

"Then do the dishes," Citrona said.

"No, not doing dishes neither."

Citrona nodded to the two girls, who cleared the table.

Two days later, he was entirely out of money. With his last quarter, he bought a package of jello, figuring it gave him the most for his money. He rushed it home and mixed it. Then refrigerated it. While it was cooling, he started his last book, The Death of Vergil. An appropriate subject. When he tasted the jello, however, it was awful. Raspberry, but sour, very sour. He took the box from the trash bag and read the label. It was unsweetened. He'd chosen the wrong box. He went back to reading, in disgust.

He had forgotten his gun, when the first opportunity presented itself. While some middle-aged sow was writing a check at the counter, as if in a contest to write the longest essay possible, he grabbed the tens from the open drawer and ran out of the store before the clerk could even shout. He heard shouting, though, as he ran around back. He zig-zagged over five blocks. He stuffed the money into a pocket, after he realized that he was still holding it. He slowed down to a walk. When he passed the C&L store, he realized that he would need a razor blade. He hoped no one would remember him. At least it wasn't the store down the block from his apartment. He had to use one of the tens. It felt like free money.

He counted it out on the bathroom sink. Forty dollars, tens, plus nine more or less in change. That meant there had been five bills in the drawer. Enough for rent. He went out for a steak.

He had shaved and cut his hair. He dressed neatly, believing it made him invisible. He was afraid to try banks or pawn shops. Super markets made him a specialist. He carried the gun in front, under his belt, and under a too large jacket. Carrying the gun was making him very nervous. The robberies were making him nervous, too.

One morning, he almost shot someone in the basement. The young man, Erardo, gave him a packet and fled. Walker looked in it and saw the fine white powder. He laughed maniacally. After all he had been through. He carried it upstairs, laughing. The basement must be a local sales district, he thought.

He snorted it. He kept coughing it back out. But, he felt calm. He was dizzy, so he went to bed, and slept for two days.

He returned to the basement and waited, reading a new book. After an hour, he heard two male voices in the hall.

"Telling you, it's nothing!"

"Fuck you."

"Dont be an asshole."

"Get the fuck away!" shouted the first one.

"You're shaking. You sick or something?"

"Something, fuck, I'm burnin up. Need it now."

Then the second one saw Walker, ""?Como te llamas?"

"Me llamo Joe. Me puedes llamar Joe," Walker smiled, pleased with a few more new words.

"Yea, sure, you can call me Nao," the second pursed his lips, thinking, cop or not-cop. "What'a you think?" he asked his companion, who was holding his arms around his abdomen now.

"Trato de no pensar mucho en estas cosas," Walker answered automatically, realizing that he really did not try to think about things too much anymore.

The first started towards Walker, muttering "fuck."

"Clamate!" urged the second, "Calm down. He might have money."

"I do," said Walker.

"Buena," said the first.

"I was hoping to trade it," Walker said.

"For what?" asked the second.

"A few moments of powdery pleasure," Walker answered.

"We can do that. We are businessmen. The rates our set by our suppliers, however. We need twenty per."

"I only have twenty," Walker fingered his shirt pocket.

"Let's trade, then," the first held a packet in his right hand.

Walker held the bill in his right hand, and they performed a little dance of grabbing and letting go. With his left hand holding the packet and his right hand empty now, Walker said, "Gracias."

The two turned and left without another word.

Walker went up to the roof and back down to his apartment.

He studied it. What if it was just powder or something more deadly, he wondered. Then, if it was poison, he would still get high, but it lowered the chances of future opportunities. Ah, well, the mark of an addict, which he knew so well from his job, was to continue regardless of wither possibility. He opened the packet.

He looked in the mirror. The mirror is cold, impenetrable, cannot get inside unless you are en muerto. I not, but have ghosts inside me, ghosts of losses and time, but also jaguars and eagles. To run, fly.

Soon, he needed coke just to get keyed up. It felt like the coke was doing all the moving and he was just getting carried along. He started changing apartments, renting just rooms, now. It was cheaper and easier to move.

He figured that he would run out of markets long before he ran out of rooms. Then he started going to movies to relax. He exhausted the good comedies and the bad comedies, then the horror movies, westerns, and adventures. Then the cheap ones and really dull ones. How could so many bad movies get made? He discovered the pornos, but the formula was too simple to hold his interest past the third one. Each cock and cunt was presented like the inside of a pump might be analyzed by a group of mechanical engineers. There was little excitement in the five hundredth view of a piston pumping up and down a cylinder.

In desperation, he began listening to music; any band, concert or singer that happened to be playing, although he hated to be with people in the light and hated to be seen by them. Walking down the street after a concert one afternoon, he heard a shout, "Hey!"

He looked around in curiosity, but saw a policeman, looking at him.

"Shit!" he expelled and took off immediately. He felt the gun like a lead weight under his stomach. Why had he brought it? Because it was too dangerous to leave in the room, stupid.

"Halt!" came the next command.

He didn't bother to look around, just dived in the bushes. He was near the river. He saw a marmot hole and rammed the gun in it without hesitating. His diaphragm hurt. He wasn't used to panic running. He circled back toward the Fifth Street bridge, hoping that the cop had dutifully tried to catch him. As he came out from the brush, he saw the cop waiting at the bridge, resting. Shit! he thought, but all he could think to say was "Hi."

The police officer signaled him to a police cruiser at the other end of the bridge. They were both too tired to run;

'Not like television' thought the officer, keeping in back of the fellow who had run from him once.

"Nice of you to come back this way for me. Please put your hands on the roof, spread your legs." Walker felt the patting remotely, he had ditched the gun; he surreptitiously wiped his hands on his trousers when he was told to turn around. He looked up at the officer, noticing that he had fine features, or features at all, hearing the words "name and address" put to him.

"Angel Zavala," he replied, relieved that he hadn't said Jesus.

"You don't look like an Angel" came the statement from another officer coming towards the car. Walker shrugged his shoulders.

"Does he fit the description?"

"Yes, I think so— Dark complexion, 5'11", dressed in brown." replied the first officer.

"Spic, y'mean, this shit's greasy enough. We're taking you in buster, hop in the limo," the second officer turned to address Walker.

Walker accepted the fact that a Hispanic name put him in a mold with these men. He wondered if he had given an English or German name, von Richtofen, instead—would he be given more respect.

"Aren't you going to read him his rights, first?"

"Fuck his rights, get in."

The ride in the car was uneventful.

"Spic limo," the driver was snickering, while the younger officer observed protocol, reading him his rights.

"But why are you taking me in?" Walker asked, not sure where "in" was.

The driver answered, "Suspicion," and snickered again.

He didn't pursue it. Oddly, he felt like a dignitary visiting the city, being chauffeured to an important meeting. The police car wove around other, slower drivers. People glanced into the car at stoplights, but he didn't favor them with a look.

When he asked again, where they were going, the young officer replied, "Jail, probably." The station was a block fortress built on a slight grassy rise—another federal building, Walker recognized. The LA County Jail, with a view of the tracks. It resembled a rest area off a turnpike or highway, surrounded on all sides with groomed grass and neatly clipped trees. The car drove around back. At some signal or code, a large door lifted, allowing the car to drive inside the lowest level. He waited until the car stopped and the first officer came back to let him out.

As he got out his heart started beating faster, his breathing becoming shallow. He almost slipped.

"Careful," warned the young officer, steadying him with a hand.

Walker looked down at the concrete floor, "Why is this so smooth?" he asked.

"Let's say it facilitates moving people to where they may not want to go," he explained.

"It's for drunks, peaceniks, commies, coons, and spics like you," added the bitter officer.

Bitter and sweet thought Walker, good team. He was lead into a bright hall, where he waited as the officers exchanged the code words and numbers that would determine his disposition.

He was led to a small room, where he answered questions about his name and address, his parents names, his occupation, and his whereabouts on certain days. He answered honestly, he thought, giving the Zavala name, an old rooming house address, New York names and addresses for imaginary parents, an occupation as welder currently looking for work; he told them he was at the library during the times for which they expressed so much interest. He overheard them describe the man they wanted; since he didn't look anything like that, he wasn't particularly worried. What did worry him was his suitcase of clothes at the rooming house. He had to get back there within three days.

He was led into another hallway, one side of which was lined with half-barred doors. He was given the third cell. He didn't notice it much, just lay down and went to sleep. The trial was short. He wasn't even sure it was a trial until a sentence was imposed. Seven years! He could get up seven years. He didn't even know what they were doing. For a car? What car? He hadn't stolen a car. He didn't even know how to drive! An officer led him from the court, hand-cuffed. When he protested, the officer said the he couldn't judge, regretfully. He hadn't waived his rights somehow, had he? He was taken back to his cell to await transfer in the morning. Walker couldn't stop thinking, now. The immediate past was like a manuscript on which the typewriter struck every other key. He could make out some of the words, but the sentences didn't make sense. He wondered when had he had coke last?

Chapter 9. In the Bamboo Dragon

The bus took the Pomona Freeway, east, from LA, out to Central Avenue, and then south. His first sight of the outside of the prison wall reminded him of a dam, a gray-white wall holding back the waters of chaos. San Ramon Correction Facility. Behind the wall, twenty five smaller buildings. From the van he was taken to the reception block. This was slow going because of the leg irons—"stupid fucking death march"—he couldn't even gesture with his cuff fastened to his belt. He was unshackled, strip-frisked, and assigned a temporary cell.

He was locked in. The cell was clean, with a steel bed on one wall; a small steel sink, a small topless toilet. In the opposite corner, near the ceiling was a camera, in a little cage by itself. The door closed with finality. He would always be able to call up the echo in memory. He put the issue on the bed and looked around.

"You'd better make that up if you want to eat," warned the guard.

He looked down at his green cloth.

"Mom wanted me to be a man of the cloth," he said testing his voice in the cell.

He listened and could hear every word spoken in every cell down the line:

"—so, then she— "

"Aw, shit! ya don' know shit!"

"—peas for dinner—"

"—then I says— "

He could identify the smells of food processed by twenty other bodies. He sat on the bed and wondered what had happened to his meager possessions; maybe they would be put in storage, until he could claim them. The sweater from Goodwill cost $2.00. He was lucky to have it; it would take time looking to find one better. His coat; the books; the new cassette player. Damn, that had cost $29.00; stolen money, but just as hard to get. What would he do for music? What would he do at all? He didn't know. He didn't want to eat. When nothing happened, he went to sleep, feeling hungry, tired, and trapped.

He woke in the middle of the night. No dope! Oh, shit. He cried out. No dope. He needed it. He got up angrily, throwing his blanket. Miserable, he drank from the sink, hoping that water would fill some of his need. It didn't. He felt nauseous. He slammed his hand on the iron, then his head. He shouted his need, but didn't hear the tired chorus of "Shut ups" and "fuck-offs" echoing in reply. He slammed his hand on the bed, again, relishing the pain.

He was assigned standard issue clothing and given a number: 18791. The number was on his clothes and in his brain. As long as he had that number, he would never have a name. He was issued one sheet and one blanket, then escorted to another cell.

Because everyone was "busy," he had to wait three days to complete the "reception process," as it was called. He was photographed for an identification card; the name 'Angel Zavala' looked strange on it, but he remembered it. He was given a blood test and another haircut. He was glad that he had cut it short for his short career as a robber, when he saw how merciless the barbers were. Later he learned that they expected to be tipped before performing their service. He was issued a pair of earphones and a copy of the prison rules, 35th edition. Before he could get a permanent cell assignment, he would have to interview with the classification committee, which made all job assignments. He didn't want to stand out in here. If he told them he had worked in astronomy or with computers, they might check that. Shit, that was the start of his troubles. But what could he do, carpentry, painting? He had told them welding, but he didn't know jack shit about welding; it had always looked hot and uncomfortable.

Better be consistent, he told himself. It didn't matter. He was assigned to the paint shop. Later, he found out that that was the only opening available and he was lucky to get that. At least he would be 'employed' and painting wasn't that hard. Painter, grade 1, $0.506 per day. If he could get transferred someday to an industrial shop he would make $0.550 per hour. Prison reminded him of the Air Force. When he had requested astronomy research or radar, they had assigned him to the medical corps. As a technician, for Christ's sake! His life had always been out of control.

Eight permanent cell blocks, each 300 feet long, 50 feet wide, three stories high. Eighty-four cells per floor; forty two in a company. At last, the knowledge would have pleased his father, he was a company man. He was assigned a closed block in B (closed meant that there was a 12 foot hall outside the cells surrounded by the barred windows of the cell block). B block was for vocational groups; A was for academic; C was farm; D was kitchen workers. He wouldn't find out about the other four until later. C and D could watch the televisions on their blocks; A and B had none. C and D were privileged because their work was considered harder and dirtier. They had more time for showers, laundry, watching, and goofing off. Inmates of all the blocks were locked in at 5:00 p.m.

All cells were the same size; six feet wide, eight feet four inches long, seven feet nine inches high— he had paced his off, even jumping toward the ceiling. The back and sides were steel plate, the front was steel bars with barred doors. There was the single bed with the steel frame

119

and foam mattress, small sink, small topless toilet, and a small steel locker, stool, and a bare 100-watt bulb in the ceiling; nothing new. His cell was on the third floor, the least desirable, in the middle, upstairs (no elevators), coldest in the winter, hottest in the summer (no air conditioning), furthest from anyone, but facing the yard, not a wall. He saw a roach. Wondered if it was anyone he knew.

Outside, there were two yards, one for football or baseball, the other divided into areas for television, cards, volleyball, basketball, shuffleboard, and weights. His first day in the yard, he was approached by a mild, little fellow, who offered to have his holiness pray for him. Irritated, Angel told him to butt off, then turned away and ignored him. He was satisfied when the little man went off and left him alone. He wondered what that cretin could possibly have done to get in here; embezzlement, he decided. Shortly after, another prisoner approached him, selling nutmeg.

"Nutmeg?" asked Walker, thinking this joker was a mad cook, "I need junk, snow, coke, dust! Not nutmeg!"

The black man left, shaking his head knowingly. When a guard offered to sell him Benzedrine, he realized that he had nothing to buy with, yet. His first day at the paint shop was an exercise in waiting. No one seemed to be in any hurry around here. Guess why, he realized. There was only one job order, and four of them waiting to fill it. Well, it sure wasn't going to be him, on his first day. The others divided it up. One checking out the paint; another checking on ladders and tarps; the third, obviously the painter, waiting for the others to get set up so that they could leave. Walker was assigned the coffee pot. They would be back in an hour or so. Would he be so kind as to have coffee and rolls for them. He would, indeed. Of course, he would. He knew where the butter lay.

Checking out of the shop was a contest of wit. The guards wanting to search everybody and account for everything. The workers wanting to smuggle paint, brushes, alcohol, whatever, back for trading. Walker learned by watching. Soon he would be trading paint for drugs himself, he hoped.

He went to dinner. Just like a cafeteria. The line; trays; overcooked food. Tonight was hamburger casserole, with bean salad, jello, bread and butter, unidentified red fruit drink, probably apple, raspberry, grape, and spit. He aimed for the whitest table, but found that he was excluded; even the vacant seats were taken. Well, he didn't fit with the blacks. That left the Mexicans, Texicans, Puerto Ricans, Spanish contingent; they were as varied as the blacks or whites.

"I guess it must be in the names," he muttered to himself. He sat down to a few nods. "Home at last," he smiled.

Ninety teeth aimed back at him. Probably all for cars and hubcaps, he thought. The blacks are all in for muggings and drugs; the anglos, as he thought of them now, for embezzlement, rape, and murder.

During dinner everyone, by some mysterious convention, talked only of food. His table wanted to add fish and pork to the menu. The blacks wanted to subtract fish and pork from the menu. The anglos didn't care as long as they got more of it. But there was no choice on the menus and no substitution; and no pepper.

"Too dangerous, man" replied one heavy-set Indian-looking man, to his question, "could blind you in a fight, could blind guards in a fight, so we don' get it."

It had been explained to him that all inmates were required for all meals, but he noticed quite a few vacancies.

"They out on business, man" was the answer, but he didn't feel like pursuing it. He also learned that everyone made the Sunday dinner. That was when the good meat was served. The only good meat, everyone agreed.

On his way out of the shower, he was surprised by a group that seemed to be waiting for him. A test, he knew, but he wasn't ready for a test.

Scared and angry with the threat, he tried to push through them, muscles so tight that he couldn't talk. Two of the bigger ones grabbed his arms and bent him over the sink. He took a deep breath, thinking they were going to drown him. But as he felt his trousers being pulled down, another fear blossomed in his chest. He pushed backwards and to each side, but they were holding him tightly. He shouted his helplessness and tightened his buttocks. But hands forced them apart. He felt something hard press into his ass, then his sphincter muscles stretched and released. His arms and legs screamed with tension. He felt it move in an out, pressing in. He tried to push away, but was pushed back harder.

"Hold him!" came the threat. Then he pushed forward into the sink, helped by his assailants, who expected him to push backward. He jammed his heel back toward his own buttocks and was rewarded with a scream of pain from someone.

He heard his assailant, "Sme, long-dick, buck bender, all night grinder, here to grind you, and remind you ..."

Another voice: "gonne be my cow, too."

Then, the intruders were gone, but he was being slammed by fists aiming for his face and balls. He pulled his legs into the sink and wrapped his arms around his head; as he was being pulled out, he uncoiled and threw his fists out past the others' arms. Then he hit the floor. He started to swing back, but it was hard to breathe, then there was no one there. He must have lost consciousness. His anus was on fire, his face was a dull ache; his arms and legs felt as though they had been stretched too far, then beaten; his kidneys felt like broken bags. He tried to stand up, but his trousers were still around his legs; he pulled them off, taking his shoes in the process. He fell over headfirst.

"That's the way you wuh bohn," came a voice, "only meybe smaller and less huhtfull."

Angel backed up against the wall, making weak fists, looking up out of eyes that seemed to have shrunk in the flesh.

"No worry, no worry," assured the voice of the old Cyrus, "Lucky, you coulda been paralogized. But, now you establish that you bad. You pass. They jus have to tes' the new fish, see where they fit in."

"Fish?" Angel asked.

"Fish." Cyrus affirmed, "New boys is fish, like outa water, dig?"

"Dig?" Angel was afraid this mish mash of jazz was beyond him. "Help me," he begged, too beaten to care.

"I'm helpin' ya, jus don' see the doc and don' tell, understan'? Best rabbit away now."

He woke again, to no one; he was in a closet or something. He dragged himself to his cell, bent over in pain. On his bed, he began to inventory the pain.

"Okay, medic, what's wrong," he asked himself.

"Just scratches and bruises," he reassured himself. One of his balls had swelled; bruises on his thighs; two fingers couldn't straighten, probably broken— he slammed them against the bed, whimpering in his throat; when they were straight, he tied them together. Throat, ribs sore on right— from the sink, probably, cracked possibly, broken maybe; one eye was swollen shut; some fluid was leaking out of his anus. He sat up on his bunk, ready to kick the shit out of anyone who came in. He was going to have to wait for lock-up like this, he realized. He was afraid— he could never be on guard all the time.

When he heard the guard, he lay on his face until the door clicked. When he woke, everyone else was up. He got up for breakfast. He was starving. He had to eat. He had to control his anger enough to eat.

But after he got his tray, with potatoes, eggs, and fruit, he saw two of his attackers at the anglo table. He launched out of control. Without hesitating he threw his tray at the blonde one and aimed a punch at the head of the other. They scrambled at each other on the floor until they were pulled apart. Angel was too tired to move his arms. He was pushed from the dining hall and he went back to his cell.

He knew from experience that eating took energy away from healing, so he decided to fast for three days, until he could control his rage. The next morning, he sat up to the scrutiny of the servant of God, who was watching him from outside.

"I will pray for your soul. Please join me." he said sincerely.

"Fuck off creep! Take your sniveling god with you!" Angel shouted.

"You are possessed by Satan," pointed the worm.

"I am Satan, worm!" he replied, getting up naked from his bed, menacing with his good eye and good fist.

He heard someone laughing as the worm hunched back to more fertile soil. Well, he thought, Satan was an angel, and I am Angel, so it's fitting. He found that he was less anxious if he was walking or moving somehow. He was careful to be late for eating or work; everyone else steamed to the front early for the best food or jobs. Regularly, he would curse God and humanity, throwing trays and paints— whatever he could find to throw— at inmates who irritated him. His Puerto Rican friends, friends by default, would warn him not to curse God. Soon, they called him Satan. Later, however, everyone called him that. Somehow, it was more comfortable than "Angel." He learned to like the regular solitary confinement; Satan with no angels to accompany him.

The penalty for breaking a minor prison regulation was a warning, or an infraction slip, if the proper attitude wasn't displayed during the warning. Infractions included spitting, loud noise, messiness. For the second infraction within 90 days, the prisoner was keeplocked in his cell until he could be seen by the Adjustment Committee. For a serious offense, like assault, he was taken to the segregation block until the Committee met. Angel remembered the first time, for the cafeteria 'infraction,' when he was cuffed before the Committee. The charges were read to him and he was invited to comment.

"Tripped," was all he could think of to say.

"But are you guilty of striking Bill Moran?"

"Oh, yes, as I tripped, yes I must have."

"You did," affirmed the talker, who must have been the Chairman of the Committee. "And your punishment in this instance shall be keeplock for a week. Are we all agreed? Yes? Then sentence is pronounced."

And he was locked in his cell for the week. The second time cost him solitary for a week.

Sometimes when he was in solitary, he would hear old 'Cryin' Curtis sit outside and sing. He could not figure Curtis out, since he seemed to move with the anglos and Spanish as well as the blacks. This time, it was from "No Rest."

"so tired of living   so tired of movin   want to park my body, and rest   but everyone say 'go!'   there aint no reverse gear   even if it stopped   no guarantee you start again   body has no battery   and no electric starter   so you keep the motor on   and you keep on goin."

He tried to thank Curtis for helping him. He spoke first, "Thanks fo helpin after da bookooing bad-ass buckras."

Curtis looked at him for a moment, and then replied, ""Doubtless you think you have learned the linguistic code of our argot, but please do not try to use it."

"What?"

"I speak several languages: Vanilla English is one. As well as chocolate, carmel, and strawberry. Just speak normally."

Angel looked at him, noticing the fine wrinkles around the neck and ears. He had no idea what to say. So, he said nothing, just nodded. Later he understood the flavors were anglo, black, hispanic, and indian. He also learned to understand the flavors automatically.

"And the music?"

"Blues is the Devil's music. Dreams as pure brothers," Curtis answered.

After he left, Angel would repeat the song to himself.

Then he was out again, back home, to his cell. Because he hadn't turned in the men who had beaten him— he never told anyone about the rape—

he had credit with the anglos. Because he hadn't gone to the hospital, he had credit with the staff; too many hospital visits for beatings reflected badly on the prison's reputation. But, as a result of his violent behavior, he was required to see the part-time psychiatrist on duty, Dr. Korswamy, an Indian. Dr. K.

After he was escorted to Dr. K's office, the treatment started.

"Please sit down. Are you comfortable?" asked Dr. K, with a crisp British accent and Indian lilt.

"No," Angel said.

"Why not? Is the room too cold?"

"No, I'm here with you, instead of working."

"But, it is free. You have to pay nothing."

"And you get what you pay for?" Angel asked too sharply.

"The taxpayers get what they pay for, rehabilitation; you pay for what you got." K. answered levelly.

"But, I didn't get anything. I don't even know what color it was supposed to be."

"What is it do you mean?"

"The car."

"Well, tell me about it, " K. invited. "But first tell me about yourself."

"It's in the record, on your desk."

"No, that is never accurate, is it? Tell me about your parents."

"They were born, lived and died."

"Perhaps if you remembered them in more detail," K. suggested, playing with his pencil.

Angel didn't feel like it; it seemed so out of place, so he tried to reverse the questions, "Why are you here?"

"I?" K. seemed surprised, as if no one had ever asked him a personal question; perhaps no one had. He did have a certain remote dignity.

While he was digesting the question, Angel tried again, "Are there many Indian psychiatrists in public service?"

"Are there? Yes, I suppose there are, indeed," And K. told him of his scholarship to Johns Hopkins, and how he stayed in the Norwegian Sailors' home in Baltimore when he first arrived, and how he worked toward his present position. "I wanted to stay. I had become accustomed to the freedom and luxury."

"You mean you couldn't have had luxury in India?" asked Angel, guessing that K. must have been a Brahmin to get any special education.

"No, not luxury, exactly, but benefits, highways, schools, supermarkets."

So they discussed supermarkets, before K. remembered to answer the one question. "The money paid for public service is far less than for private practice, where I could charge $75.00 an hour or more. But to an Indian or Pakistani, it is harder to start privately and build up a stable of clients. The money for public service, of course, is far more than I would have earned in India."

Angel dreaded the conversation turning to him. K seemed to realize that and steered obliquely away during the first session.

But he did ask Angel to consider how he spent his time in prison. "You should improve yourself. Ninety-nine percent of the inmates dedicate themselves to making their stay comfortable. Like American tourists in Europe," he smiled to himself, "they never learn more than they have to. Take courses, learn a trade or skill. If not for yourself, then for the parole board, who love to report real cases of rehabilitation. You might consider being less violent and less anti-religious. The board likes its prisoners to have religion, also," he concluded sadly.

Shit, Angel thought. Another suggestion; another no-choice situation.

Walking back to the cell, he noticed how comfortable some of the 'homes' were; many prisoners had extra pillows, rugs, paints, typewriters, brushes, shampoos, hot plates, dress shirts, calendars. Calendars; everyone seemed to have a calendar of some kind, with a young woman in some state of undress. Some of the centerfolds were true down to the hair. Then, he noticed that most of the cons were healthy, not bent over or worried, ulcerous or overweight, like the guards. He caught the attention of a guard and asked to be locked in. He considered the guards good-humor men, with keys. Their rounds were so regular, it was like living near a subway or train station. He hoped that he never crossed one of them. Most of them seemed okay, although some dealt dope and sold favors.

The mail came around again. Again, he got nothing. But, then, no one knew where he was. Inmates could receive two packages per month from persons on an approved mailing list. The package could contain food, clothes, sundries, and five cartons of cigarettes per month. Cigarettes were limited because of their value as currency inside. He was able to trade paint for cigarettes, and retrade the sticks for fruit or wood— for his bookcase. Some of the cons got cash, wrapped in aluminum foil with chicken in their packages, or dope mixed in tea bags. He had finally gotten some marijuana, too late to do any good, but satisfying just the same. He couldn't afford to have it as a habit, though.

During dinner once, he derailed the talk of food by asking every man's second favorite question, "How'd you get in here, Jorge? Juan?" Cars, cars, cars, all right, with a mugging or robbery for spice. The talk switched to the difference between street criminals—his club—and chair criminals, the anglo white collar nabs. He was in the five-to-seven society, for cars. But, a stock broker who had stolen millions from the mutual funds of old ladies might get only four months to a year, some of it suspended. Maybe the judges identified more with the Harts, Schaffner and Marx set. Most of them at the table were serving indeterminate sentences, two to four, five to seven, five to fifteen. He himself might get parole after three and one half years. Juan told him he might try collecting good time, ten days for every thirty days served on good behavior. Good time? He had never heard of it. He was also told about conditional release, CR, where the rest of the time was served on parole.

He was in, no getting around it. Better adjust. First a picture, then a journal, then a trade, then a class, then parole, then freedom, a restaurant, apartment, profession, friends, success, fame, all mapped out— normal ambitions, not too much to hope for. He took K.'s advice and signed up for classes.

The photograph was a Miss June, from Playboy probably, costing four cigarettes. She was lying across an air mattress away from the camera, the swell of bare buttocks rising from a string bathing suit pulled half-way down, her face turned back to the camera in surprise, one plump breast hanging down almost to the mattress. He liked it; it was modest and tempting, not open and vulgar. Beneath her leg he penned 65603. She had no real name, but he could give her a number, too.

The journal was only three cigarettes; possibly because it was all blank paper. He wondered if they sold pre-written diaries for dull people. He started it immediately, ambitious to record all of his observations and feelings.

History of Angel Zavala Arrived 6/12; overcast day

Daily schedule

6:30   wake up; exercise. 50 sit-ups, 25 push-ups, 25 knee bends, 25 windmills.

7:00   bell rings, length of ring depends on who is on duty

7:15   doors open; rush to breakfast to avoid crowd; eat fruit if available

7:30   proceed to work; frisked at checkpoint, sign logbook, leave pass with CO.

7:45   Arrive at shop; go over list of areas or items to paint; spend day reading in shop if no assignments.

8:15   CO checks in, Officer Kowalski, easy to get on with, good joke teller; today one about dying rabbi (in back of journal)

11:00 skip lunch, or dinner as it is called here— barbarians— since it is main meal. Visit kitchen room in shop area. Meckley is cooking small stakes, fried potatoes, onions and green peas. Always hated peas, but pay 40 cigs for small part. Excellent cooking, pity others eating jello.

11:40 back to work; repainting part of E cell block, gray of course. Sell quart of black to Jefferson for bench for $2.00 Cash!

2:25 finished, clean-up.

2:55 leave job area, get pat frisked, pick up pass and back home

3:05 arrive home, change clothes, wash up, smoke, lie down to listen to soft music on hard headphones

3:54 get up, smoke, try French inhale, fail, cough, regard course in geography, looked better than accounting but usefulness questionable; skip meal

5:00 bell rings, horses in stalls, doors close, body count, keep reading, don't bother getting up

6:00 go to night class in geography. Learn that it is cultural geography; cities, not soils; learn of birth of cities, trade routes, cultural centers. No mention of human   disposition to live together in ant hills.

8:35 back home; leftover cheese and tomato sandwich, read about citrons (fruits), smoke, think about sex

10:20 masturbate to the bottom of 65603, wishing her mouth were here at least. clean up, lucky no traffic write bout exciting day in journal.

Writing was hard work. It looked so shallow. After months of holding out, when he first started masturbating again, it was only safe in the dark, too many surprises otherwise. One of the most popular greetings was still "How many times, man?" He'd heard that some of the more social types engaged in "cuming contests" much like spitting contests.

By the next day he was desperate to write something interesting. He started with a typical menu, being sure to go to all three meals for research purposes only.

> Typical menu Breakfast Hot oatmeal   stewed prunes jelly donuts
>   coffee or milk roll or bread
> Dinner seafood patties   boiled potatoes spinach   bread   milk
>   sugar cookies Supper franks on buns bean salad   jello   bread
>   apple drink

Usually it was apple, which was the cheapest of juices; mixed with water, the cheapest of fluids. He wondered how many men had to go to all three meals because they had no friends or packages or cigarettes. He had too much time. The work day only lasted four hours or less, depending on the work. Maybe there was more work, but it didn't get done.

He added in the journal, "It's a dandy idea to curb unemployment; reduce everyone's work period to half. Women, the poor, the unemployed would all have work then. What's the catch?" He had read Catch 22 recently, and realized that everything had a catch. He began numbering the catches to his own reasonings. Catch 1 was government interest, which used unemployment to its own advantage.

Then he began numbering everything. The daily format of the journal was buried permanently.

> 4 of 5 cons have bad teeth
> 67% have tattoos;
> 80% of those on arms
> 71% have nicknames like Popeye or Dorkface
> 39% have relatives in prison
> 21% were identifiable as homosexuals
> 92% say they were innocent
> 14% were innocent in reality

He fitted into some of those categories; he had a nickname, and he was innocent, at least of grand theft auto (was it poetic justice, a miscarriage of justice, or fucked by the odds?) He wasn't sure of the homosexual percentage; it was hard to find out. Probably some had been converted the hard way.

He learned that the answer to any insult was to beat the shit out of the caller, who was usually new and anxious to prove himself. The ones who let remarks about their mothers and fathers pass, especially among Latino units, were considered trash. And treated that way. Once he proved himself sufficiently classy, by punching the time clock of some new-element druggy, he was left alone.

At first being a Latino was a new perspective. He had never understood minorities. Now he thought he did. The Latinos were outnumbered by blacks three to one; by anglos two to one. That meant they got the fewest concessions for food and dress, for recreation and church. Even native Americans got sweat lodges occasionally. Latinos called themselves Latinos, but everyone else called them spics; blacks called themselves blacks, but everyone else called them niggers; whites didn't call themselves anything but everyone else called them honkeys or fays.

He went to Catholic masses, for friendship and appearances, but faithfully recorded his impressions in his journal. He even confessed his lusts. At the same time, through the library, he got copies of Bierce, Twain, and Cioran. The Devil's Dictionary, Letters From Earth, and The Temptation to Exist. Those books restored his perspective. The journal cemented it.

"If we lived in heaven as described, people would turn to crime in desperation. All that is distasteful and dull in life we have put in heaven"—Twain saw that—singing, praying, loving God, playing harps. Could we sing without eating, love without touching, live without uncertainty? When time was dead we would kill ourselves in grief.

What sacrifice did Christ make? He took his life back three days later. Where's the sacrifice in a temporary inconvenience? Where's the responsibility in going back to heaven? .

Be fruitful and multiply was a criminal injunction. Flesh perpetuates like the plague; procreation is too pleasant. 'Be rare and stay valuable' would have been a better order. And harder to follow. .

Satan is the lord of the earth. Would not Satan, aware of the harmfulness of one of God's creations toward the others, cause it to perish? If Satan had power? .

A tale from Ambrose Bierce: Some explorers touched upon the shores of America, and one who professed to have penetrated a considerable distance into the interior, thought that God, Gold, Mob, and Dog stand for distinct entities, but "Frump insists that the natives are monotheists, each having no other god than himself, whom he worships under many sacred names."

Cioran had such an elegant argument for suicide that Angel had drafted several letters to announce his suicide to prison authorities.

Cutting the wrists was the best form of suicide; you are conscious, the risk is not great if the cuts are not too deep, it is always recognized as an attempted suicide, and it often achieved the desired results. The hospital seemed to have one suicide attempt in residence most of the time. Angel thought that starvation would be a better way, taking more time, being more reversible, indicating a more serious attitude. He fasted for five days. In his body in his former life, the one in Hawaii, the Greek ideal had been larded over with residues of fats and sugars, untempered by exercise. The ideal began to show through with unemployment—now it was chiseled in his flesh. He drank juices for two days before eating solid foods. He was pleased with the changes. Unemployment had cost fifteen pounds, prison twenty. He considered writing a diet book.

One day Cyrus brought around a memo for him to see. It had been stolen from the warden's desk. The memo dealt with changing the public image of the prison through use of proper terminology. The prison had already been renamed a correctional facility, but the hospital was to be referred to as "an in-patient component;" a sick-call was "an inmate health encounter;" a fight was "an anger-type situation;" and a riot was "a possible self-destruct scenario." Angel started laughing so hard he pounded his bed. He was still laughing as he entered parts in his journal, tears of humor staining that page. Cyrus began singing a song, called the terminal blues. Angel transcribed it.

"comin out aint goin out if ther's no way back
goin in may be comin in if the lines are track
guess id better be gone now thumbin out o town
disappearin down a smokin hole see me goin down
some words just wont do baby, not a two-way street
some words make a fire, some words fan the heat
but less you got more to cool em, ice em stop em,
aint no words get you out, oh no, none, uhh, ummm.
i got a case of the terminal blues long-term, life-time
terminal blues i didn't even lie, jus sentenced for some crime
nothin bout a trial just sentenced given life
wish this prison had some walls, a place to go
and if i ever got there, baby, id just know
i got a case of the terminal blues miserable cold,
never too old, terminal blues—

He liked that. He wondered why old Cyrus came around him. It wasn't a good idea. He asked him about it.

"You almost black. Next best thing: brown. Maybe you have a black grandma."

"No, but my father thought there was Chinese somewhere. Doesn't matter, though, does it?"

"Naw, doesn't. Les try the song again:

illinois central out of track,
no soft bed for this poor black.
bus station bus end of the line, no more money no way back;
got to walk on to get past too tired too late to get on, too dark,
don't know where i am, can't read signs, got to lie down,
don't care cover me with paper something say i can't last oh,

> long-term life-time terminal blues wish i had warmer shoes,
>   more pages in the news "

"Teach me to play?"

"Ask me again next month. That way I gage your seriosity."

Once, he had asked Cyrus why he was in. He pretended not to remember, but Angel persisted.

"Murder. I killed whitey."

"Murder?! for what?"

"Don't matter." was all he would give.

"You're right, it doesn't. 'To kill is just to create a vacancy without nominating a successor' said Ambrose Bierce."

"What? What's that mean? Who's Bierce"

"I don't know. He was a newspaper man. Bitter Bierce. I have the Devil's Dictionary, Want to read it?"

"Naw, don't read; you just keep quotin' him."

On the next Sunday, with Curtis, he went to one of the services favored by blacks. He sat beside Curtis and listened to various conversations: "What happened?" "Preacher preached an' sisters moaned. Clapped and slapped, chanted and hummed all night til that nigger was funeralized good. He's gone and dats dat. Meeting broke and followed home."

"You here to pray?" "Just play play, ain't doodly-squat."

"He doggit, but it don' signify nothin—"

"You so dumb you always callin' fifty-cent cash money." "Don' meddle me." "You so stupid you journey proud be in jail!" "You loud talkin me? Bitch!"

"Need some jam." "Pay this time?" "Chip a few nickles later." "After—"

Then the room settled down. The minister, who looked more like a pro-wrestler ending a mixed career, started speaking with an imposing thunderous voice, "Noooo, you WILL not gamble. That way leads to HELL!"

Angel listened to the rhythm of the words.

"They set you 'gainst your best friends lead you into numbers racket. Use dirt and filth, gravel dirt dead finger. Do NOT abide them," the preacher continued.

Angel looked around, without moving his head. Many were frowning, although Angel could not figure out why—virtually all of them were doing worse things every day. A few were smiling, but that may have had more to do with their immediate business dealings.

"Lucifer fell into a world of darkness—that's the world spiritualists penetrate."

Angel sat up, thinking well, that's the world the morning sun penetrates too. The preacher went on but did not mention Lucifer again. Apparently the sermon was on gambling and visiting the dead.

The preacher finished with a directive: "Take the bible. Ah want chew to read de Ninth Chapter of Psalms. Read it ovah three times for tuh bed. Sleep wi dat Bible under yore pillah."

The choir, only a few men, began to sing, so Angel joined with the others and sang spirituals. A mystery, that the human voice had such a range, and was used for so many unbeautiful things as well.

He took a journalism class. Awful, just awful. It was just like writing out of order. Putting the most important facts first leading down to the least important. Nothing every developed logically in a newspaper story. The headlines just got smaller until they disappeared in two-point type. One assignment was to interview someone. Angel decided to interview Patric Dixon, one of the guards; one who seemed honest and thoughtful. Dixon didn't like journalists.

"None of the guys like journalists. Those creeps show us up like sadists, then treat the prisoners like good guys, as if they were just here by accident or something."

"Why are you a guard?"

"Cause I couldn't hack it as a nuclear physicist. I couldn't get through the math. Why do you think? It was the only job I could get. I used to sell greeting cards, can you imagine, greeting cards. I got married to a girl, Yolanda; we had three beautiful kids."

"Do your kids know what you do for a living?"

"Sure, it's like being a policeman."

"Wouldn't you rather be a policeman?"

"I am a policeman, I police you don't I?"

"So you do, Who else don't you like, besides reporters?"

"Lawyers, those jerks are paid big money to get you cons out. Why shouldn't I be paid more to keep you in? It's harder. It's dirtier, it's thankless. Well?"

"I don't know. You don't hate baseball players, do you?"

"No, why should I?"

"They get more money than lawyers, they steal without getting caught."

"Ha, ha, ha. They're famous. Famous people always get more."

"Who else don't you like?" Angel asked, wanting to pursue the big money, America rewards its stars theme, but not wanting to spoil the interview.

"Social workers, those floppy-boobed cunts romanticize every con they see; and you romanticize them right out of their panties. All social workers should be over sixty, and paroled, not dumb college girls."

"Do you like cons?"

"Some, why? Quiet ones, you know the kind, don't talk, don't profane God, don't fight."

"I don't profane God," he started, winding down to a mumble, "just churches and their instruments." He pulled himself back to Patric, "Do you like anyone?"

"Yea, people, the victims. We're the ones that think of the victims, the ones that are left with the crimes, the ones without social workers, prisons, and rehabilitation programs. You guys got it easy. You just can't go out and get a beer, like I can; that's all."

Angel was silent for a moment, reflecting; Patric was right, but how would he conclude the interview. "What would you do for prisons, then, to improve them?" was the general question.

"Have a uniform national code, I guess. I don't know. Make the prisoners build their own walls, grow their own food, so taxpayers don't have to support the same people who attack them. Why should it cost $40,000 to support you for a year—I support four on $22,330? Besides, a lot of these guys know the inside—hell, that's all they know; it's a lifetime for them, even if it comes in chunks."

"Thank you, Officer. You have been very frank."

"We're finished, huh?"

"Yep, gotta go write it up for the Daily Globe. Be seein ya." Cornball, pure yellow journalismal cornball.

Walker never knew if he was making progress with Dr. K. All they did was talk, exchanging life stories and experiences. It was Dr. K's turn.

"I went to visit a friend of mine, on scholarship, at The University of The South," pronouncing each article as the most important noun. "in Tennessee. We were driving down from the college—you know, even in India and Europe, all colleges seem to be located on hills, perhaps for defense; you know this is not true in central and south America, where the colleges are in the center of town and the peasants and peons are permitted to live in the hills with the views of the town—I wonder if that is a cultural difference, perhaps it is just geographical, you—ah, where was I?"

"The The," Walker answered.

"Ah, yes, quite right. We were going down to the town for some beers. The driver, Jay, was not as attentive as he could have been and the car attracted the attention of local law enforcement officers. They stopped us and flashed their lights into the car on each of our faces. The officer with the light stepped back, drew his gun, and spoke to the other officer, "There's niggers in there," and then to his partner, "Cover me!"

and then to all of us, "Step out of the car and place your hands on the hood." I remember that well, since I mistakenly placed my hands on the roof and not the bonnet. They were very rude to us, calling us niggers and coons. One of the other students, Alan I think was his name, spoke to him, pointing out that our features—our noses and lips—were as fine as their own, that our hair was not woolly and that our bodies were smaller. He worked hard to explain the difference. The officer without the flashlight and gun laughed and threatened to lower our trousers. The other laughed and said something about fine niggers taking the place of hard-working whites. I did not feel that any whites had to work as hard as we did, but I held my tongue. After that, I did not return to the Southern states."

"Yes, I know what you mean about mistaken identity. Just a suntan or a name can determine so much of your life."

"And will you speak of yourself to me?"

"All I wanted was to study the properties of light,"

Dr. K. frowned and leaned forward, "How are you doing in your classes?"

His philosophy class, 'Introduction to Modern Thought,' wasn't very satisfying. To begin with, the instructor was a wimp. Dick Myers; mandatory beard and long hair. You could tell this guy was going to toilet train his kid right, had bought the biggest Swedish stereo available, and still conducted all-night think sessions on the meaning of life. He referenced all philosophical thought to his grandmother's visions and to his own philosophical niche, the later Marxist influence of Sartre. Philosophy was such an anemic discipline, too tired for activity, a refuge for the timid, who pursued its rational limits in their soft comfortable chairs, like Dutch burghers, not understanding that the universe was expressed by living, not argued tautologically for a conclusion.

The class started badly.

"Does anyone know the meaning of philosophy?"

Angel sat right up. "Philosophy is the love of wisdom."

"Very good—"

But Angel wasn't finished. "And wisdom is a function of exhaustion; rest transformed to vision, in the twilight of reason."

"Well, uuhhhm, that's a very, uhh, sophistical answer. But I don't really think you understand philosophy."

Angel could see the "C" forming in the grade book, so he shut up, happy that Dick—"just call me Dick"—had not recognized the paraphrase of Cioran, the French nihilist. As Dick droned on, Angel wondered if his wife called him "Dr. Dick." Maybe "Dr. Dick" was stenciled on his pajamas. Surely, Dr. Dick wore pajamas; and probably muffies on his feet. He started to fantasize about Dr. Dick as the hour wore on, past Descartes and Bacon, past Nietzsche and Kierkegaard, past the Tuesday night movie.

Introductory psychology was so interesting that he immediately wondered if it would make a good major. That was before he understood that everyone who took psychology did so to understand themselves better. Certainly that was the case with Rose Davis, who taught the introductory course. He was certainly interested in her mind also, and wanted to get there through her body. He was disappointed. She was not interested in his mind or his body, or anyone else's. She was a solipsist. No one else was real to her; other beings were cardboard props in her universe. And her universe had a decidedly ratomorphic flavor. Pavlov and Skinner were her Gods, but just bigger props, since they had essentially the same ideas that she had, just sooner. In fact, she would end every disclosure with the statement "See, here, Skinner says the very same thing, on page 37 of your text." A text that she had edited, of course.

Rats were larger than life. Rats were the totemic idol of psychology, although there were some who said that the pigeon was greater. Rats were bred, stumped, tortured, and killed for science. And vast tables of numbers were erected in their memory, of perfect Pythagorean numbers from their lives, and these numbers foretold of the human condition, of human needs and purposes. And the students in Psych 101 learned those numbers and learned to draw the right conclusions from them, and passed forth from the class with true knowledge and deep convictions.

In fact, Angel liked the experiments that could not be explained much better than the expected ones. The experiment on the experimenters, the experiment in the factory. What psychology couldn't explain was what attracted him to it. So he took the other courses, on the various degrees of human abnormality: pathological abnormality, learning abnormality, social abnormality, perceptual abnormality. Only once did he read about normality, in Maslow, but that seemed to be the future of psychology and not its past or present.

He took a poetry class to avoid another Shakespeare. Then he started writing poetry. And he realized that everyone wanted to write poetry. The urge to express was as great as the urge to reproduce. Maybe it gave more pleasure because it was harder (and had fewer taboos). He talked to others who wrote poetry. Everyone wrote prison poetry. It was what they knew best, themselves and their problems. He wondered if the suburban housewives who took the same course wrote a poetry of middle-class love, dish-washers, and beauty. He wondered what that was like. Most of his poetry also reflected the physical and psychological horrors of confinement. The lack of privacy, the smells of hundreds of open toilets, the cries of despondency, the violence, the rattling guards every two hours. One poem of his that he felt strongly about, because it evoked his Vietnam experience, he entered in his journal.

"eaten by a bamboo dragon captured by teeth and claws
and pulled down stomach passageways to lie in the humid darkness.
concrete walls and concrete floors planed smooth to ease resistance
iron stand with iron bowl iron bed with nylon covers that fall
when i wake exercise and clean memorize the grains repetition

without end — all life entertains changing guards, changing
seasons, changing me.

It had only gotten a B, even after he explained it. The bamboo prison
was a cong cage; it was also the Chinese ideogram for prison. But
Winston Mars liked iambic pentameter with masculine rhymes. He also
liked to toss his long white hair dramatically. The B grade stood.

He took the standard physics courses that he should have taken in the air
force. He learned how to describe the motions of projectiles and rotating
cylinders. It was necessary material.

Rivera interrupted him that night as he was working on his journal.

"Hey, man, the next sermon is on you— Satan."

Angel asked, "What do you mean?"

But Rivera only repeated, "It's on Satan. Be there. Be it."

Walker went the following day to the meager library, for research.

That Sunday, he went to a sermon on the 'Origins of Satan,' by
Reverend Miller Shehan. He arrived late and stayed in the back. The
reverend, in black, had already been introduced and had mounted the
low platform. He gazed in challenge at as his audience.

"Few of us," his voice projected through Angel, as if to reach the
men outside the room, who did not attend, "realize the part that angels
play, yes, still play, in human events. Even today, there is bitter conflict
between the holy angels faithful to God and the those allied in darkness
with Satan." He paused, glancing upwards dramatically.

"Once Satan, an archangel of God, was called Lucifer, 'the son of the
morning.' He, with Michael, was one of two archangels, the highest to
serve God, our Lord. But, he became jealous of man; he challenged God.
So, he was cast from heaven with his rebel forces by Michael. Although
he continues to fight, and may be winning some battles, the final
outcome is certain. He will be defeated and God will shatter the power
of darkness." Shehan glared as if daring anyone to defend the powers of
darkness, then continued.

"Many men have asked, 'How could this conflict disrupt God's perfect universe?' The Apostle Paul (II Thessalonians 2:7) calls it the 'mystery of iniquity.' While we have not been told by God, one thing is sure, the angels fell because they had sinned against God. The Scripture says (II Peter 2:4), 'God ... cast them down to hell, and delivered them into chains of darkness, to be reserved unto judgment.' A passage in Jude (6:4) puts the responsibility directly on the shoulders of those angels, who 'kept not their first estate, but left their own habitation.'

"The greatest of all catastrophes in the history of creation was Lucifer's defiance of God. One third of the angels joined him in his wickedness. And all this happened—"

Angel's attention wandered: so what did Lucifer do, tie a knot in God's shoestrings? Was Satan the same as Lucifer he wondered? He went out for a smoke, but soon looked back in.

"—and the great dragon was cast out. (Revelation 12:9) Now this battle that rages in heaven, rages on earth. Satan and his demons promote discord, start wars, spread hatred and murder and all foul things. They are dedicated to destruction."

Angel closed the door, again. This guy was using the Bible like a Hollywood script for the future. He would have to read it. He peeked in again.

"—committed the sins of covetousness and pride. The sin of pride has caused the downfall of many men. So strong is pride that it brought down the third of the heavenly host. So we mortals must be on guard against pride, lest we repeat the pattern of the demons."

He stood back and lit another cigarette. Would this buffoon never be through? He snuffed out the cigarette and went back in.

"— to raise doubts! It is deadly to doubt the Word of God! Satan's dastardly strategy is to persuade us to reason, as he did with Eve. Eve reasoned with the serpent and began to doubt the Wisdom of God! Satan went to work and the subtlety of his tongue, the clever 'ifs,' the if of this, the if of that, drove a wedge between Eve and her creator. With consequences for all history. This is where death began! And sin began! And we are depraved by nature! We inherit it from our parents (Romans 3:19). We each bear the sentence of guilt and the stain of sin. And Satan is still working to make us think 'if:' if I live a good life, if I go to church, if I do not covet or steal, if I help others! But! But these ifs do not meet God's requirements for salvation. Jesus said 'You must be born again' (John 3:7). We can only find eternal life in Jesus Christ. Say yes to Christ, now! Come to Christ now!" Shehan bowed his head to pray.

Many in the audience did. Angel wanted to see this man up close, but decided to wait. As he headed around back, he remembered a comment from K.: "Christianity is the only religion where the adherents are born into the church. When the Hindu, Jain, or Buddhist is born again, it is out of the church."

He met Shehan afterwards, armed with his research.

"That sermon was a lie," he started.

"Oh, how—what do you mean?" Shehan did not seem to be upset.

"The fall of Lucifer. That wasn't so."

"Oh, and, uuhhm, what is the truth then," Shehan smiled, because he liked a challenging argument.

"It goes like this: When God made Adam, he told the angels to bow down and honor his latest creation. But the archangel Lucifer refused, saying 'You created us from light, from the splendor of your glory; would you then have us adore a being made from dust?' God answered that Adam surpassed even Lucifer in understanding. God was so proud of his creation that he boasted without being sure. From his own pride, Lucifer replied that if this was so, then God should test him against Adam to increase his understanding of God's creations. God was forced to accept this challenge, and sent Lucifer to earth to name the beasts and birds as God would have had them named. If he succeeded then God agreed that Adam would have to reverence his wisdom, but if he failed then he would have to praise Adam's understanding. The angels witnessed. But when the animals passed before Lucifer, he could not speak. He failed with the ox and cow, the first two to present themselves, and he failed with the camel and donkey. Then God turned to Adam, questioning him about the names of the same animals, using the first letter of each question to point to the beast's name; and so Adam named each creature. That is the divine comedy: that God cheated, giving Adam the advantage. God was jealous of his creation, and protective. When he saw this Lucifer yelled at God in frustration. Jealous of the position of Adam, stung by unfairness, Lucifer refused to praise Adam. Then Michael and over half the angels demanded that he do so. He refused, and fought, and fell."

"And what do you make of this?" asked the preacher, mildly amused, maybe irritated at the coherence of the story.

"God taught Adam to recognize the signature of all things. Lucifer, at a cost, learned this better. Dust, which had been the furthest thing from divine light, nevertheless, closes about a mystery and expresses the infinite in its own way, with language. Now, we have come to understand that dust is an aspect of light; frozen light, solid light. Furthermore, the whole thing could have been avoided if both God and Lucifer had not been consumed by their own pride—at least as it was reported by the human reporters." Angel was possessed by words himself, not having thought of them before he spoke. He was riding the words, as surely as an ocean current.

"And who are you, who knows so much, and is in prison?"

"I am Lucifer," he answered simply.

Neither spoke for a moment. Shehan's imagination was scattering clues in all directions. He could not speak. He looked at the eyes of the other, bright, perhaps from insanity.

Angel was amused by the sudden stillness. "Did you expect something from the inferno? Three heads and bats wings, tears mixed with blood and pus, rake-like teeth under matted hair and frozen crusts, pinched and prisoned in ice? I too sleep under the stars. What are walls and bars?"

When Shehan was still silent, Angel quoted from Ecclesiastes, "Truly the light is sweet, and a pleasant thing it is for the eyes to behold the sun."

Shehan had concluded that the young man was mad. Madness takes odd forms. Perhaps he was in league with Satan. He would humor him for a moment, and then—"Well, Satan—"

"Not Satan, not some small Babylonian king. Lucifer, 'the son of morning,' bearer of light," Angel corrected.

"God is omniscient and all-powerful," Shehan started, forgetting the big word for all-powerful, and hesitating, "He would know about Lucifer, his pride." Shehan didn't like the thought of pride associated with God.

"Yes, then Lucifer acquired more understanding than Adam." Angel began. "He turned Adam's strength against him. Consider what happened to Adam afterwards. Because of his naming the animals, Adam noticed that he alone was unpaired, and lamented his dissatisfaction. God was moved to create a mate for him, not out of dust, but out of sediment and filth. He created Lilith and presented her to Adam, who was overjoyed and pushed her down before him, to mount her like an animal. When she refused to be dominated, Adam tried to force her, but she would not be forced, and spoke the magic name of God, 'Shem hamephorash,' the Ineffable Name, and rose into the air and away from Adam. As Lucifer had revolted against God for unfairness, Lilith revolted against Adam. Poor Adam. God made another woman under Adam's childish gaze. But when Adam saw how the woman was made, dust and water to flesh and blood, he was offended. And he rejected that woman, too. So God put Adam to sleep and made a mate out of part of Adam. Poor Adam. She he mounted, but she was seduced by Lucifer with the same language that Adam used to defeat Lucifer, the language of reason. So, Eve was blamed for using reason? Was God too weak to withstand reason—"

"Enough, enough! A cute enough story," Shehan began, knowing he could call upon authority to dispense with this upstart. "But the Bible tells us how God created Adam and Eve, and drove Satan from heaven with lightening. God is perfect. He has no pride."

"But that's it, you see, God was perfect. How boring. What a dilemma. The perfect God creates the perfect universe, peopled with perfect beings, angels, that is. They all love him; he loves them; they all love the universe. But God can imagine its undeviating movement for eternity. No surprises. God wants more. He puts the seed of doubt in his brightest angel. He puts the seed of chance in the apple of the universe. The universe is seeded with light. He slows down light, and matter precipitates from light. The universe is a little free from God. Will it be predictable? Will it love God or not? Will freedom drive it from him. Perhaps he does not care. He has made something that is going beyond himself. Perhaps he engages in the sun, in whales, or men, men like Christ, Mohammed, or Buddha, or women like Lilith. His first step is to create new beings from dust and place them at a distance from his radiance, on a mote of dust. This step alone creates dissension in heaven, revolt, as Lucifer and others bring freedom and reason to the beings of dust. Then God balances the evil brought about by freedom."

"This is ridiculous!" Shehan interrupted.

But Angel is rolling and rolls over the objection. Shehan stands fascinated, is if by a serpent's dream or a horror story of madness. "Perhaps God discovered a way to push creation along on its own. Then to disengage from that creation and let it live its own life. Consider, with matter unrolled, time unrolls. With disequilibrium on heaven and earth, there is transformation and evolution—yes, evolution is God's ball, he rolled it and not even he knows where it will come to rest, if ever—existence is polarized, life advances creatively. There is unforeseen novelty. Light battles light, light battles matter, and matter battles matter. The universe spins and unfolds, accompanied by pain and limit, joy and death."

"This is rubbish," Shehan would not be denied any longer. "The Bible has nothing like this. It is very explicit. God is omniscient. Lucifer rebelled. And there is no evolution. That is Man's folly. And now, if you will excuse me—"

"I like the Bible." Angel admitted. Shehan held his breath to see if it was a trick. "It is poetry. An anthology of poetry, anyway; some of it is better than other parts of it. But it tends to be repetitious, like the worst of Elizabethan poetry: God is almighty, this person obeyed him; that one didn't; this one lived and that one didn't; this one begat and begat and begat; and their seeds begat and begat and begat, ad infinitum; very repetitious."

"The Bible is the word of God. How dare you," Shehan sputtered.

"Yes, but it was recorded by men and women, and men and women use repetition to help their memory. I'm not saying that there is no good in the bible. There is. One of the main themes of the Old testament is freedom. It is a paean to be free, to leave what you have, free yourself from fetters of all kinds. Abraham is commanded to give up his country and clan. Moses is charged to liberate his people."

"And are you free? in here?" Shehan interrupted with a sneer.

"Yes, more than most. More than you are probably. You have to be here on Sunday. On the Shabbat, the day of pure freedom, where one—"

"I will not stand for this. Larry!" he shouted.

As Angel started to continue, a large con in a workshirt came in, eyebrows raised.

"Get him out, get him out, now."

Angel shrugged and moved toward Larry as he moved towards him. He looked at him and said, "I'm going." Then he turned to Shehan, as he moved through the door. "I am not tempting you. You have already succumbed."

Then he was into the hall, listening to see if he was being followed. Angel was happy with his interpretation of the universe. He had read everything he could find on Lucifer and pieced it together logically. He could identify with Lucifer.

The next month, the Presbyterian minister offered his version of the Fall of Satan. Angel went to that service on time and sat in the back of the room again, for convenient escape.

"This sermon concerns the origins of Satan," the Reverend Paul Smiley began. "When Job fell on hard times and questioned God's judgment, God responded with questions designed to show Job, uhh, that he didn't have enough wisdom to judge his creator. 'Where were you when I laid the foundation of the earth! Tell Me, if you have understanding, Who set its measurements, since you know? Or who stretched the line on it? On what were its bases sunk? Or who laid its cornerstone, When the morning stars sang together, And all the sons of God shouted for joy?' (Job 38:4-7) In this description of creation, uhh, God refers to the angels as morning stars. Angels remember are higher beings than man; they have personal audience with God. Now, uhh, when God created the universe, these spiritual beings, uhh, all shouted for joy, in complete harmony." Smiley had a gold tooth in the back of his mouth.

"The most exalted position among the angels was held by Lucifer, who was perfect in all of his ways. Thus, uhh, said the Lord God, 'You had the seal of perfection, full of wisdom and perfect in beauty. You were in Eden, the garden of God; every precious stone was your covering: The ruby, the topaz, uhh, and the diamond; the beryl, the onyx, and the jasper; the lapis lazuli, the turquoise, and the emerald; and the gold ...' (Ezekiel 28.11-15). He had the pattern of perfection, was the most beautiful and wise of all, uhh, God's creations. How perfect? He was the 'anointed one' which indicates supreme favor. The Messiah, by comparison, was God's anointed king. Lucifer was the leader of all the angelic beings. With all of the fabulous jewels indicating, uhh, his exalted rank, he had walked on God's mountain, on the holy mountain of God. He had walked 'in the midst of the stones of fire,' which was

God's holy presence. Lucifer was the greatest, uhh, being God ever created. He had unequaled strength, wisdom, beauty, privilege, and authority. According to Isaiah, he was, uhh, the 'Son of the Morning;' his name means literally, the 'shining one,' a word for great beauty.

"Why then is he not by the side of God, even now? How could Lucifer, created blameless, uhh, and perfect, fall? Created without any form of evil. What happened to him? Hmm?

"In Isaiah (14:12-14), Lucifer was perfect until 'unrighteousness' was found in him. This unrighteousness, uhh, introduced all suffering into the universe, by saying in his heart, 'I will.' 'For thou hast said in thine heart, I will ascend into heaven, I will exalt my throne above the stars of God, I will sit also upon the mount of the congregation, in the sides of the north, I will ascend, uhh, above the heights of the clouds, I will be like the Most High.' And here is the real description of evil, that sin originates in the heart, that Lucifer, the shining one, created in the glory of God, said five times in, uhh, his heart, 'I will.' He filled his heart with the violence of rebellion, with the desire to act independently of God. He thought, and felt, that his power, his magnificence, his beauty, was worthy of worship." Smiley read his notes without looking up.

"God took a risk when he created angels with intelligence and, uhh, self-determination, so they would respond to his love spontaneously and with joy in their hearts. And Lucifer, inflated with power and pride, broke the fellowship of God. He rebelled against God, enticing many other angels to his ranks!" The reverend Smiley punched the air vehemently.

"But, uhh, when he rebelled he lost the most important trait for perfection, a personal relationship with God. When he fell from his high position, the perfect universe became impure. And so God brought him to trial and pronounced judgment upon him and upon all the angels who rebelled with him. He charged him Satan, the 'adversary' and sentenced him to eternal banishment. But God had a plan, and, uhh, that plan was to resolve this rebellion on earth. To allow Satan to throw his strength against God and his creation, until he could throw no more, until his heart would heal, until no more would he say in his heart, 'I will', and Lucifer would be born again to sit below the throne of God."

The preacher paused, overwhelmed by the sadness of the desolate picture he painted for his flock. Would they understand how close evil was to God, how much Lucifer could have meant to God, his son of the morning?

He concluded: "Next week, we shall see how Satan wounded God in this terrible contest, how Jesus lived, and was, uhh, tempted, and died on the cross for our sins. And perhaps see why God created the parents of Man, and how Satan changed their lives and those of all their descendants," he baited his hook. Smiley swept from the stage with his robe trailing.

Angel waited eagerly for his meeting that afternoon. "Thank you for letting me see you. I had several questions about your sermon this morning."

"Yes of course," answered the Reverend Smiley, who seemed curiously deflated from the presence on the podium.

"When Satan said, 'I will' it was only after Michael had addressed him thus: 'Give adoration to the image of God! But if thou do it not, then the Lord God will break out in wrath against thee.' To which Lucifer then replied: 'If he breaks out in wrath against me, I will exalt my throne ...' Then God flung Lucifer to earth. When Lucifer said, 'I will' how was that different from the 'I will' of God, who would make creation and exalt it? Was there a different wickedness and scheming taking place?"

"We do not always understand the ways of God. He tells us only what we can understand. We know so little of how Satan fell," Smiley said, unperturbed.

"Why do you keep calling him Satan? Satan was a Prince of Babylon, who, because of the brilliance of his wealth, surpassing other worldly monarchs, was compared to the brilliance of Lucifer. Lucifer is not Satan. That is just a poor interpretation of the passage."

"Did you come to lecture me, or ask my help? Yes, I know, St. Anselm, the archbishop of Canterbury, used Satan as a synonym for Lucifer. The interpretation has to do with Satan as a prince of the earth. Lucifer fallen is not Lucifer the archangel, merely a prince of the earth, a rebel beaten."

"Why did Lucifer rebel?" Angel asked. "The desire to sit on God's throne, in God's absence, or in the place of God? Not likely. His envy of Adam, perhaps? The desire to think for himself and not take all on authority? What if Lucifer were the symbol for freedom from tyranny? Even perfect tyranny? The incarnation of the spirit of individualism, of liberty and spontaneity? The light and benefactor of the world? The modern Prometheus? Perhaps God, the dull weaver of stodgy similitude is the villain; the creator of chance who did not understand what he had created?"

Smiley narrowed his nostrils and focused on them. "The Bible was quite explicit, but I understand what you want to do. You want to romanticize Lucifer. Make him the 'Modern Prometheus,' the hero of heaven. Well, it won't wash, young man. Satan was the loser, and a poor loser at that. He is responsible for the evil in the world!" Smiley's voice rose as he made his accusation.

"Did you learn that from your personal relationship with God?"

Smiley pointed a long forefinger at Angel, "You will not question my relationship!"

"Why? How do you have a relationship with God? Is she human, personal? Must be a one-way relation. You do all the telling?" Angel spoke faster, irritated at the stupidity of a personal God. "You don't experience God, or encounter him, even if he is. You experience nature, and you can't even have a personal relationship with nature."

"You are a fool, get out!" Smiley exploded.

Angel paused, shrugging his shoulders.

"Get out, damn you!" Smiley repeated.

"The God you love is a political hack, who rules through violence. Even your Jesus was always threatening to use his 10,000 legions. Is this so—"

"Go to hell!" Smiley interrupted, face beet red, unconsciously clenching his hands.

Angel stepped backward, as Smiley stepped toward him, in an awkward kind of dance. He quoted Milton's Satan to Smiley, before leaving. "The mind in its own place, and in itself Can make a heaven out of Hell, A Hell of Heaven. What matter where, if I still be the same, And what should I be, all but less than he, Whom thunder hath made greater? Here at last We shall be free."

He engaged in his routine for a week, studying in the library. The library was geared to law and religion, as if these were the most important thing to the prisoners. He continued his courses.

The next Sunday, he listened to a part of Smiley's continuing sermon.

"— the serpent was more, uhh, subtle than any beast of the field."

The word serpent in Hebrew meant something shining and beautiful, much like Lucifer, Angel knew.

"Obviously, Satan studied man and woman in the garden of Eden, to see how he could make them, uhh, rebel against God, too. By waiting for Eve to come by the tree of knowledge of good and evil, Satan played on her natural curiosity, a trait that brings trouble seemingly, and planted the question in her mind, 'why doesn't God want us to eat from this tree?' That is, uhh, how Satan works, by ideas, innuendoes, questions!" Smiley accused.

"In this garden, then, man gave the deed to the world to Satan. The human things of the world—art, music, philosophy, science, uhh, culture—are not intrinsically evil, but have been used by Satan to divide man's attention from God. By rejecting fellowship with God, man

153

turned over legal ownership, the authority given by God to Adam over the fish and the birds and all creatures and elements of the earth, to Satan. Satan won the legal rights, in fact, he tempted Jesus with that domain, by showing him all the kingdoms of the earth in a moment."

Angel couldn't take anymore relationships or temptings. He left. So, Lucifer was the legal owner of the earth. The landlord. Why shouldn't he make the rules? Raise the rent? Angel smiled.

He continued to learn everything he could, determined to get back and study stars. Slowly he realized that he was becoming more interested in how he knew things than in what he knew. Four months before he got out, he overheard a new 'resident' describe the auto theft for which he was convicted. In perfect detail. He also knew why he had been allowed to overhear it. Someone knew his record. But why tell? Why this? For weeks, he figured out ways to kill the bastard, Hernandez; it was too close. Then he concentrated of ways to force a confession. He wanted to be released immediately, then.

He didn't do either. He walked to Hernandez' cell and started punching him. "Hey, wha, Heeyyy!" Hernandez started, then ducked. Angel hit the wall; he was sure he had broken another finger. He hit the larger man twice more, for good measure, then left, feeling much better. But, he was tight to leave this place. He was easily distracted, now.

Hernandez reported running into his own door. Angel mentioned that he had slammed a door on his finger. The image of both rose slightly among the others.

The days passed like calendar pages in the wind in a movie scene. Finally, he was close to getting out. He took a day to prepare for the parole board. He had been warned that the board liked to ask, "What have you done for yourself in prison?" He had finished his degree in physics and astronomy, finishing with more courses in psychology than in stellar structure, but at least he had finished what he started. Then, also, he had worked at a trade, painting, for over three years, learning good habits; habits like two-hour lunches, pacing his 'output,' 'liberating' supplies; he wondered how much the board really knew.

He had worked for short times at other shop skills, as he had gotten chances. Welding was an appropriate skill, but boring. It was a 'repetitive' skill; learn three basic positions, repeat a million times. He didn't like welding, though; trying to see through the smoky window, he had almost cut off his fingers. He had spent some time in the major appliance shop, learning to repair toasters, televisions, and washing machines; more importantly, he had learned to wash his clothes in comfort, at his own convenience. In the machine shop, he used the lathe and milling machine to make, and sell for handsome prices, copper and brass candle holders. The automotive shop had been too popular to get into. Maybe someone thought he would steal an engine.

The informal courses were probably even more valuable. Many of the cons were skilled in lock-picking, safe-cracking, fencing goods, modifying guns, and scams. Neither were they reluctant to impress other cons with their knowledge. He felt extraordinarily well prepared for his freedom; prepared for any eventuality. The parole board was mercifully brief. They were impressed with what he had done. Their only concern was with his list of solitary confinements, his nickname of Satan, his disposition to violence.

"What guarantee do we have that you will not express this violence upon the public?" asked the youngest member, a used car dealer in business with his father.

"Why, the guarantee that I was never violent before I was invited here." He noted the expected chuckles, few had ever refused such invitations. "When I was here I only fought in self-defense, to save myself from aggravated assaults."

"Do you think this prison is a violent place," asked the one female member of the board.

"No more than any prison, segregating some violent people from the public." He replied politically.

She continued, "We notice a report here that your nickname, encouraged by you, was 'Satan.' Is this indicative of something?"

He smiled at her. "My name is Angel. There aren't many angels in prison. It was a natural nickname, like 'lefty' or 'scarface.' I am a good Roman Catholic."

Some concern was expressed because he didn't have a record of any kind. But he assured them, that was because he had never been able to find a good job, a full-time job; and because he had never been in trouble with the law before.

"How do we know that you will be able to find a job, now?" asked the one with his pencil chewed.

"I intend to—" Angel broke off, realizing that he had started to tell them that he was going to get his job in Hawaii back, again. No, no, too late for any contradiction or unexplained leads, he thought. "I guess I'll apply for any job for which I am qualified. I did finish my degree." He added unnecessarily, sure that they knew and were impressed; and sure that they didn't care how useless it was in the market place. Shit, Ph.D.s had been laid off when he was. That was how useful the degree was.

"I wanted to compliment you on your excellent use of English," began the woman, a Mrs. Hunter, "I used to be an English teacher, so I can appreciate the proper use of who and whom."

And that seemed to wind down the meeting. He felt confident that he was on his way. He was 29 years old. His birthday was in two weeks.

Chapter 10. Road Kills

The eyes had burst. The whole body was like a ruptured bag, leaking fluid over the blacktop. He was outraged for the gravel-crusted fur. He pulled the emergency cord on the bus. Not even speaking to the driver, he picked up his bag and walked back to the cat, hearing the bus roar off toward its destination. It—already an it—had probably been a beautiful friendly cat earlier in the day. He picked it up carefully and set it in the weeds, reflecting that his hands were as unknown to it as the ones on the steering wheel that ran it down.

"All animals need a private death, a private place to turn and lie still." He wanted to say more, but choked on the words. He wondered if the highway gods demanded payment to keep the highways smooth. A car swerved a little as he started walking north. He saw the eyes behind glass, fish eyes, fast-moving fish eyes, whose lives were measured in miles, he thought bitterly.

He didn't know what to do when he got out. He had gained $133.85 but lost almost four years. He wasn't sure who he was. Angel had become more comfortable than his own name, George. He had to decide if he was an educated con or an uneducated 'sheep.' Phil Garcia had given him the name of someone to stay with in San Francisco, a sympathizer. He would see, first. If he could ever get picked up, again.

The car was a 63 chevy. He saw it from the back as it passed him and braked, hopefully in response to his erect thumb. Four greasers were inside. He hesitated, then sat in the back, as one slid reluctantly over.

He answered the "Where to?" with "Frisco." No one talked. Everyone sized him up with nonverbal cues. He was happy for the ride. He thanked them in Spanish for the ride—that opened the floodgate of words.

When they got tired of talking, they left him off on the highway; he still had to walk into town. No one gave him a ride in the city. It took him six hours to walk to the address Phil had given him.

It was a small townhouse. A nude brunette let him in, and led him to a room in front. And left him there, without speaking. He knew he would like it here. He pushed aside some of the coats on the bed and lay down.

When he woke up, he saw blonde hair on the pillow next to his. He stepped silently into the living room.

"Angel?" came a voice from the hall. He turned and walked toward the voice. It was Ramirez. He was hard not to recognize, a pyramid turned upside down; a wrestler's chest mounted on a dancers hips, over a swimmer's ankles. He was sure that not much of it was fat.

He respectfully asked, "Al?" not ready to use the nickname 'Gordo' without permission.

"Hey, man, glad you could make it. Call me Gordo." They slapped palms.

"So, how you been, Satan?" Gordo asked. Angel winced, thinking of the parole board. "We got a surprise for you tonight."

"Food?" Angel asked.

"No. It's in the icebox." Angel headed for refrigerator, aware of the other's scrutiny.

"No, it's a mass in your honor." Angel turned and raised his eyebrows. "Black mass." Gordo explained cheerfully. "Because of your name, and your reputation, Frank and I thought you might like it."

"The group last night?" he wondered out loud.

"They was here for a lecture. No one gets to be a member until they been to three lectures, had an examination, and an interview with the Council of Six."

"You on the Council?" Angel asked, dreading to go or refuse.

"You bet."

"Tell me about your group."

"Our church, man, our church." Gordo motioned for the orange juice. Angel handed him the carton. "We worship Satan, who has more power on earth."

"And God?" Angel was curious.

"He's a force in the universe," Gordo answered pronouncing his words like an Irish Catholic, 'farce,' 'uni verse.' "We believe Satan should be restored to the throne."

"Is that what the Mass is for?"

"To worship him, as he commands."

"And what else do you believe," Angel inquired, trying to keep his voice from getting dry and cynical.

"The iron rule: do unto them before they do unto you. Love your friends, but hate your enemy. Don't turn the other cheek, smash his. The world is a jungle, man. If we don't dominate it, it dominates us; so we choose to dominate it." Gordo paused to wash his roll down with orange juice. He handed the container back to Angel.

As he put it back on the shelf, he asked, "What will I have to know?"

"Nothing. We don't make anyone do anything. We're into self-indulgence."

"Self-indulgence?"

"S-M, madness."

Oh, great, I should have gone south to San Diego, thought Angel.

"Wait 'til you see the congregation tonight," enthused Gordo in his high voice, "We're dressing up like bankers, gonna to piss on twenty dollar bills!" he started laughing so hard he rolled off the chair.

Angel looked puzzled.

"Doncha see. They's sacred cows. We step on sacred cows, different one each week."

Angel smiled, "Not afraid of sacred cow shit?"

"Hey, that's great." Gordo struggled as he put both hands on the table to heave himself up.

The blonde came in, wearing only jeans, turning a blouse inside out as she walked. She raised her arms to put it over her head. Angel hadn't seen breasts move in his life, it seemed. Pictures don't move. He noticed her nipples were flat and soft. He hoped he'd fucked the brains out of her, last night, but he was sure he'd slept.

"What's so funny; you woke me up?" she complained.

"Angel. Cindi, this is Angel" Gordo waved.

"Angel? Like flap, flap, come back?" she smiled at her private witticism.

"Yea, like hosanna, ho, to the clouds we go," he replied, thinking that his mouthing was as senseless as hers.

"So, what's so funny?" she turned to Gordo. Angel had fixated on her breasts; they bounced a little when she moved. Gordo slapped her hard on the hip, more intent on the seams of her crotch.

"Angel, he was warning me about sacred cow shit," he turned her around and pulled her down on his lap, pulling her back with his hands across her breasts, smiling. Angel was sure that he could hear sperm cells screaming, somewhere below his abdomen.

"Show me the neighborhood," he suggested, hoping for feminine contact.

The church was two blocks away, in a nondescript residential hotel, a wooden building.

Gordo introduced him to Albert Horton, who assured him, "You won't need to say anything. Just be our guest of dishonor." He offered a hand to him, index and little finger stiff.

Angel had watched Gordo, so he shook hands, awkwardly, though. The three of them went upstairs, to a small room, off an auditorium or some larger room. Three other men were there already, undressing. Before he was completely undressed, Angel was handed a black robe. He donned it and followed them through a door.

The auditorium was completely draped with dark fabric. It might have been a theater at one time. There were two aisles leading to the stage. Ten or eleven rows of wooden seats had been removed, not recently, judging from the condition of the floor. They all congregated before the stage. First, informally, new members, who had passed the tests, were admitted. Then, everyone lined up to pay homage to Satan. Bowing and scraping before planting the ritual kiss on the devil's buttocks— Morton bent over with his robes lifted. Then everyone arranged themselves in a loose circle, kneeling or sitting on the floor. Chanting began.

As Horton was going up the three steps on the left, a nude woman, the brunette again, walked up the other set of stairs, as if in a light trance. Her body was lightly oiled; she was slim; her breasts didn't bounce, Angel noted. Her nipples were lighter than he would have expected, and excited, from cold or anticipation. The altar was a coffin-shaped box set on two chairs that had their backs removed. She draped herself on the black fabric over the coffin.

He shifted his gaze to the black, inverted cross just in back of the altar. It was a large, crude cross, painted black, bolted out from the wall with one-inch bolts. Hanging from a curtain to the left was an inverted pentagram, the symbol of evil, two points jutting upward, one pointing toward hell, through the floor. All of the other artifacts were painted black. There was a skull—

"For man's material nature," Gordo whispered, "the symbolic phallus is for blessings, the scourge is for whippings, the bell for purifying air, and sword is a symbol of power."

Angel also noticed the goat motif, laid on thickly; the goat's head, the goat's foot candle, a hand of glory, waxed and ready to be lit. Morton was waiting by the altar, dressed in black, with a red-satin lined cape and black cap with a silk widow's peak. He was watching another black-haired woman approach the altar. Angel supposed she was an acolyte.

Gordo leaned over and said, "She's a prostitute; the one on the altar is a virgin."

Another figure in black—"The master of rituals," Gordo identified him—picked up a ring from the altar.

He passed it through the flame of a candle once, saying, "Fire, cleanse away all malice and evil toward our brother Judas, adhering to this ring."

He passed the ring through a bowl of water, with a ritual to cleanse all evil from it; the ring was held above his head. Gordo was too busy feeling the thigh of the woman on his other side to tell him the meaning of it. Incantations were exchanged as the ring was given to another young man— Angel guessed this guy really was a banker in 'real life.' The bearer of the ring carried knives to the altar. The knives had been exorcised and all the equipment dedicated. Morton held up a black cat with his left hand. Suddenly he slit its throat with the knife in his right hand. Angel groaned involuntarily. Morton's eyes flicked toward the sound.

Gordo leaned away. "Just a stray cat," he mumbled.

The ceremony continued. The acolyte held a chalice under the exsanguinating cat. The blood came in spurts, from an artery. Angel felt a rumble of rage start in his intestines; his fingers curled with strain.

"She's urinating on the host," Gordo explained, leaning over again, "It's a consecrated host."

The chalice had been placed between the breasts of the virgin, several trails of blood leading to the center of her chest.

"The sacramental materials are bodily, not spiritual," Gordo continued.

Morton was speaking. Angel recognized the words, Latin, but not the sentences. It was the Catholic missal, he realized, but read backwards. The name Satan was substituted for God.

Angel started to blank out. Gordo nudged him, "The mass is over. The best part's coming up." Angel struggled to look up. The virgin altar was getting up. Morton was already at a long table at the foot of the stage. He had killed a duck and put it on a silver bowl to bleed. Someone had brought in trays of food, expensive breads and wines. He heard violin music. Black robes converged on the food. He went over, but could not eat. His eyes sought Morton.

The blonde, Cindi, had started to dance. The violin became more frenzied. Two men started to dance wildly around her. Angel saw Morton stepping down from the stage, a large leather phallus tied underneath his robes by a belt. Cindi clung to the shoulders of her two enthusiasts and lifted her legs up. Morton walked right into her, impaling her on the leather; she started pulling and pushing with her shoulders. Then Morton repeated his copulation with every woman present. After their surrender to the instrument, the women started grabbing men in a mad frenzy, a frenzy that the men encouraged. The violin had worked to a fever pitch. The ritual was a prelude for perversion and lust—an excuse for many of them. He saw Gordo tackling Cindi. A woman came at Angel clutching, but he punched her in the throat, and she collapsed, gasping.

The little banker came up, "Hey, she's not into that!" he protested for her. Angel gave him a quick kick in the balls and he fell on top of the woman, groaning.

Good, Angel thought, looks like passion.

He saw Morton in back of the altar, relieving himself of the phallus. Angel approached him, throat tight with anger. "What makes you think it's fun to kill cats and ducks?"

"What?" Morton looked up, not understanding anyone's concern. "They're sacrifices."

"No, they're living beings," gritted Angel.

"No. They have no souls," smiled Morton. "Saint Somebody made that point and we believe what the saints say. It's right there in the Bible."

"So, you're ignorant of life" Angel said, expressing the menace he felt.

"So, God accepted animal sacrifices from the Hebrews. Satan needs them, too," Morton talked faster, justifying the kills. "Since his fall the archangel has been in pain. The pain our rituals create make him feel at home."

"I'm not at home here," Angel blurted. "Peace and beauty are the balm for pain, not more pain."

"So, who are you," Morton challenged, knowing only the nickname of 'Satan' and some of Angel's reputation.

"Someone who can tell you that everything you read in the Bible isn't true—it was written by men."

He moved toward Morton, who wanted to take no chances.

"No, Satan cannot take a life," he hastened to say, "he can have power over our fortunes and possessions, our jobs, happiness, but he cannot take our lives!" He moved toward the altar, sweating profusely. "No! Remember, 'he is in thine hand, only spare his life.' "

"Ecce in manu tua est verum, tamen animam illius serva—Job, Chapter 2, verse 6—I remember. God gave the gift of life and only man can throw it away, but there are so many ways to forfeit it," Angel said softly.

"Who are you!" Morton looked past him, hoping someone in the orgy would see them.

"I am he who ranges to and fro in the earth." Angel answered simply.

"Keep away from me! I have power!" threatened Morton.

"I am your power," hissed Angel.

Morton backed against the cross, listing the men he knew, the police chief, mobsters, inflating his importance, threatening retaliation, "I'll have you ruined, jailed; you'll never work on this coast!"

Angel glared through him.

"Oh, God, forgive me," Morton began.

"Too late you miserable fuck. You play with evil for excitement, before confessing and praying for forgiveness, hoping for heaven anyway. Tonight pay first."

Morton's fear exploded in a flurry of kicks and punches. Angel backed off quickly until Morton was off balance, then he pulled his legs out from under him. But he didn't account for the desperation with which Morton grabbed his legs. Then he fell on Morton, both bodies grappling for advantage. Angel rolled off and kicked Morton in the face. Gordo loomed over him, reaching down. Angel kicked him in the chest; Gordo was thrown backward off the stage. Angel reached over and picked Morton up, upside down, and slammed him against the inverted cross. He wrenched the legs around the post; then broke the arms over the bar.

"Why?" cried Morton, beyond pain.

"Because, I am Lucifer!" Angel screamed behind his teeth, and cut Morton's throat. He ran off the stage, kicking Gordo down again. He locked the door to the dressing room, and dressed. Someone screamed behind the door. He knew they were milling around, trying to decide what to do. He raced back to the house, gathered up his bag, and left for Oregon. His teeth hurt; his arms hurt, whether from tension or being struck, he couldn't tell. He knew who he was, now.

He was excited and horrified by what he had done. But he wanted to be Walker, again, purged of violence and lies, and angels. He had been on the road for a day and a half, passing through Portland. The bus came into Seattle at ten at night, so all he saw at first were the lights rising out of dark land and dark water. He stayed at a hotel two blocks from the bus station. Seattle had been founded by five families from Illinois, on one of the low points of land in the sound. It had grown up the sides of hills, leveling other hills with the weight of its growth.

The next day was June and sunny in Seattle, which was a nicely laid out, but a dirty city, with too many cars. He walked by the unemployment office, determined to do things in the proper order this time. The employment office was in a low building a block under the Space Needle, towering 600 feet over the old World's Fair Park. Groups of men milled around. He heard that Boeing had laid off men again.

And where Boeing went, there went the city. The park looked like it had been made into a museum of the 1962 World's Fair. After only four pages of forms and an hour's wait, he was interviewed by an earnest young man.

"My name is Holmstead. Please sit down. I haven't had a chance to read all of your application, so why don't you tell me a little bit about it?" Eric Holmstead asked, sitting down, and starting to read the forms.

"Most of my experience is as a research assistant in astronomy. I was responsible for making observations as well as data reduction." Walker started, after deciding to re-enter his former life—a life without a prison record.

"Did you use a computer?"

"Yes, I had access to an IBM 1130 for six hours a night."

Holmestead was scribbling away, but managed, "Go on."

"I had to learn FORTRAN to do the necessary programming."

"You are a veteran?"

"Yes, Air Force."

"And what was your specialty?"

"Ahhm, medical corpsman," Walker admitted, "but I'd rather not work in a hospital, or any medical field."

"Even if you have no other choice?" Holmstead smiled grimly. "Astronomy isn't a very big field in this area."

Walker could see the future clearly: hospital orderly, cleaning bed pans, tilting patients for spoon-feeding— but he answered, "Yes, if I had to, I would."

"Good. Going to school?" the interviewer asked thoughtfully.

"No, but I might like to later." Walker watched the codes appear on his card, for astronomy, computing, medical support. He was given an orange veteran's card, with his name and specialties on it.

"You listed the Kennedy Hotel as your address. Do you have a permanent address, yet?"

"Ahh, no. I'm going to look, now."

"Well, call me when you do, and give me a telephone number where you can be reached. Good day." Holmstead concluded, placing Walker's folder on top of a pile, and getting out the next.

Walker could feel the attention being turned off, so he put on his coat, thanked the receptionist, and left.

It looked like the same group of people outside on the sidewalk.

A healthy young black man came up to him, making eye contact, and asked, "Any spare change, man?"

"No, sorry," Walker answered honestly, knowing that he had no spare and he might be flat on the highway of life soon enough himself. He took a bus out to the University district. On the way, he had to decide whether to stay or move on to a city with more jobs. If he left, the travel costs would probably deplete his reserves. California was out. That left the midwest. Or East. He decided to stay. He opened his Post-Intelligencer, and looked for a room.

The bus dropped him on 45th, the center of the district, teeming with banks, fast food places, book stores, and movie theaters, his favorite places. He walked north on the street. When he saw the A&P, then the Safeway, he knew he could stay. So he turned east, and started looking for rooms. Most of the streets had fine old, residential houses; many of them had signs advertising rooms for rent. He went up 20th, over a block, and then down 19th. He heard music coming from one of the three-story houses. Yellow. And there was a sign on the porch: Room for Rent. The house was a three-story, yellow side-board affair, sandwiched between two just like it, but painted different colors. It was set up off the street by one flight of stairs. In back of it was a large gravel parking lot. Some of the houses were obviously kept up better, but some were worse.

There were two rooms for rent; one on the second floor for $15.00 a week, a smaller one at the end of a hall—a hall like a rat maze—on the first floor for $10.00. He paid two weeks rent on the smaller.

"Hey, what's your major?" asked the short, serious, young man with the black beard.

Walker looked at him; he had the air of a serious scholar, a sort of mania that excluded humor and recreation. But he answered, "Haven't decided; yours?"

"Japanese Literature," came the prepackaged reply.

"Well, thank you, see you around."

"Wait, you'll need refrigerator space. Everyone is responsible for their own food, cooking and cleanup, unless you go in with a group."

After a tour of the three floors and the basement, Walker went over to the pay phone and called the Employment Office; he left his new address and message phone for Holmstead, who was with a client.

He threw his bag on the bed, and rushed upstairs to the bathroom. Aware that the house was coed, he knocked once, rushing in without waiting long for an answer. It was empty. He locked the door and defecated, happy that the small dark round turds came out so cleanly. He flushed, and watched them spiral down the beginnings of their journey back to the earth, through miles of pipes, until it probably emptied out into the Sound. He went back to his room, and rearranged it. The bed was put under the window, looking across to the sorority house next door. The pine dresser was moved facing the door; the small writing table and chair between the other two. That was that. He felt it was time for the Midnight Acquisition raids. He borrowed a lamp and cover from a second floor room. He found a wastebasket in the basement. Over the next two weeks, he liberated a chair cushion, hat rack, and painting easel from various university buildings, left open late for the convenience of students. He spent the rest of the day looking over the campus. He rejected the swimming pool as too crowded and dirty; he might try to swim in Lake Washington later. The libraries were spectacular; the Odegaard Undergraduate Library was a carpeted cube with beanbag chairs and a dining area underneath; Suzallo library was a gothic network of mazes to different subject areas. He headed toward the new physics building. Physics always flaunted its money. The chairman was out, but the faculty member in charge of admissions, Fred Morton, was in. He seemed bored, but gave Walker an application and explained the process. He had a motorcycle footrest on his desk and it seemed to captivate his glance regularly. Walker said he would come back with the forms and left the man to his dreams of motorcycle glory.

The Psych department was being revamped. He went in. There was a faint aura of pipe smoke and musty papers. A secretary was straining over some pages of typing. He expressed his desire to be a student in the department.

She snapped her gum intensely, "Yea? Just a sec."

She dialed a single number, "Dr. Gerber, I have a student here," she paused, listening to the inaudible reply. Walker was amused by the sudden tone of reverence in her voice.

"You may go in," she was already turning to her typing. Walker crossed to the door and knocked. He didn't hear a reply, but he went in anyway.

In a moment, he observed the tall, gawky man with a pencil mustache and balding pate, seated at a conference table with a shorter, younger man, with long hair and a beard. He noticed the book shelves, the old pipe and milk-stained papers on the desk.

Then, Dr. Gerber was coming toward him, hand out. "Pleased to meet you. Arvill Gerber."

"George Walker."

Gerber gestured to the seated man, "Nick Gillis." Nick nodded. Doby's younger brother, Walker thought, of course. They smiled at each other for different reasons; Walker at his own dopey humor; Gillis because he thought Walker was friendly. It was like an encounter between a castrated male dog and an alpha male dog. Both were unaware of their reasons for being friendly, but the meeting went well.

"Are you a student here?" Gerber inquired.

"No, sir." Walker replied with appropriate humility, "But I would like to be."

Realizing how easy it was to manipulate people with respect. You could think anything you liked, just so you acted and dressed like everyone else.

He just caught the end of Gerber's reply, "background?"

"Well, mostly in physics and astronomy. But I have been interested in psychology for quite some time. I wanted formal training, now," he concluded, adding for his own benefit, 'especially since I became a vicious killer of Satanists for misrepresenting me. I took courses in prison, but that doesn't count, since I was incarcerated unfairly. You're damn right I have an alibi, I was robbing a grocery store at the time, not stealing a car.' Some things really were better left unsaid.

Gerber asked suddenly where he had been the past four years.

Walker simply said, "I inherited money from my father, so I took that time off to work on a book—you have that address in Hawaii, after the Observatory work." He was sure the lie would work; it was simple.

Gillis immediately asked him how he wanted to concentrate his study.

He replied steadily, "Humanistic Psychology— Maslow, Rogers, Festinger," hoping it would close the door on further inspection of his recent past.

But, Gerber asked the topic of the book, and Walker answered that it had to do with the psychology of religion; he would let them review it, if they wanted, when it was finished.

For the next hour, they talked about the different schools of thought. Gerber expressed reservations that he could be let into the doctorate program without a bachelor's, but Gillis prevailed, by pointing out Walker's maturity and interest, as well as his obvious self-education. Walker found out later that Gillis needed a graduate student to keep his own status up. But he was happy, anyway, he would get a chance. And his two classes that summer would be with Gerber and Gillis. He decided to go by the philosophy department just in case. When he thought about it, all the subjects here that he was interested in began with the letter 'P.'

Perhaps, he should hit political science, too, and make it complete. No, too much. Besides, he was in psychology.

The next day, he had a message from Holmstead. When he called back, Holmstead wasn't available, but he was told to talk to Alice Adams in the UW library administrative offices. Her desk was the farthest from the doors, indicating higher status, he assumed. She explained the veteran's program to him. The federal government would pay two-thirds of his salary for the next year; the library one third. One third of $2.10 an hour was $0.70. They didn't seem to have checked his previous library job. And, thanks to the feds, he was getting work and the library was getting a bargain. She had him fill out several more forms, and turned him over to the supervisor of shelvers. Michael Johnson.

Michael Johnson was happy to have someone to show, and order, around. The books were all in call number order, using the Library of Congress classification system. Each subject had a one, two, or three letter subject designation, "BF" for psychology, "QA" for physics, "PZ" for science fiction (modern, American). He was as bored as Johnson in five minutes. Worse, he was expected to shelve the books sideways, so that Johnson could check his accuracy. He was hypnotized by his own physical movements. When it was dark, he went home, poor, but employed (barely), enrolled (almost), honest (in a way), and hard-working. The last thing he thought of, before going to sleep, was red blood draining onto red satin, the black figure on the black cross, surprise still registering in the unfocused eyes.

College campuses always seemed to be such peaceful enclaves of unreality. Most of the faculty and most of the students were dorks. He was sure Gerber was a dork, but needed his courses. The course this summer was Sensation and Perception. Gerber's lectures had been memorized. In fact, he kept a written copy of the lectures on reserve at the library. Once Walker took them out before class and traced the flawless execution directly, reading from word to word. The pauses were not in the copy, however, so just as he was sure that Gerber was about to forget a word, it came tumbling out.

Gillis' class was just the opposite. There were two other graduate students in it. Abnormal Psychology 634. Gillis was eager to show that he was learning too. "We're going to learn a lot, this summer. Summer is for the serious students."

His first payroll check was $250.73. He had to pay back $50.00 to Financial Aid, to pay off the loan for tuition. To splurge properly, he skipped his classes, and took a bus downtown. He filled up on croissants at the Frederick and Nelson store, went to a Clint Eastwood movie, then ate at a French restaurant housed in the Pike Place market. He watched the ferries come in for three hours.

He decided to keep a journal again. He had thrown his prison journal away in San Francisco. He needed the discipline; otherwise he wouldn't take very good notes. He had read each text-book the first week. Psychology was so much common sense, unlike physics, where common sense was exposed as a thin veneer of organic misdirection soon corrected mathematically.

That summer, he took three undergraduate courses by examination, getting two 'A's and a 'B,' neither of which would show up on the transcript, which just listed the credits as pass. Gerber gave him a B in his course; Gillis an A. He learned that he could not ever doubt or challenge Gerber. Gerber was right by divine fiat; all the facts in the world could never change Gerber's rightness. Nevertheless, in spite of his academic rigidity, which had apparently set in before 1952, Gerber was kind and thoughtful outside the classroom. He had been invited to dinner by Gerber and then Gillis. He had bought a twenty-dollar stereo from Gerber; probably, an old one that belonged to his daughter.

He returned to the house with a wooden bookcase with a broken side from in back of the library. Although he felt conspicuous carrying it, no one questioned him. That house. It seemed to be the preferred way for the misfits to live, the poor graduate students, independent women, musicians, students with pets or drugs, or just strange students. There was a large kitchen with refrigerator space for twelve people; four refrigerators, and cupboard space so everyone's cereals would be separate. Some people would get together for dinners, rotating the cooking or cleaning chores. He preferred to eat fruits and cereals by himself, although splurging every month on a filet mignon, which he cooked reverently, knowing what the animal gave up to "produce" it. If only it didn't taste so good. If only it didn't symbolize being out of prison.

He remembered the first night without sheets or pillow, his bag on the dresser and not put away. Now, he had sheets again; his star was rising again.

He enjoyed the people he met, the black biologist, the Indian engineer, the intense fellow who was studying Japanese culture, the women, who all seemed to be in nursing, English, or education. The expansive Jewish student, Nathan Silverman, who taught him how to bargain at the Safeway store. The first time, they had bought eight very soft, black avocados for $0.05 each; Nathan had explained to the produce manager how important it was to have fresh-looking produce and how willing they would be to take the substandard material off his hands at a fair price. It was Nathan who led him behind the store ten minutes later to collect the outer leaves of lettuce, which were thrown away because they were bruised or browned.

That night, Nathan fixed a wonderful, very inexpensive, guacamole with corn chips; since the corn chips were all broken, Walker assumed that they were the fruits of an earlier expedition.

Cliques formed naturally. He found himself in a group with Nathan, Deirdre, and Lisa. Deirdre was an education major; short, dark, and chubby, but with a beautiful, angelic face. He had an instant crush on her. She was properly Italian, and Catholic; and she had a crush on Nathan. Walker was sure that Lisa had a crush on him. Lisa had graduated as a nurse, but was now taking graduate courses in English, while working in a nursing home. She wrote poems for him. He hoped Nathan had a crush on her; that would make the circle perfect. The guacamole was for the four of them. They talked until three in the morning, about politics and poverty.

He went running in Ravenna Park. He sat in on classes in English, to see what his acquaintances were studying. He was surprised at how quiet the class was. No amount of prompting by the professor would elicit a response. Better to say nothing and be right than to risk an error, he figured. He sat in on a poetry writing class, for a while, but left when a Spanish surnamed poet mixed English and Spanish in bad poetry, and expected sympathy to overcome the deficits of his poetry. Walker spoke to him about his poetry in street-Spanish. The dislike was mutual and thick.

That fall, he took Industrial Psychology, Personality, History of Psychology, Learning and Motivation, Advanced Social Psychology, and a Seminar on Proxemic Behavior. For fun he audited some of the parallel courses in Sociology, which even used the same textbooks. A few of the geography and anthropology courses were also close in content, but he couldn't fit those in and still work.

Every month, before an exam, he would look through his journal. It looked too much like an outline, but it served to remind him of what he needed to know.

> Concepts of Motivation   Fear   Aggression
> Aggressive responses can be elicited by stimuli that produce frustration and pain.
> Painful electric shocks, administered to rats in a cage, will produce aggressive responses.
> Rats will attack one another, or even dolls. (the grid on the bottom of the cage is electrified)
> Freud: id, ego superego; sex drive; five stages; tens-reduc

Jung: unconscious; functions; unity; ambitions (dreams)

Adler: consciousness; creative self; social force; ideal

Erikson: structure? dynamics? development? motivation?

Fromm: social env.; love; social factors; needs

Post-Freudian   Skinner: behavior; reinforcement; events; drives

Rogers: sep. systems; harmony; interaction; maintenance

Maslow: plastic nature; will; needs; actualization

All theories too mechanical. Humans form images of selves, and
    environment, then act accordingly

Social Psychology   Authority   Milgram on legitimate authority:
    experimenter sets up situation mock situation on effects
    of punishment on learning with learner to memorize pairs
    of words and subject to administer shock for each mistake;
    each shock greater than last, approaching fatal levels. (no
    shocks were really administered.) 65% of the subjects obeyed
    experimenter and increased shocks to the end.

Does a child get more rewards than a rat? Read about pupil
    dilation and interest ... Male pupil expands for car or woman;
    female for child or house etc.

Is it learning that changes lifestyles, or the reinforcements of
    learning (money, diploma etc.)

Before the winter quarter, he got a second part-time job in the
department, tending animals for the teaching labs. He was in charge
of the rats. He became quite attached to them. So much so that it hurt
him when they were used for the undergraduate labs. These rats were
referred to as sophisticated, since they had been used before. The rats
used for faculty experiments came from a breeding colony outside of
Chicago. These rats were naive, unexposed to the joys of psychological
investigation.

Feeding was a simple mechanical operation: Fill the cups with dry pellets and water. He talked to them as he swept up under the wire cages. He started naming them after famous psychologists; Descartes and Skinner he reserved for his least favorite rats, who were greedy. He started taking breaks with the other lab assistants, so that they could trade rat stories. Benito Pexotto usually had the most interesting stories, since he had been working for the department the longest. The first story from Benny was one of his favorites. Mark Collins, as assistant professor out of Yale, was working on a strain of smart rats. At one point in his studies, he had the rat Alpha34 run three different mazes perfectly. He was sure that he had a genius strain. He even started theorizing about the genetic imprinting of learned behavior. Inherited learning. NeoLamarckianism. He asked Gerber and several others down to witness this triumph of breeding and learning. He put Alpha34 on a fourth maze, which the wonder rodent negotiated perfectly. While the others were listening to Collins spell out his publishing future, Rad Tagore, another lab assistant was watching Alpha34's movements carefully. When he was sure of himself, he coughed quietly, his eyes showing the strain of trying to contain hoarse laughter. He told Collins that he knew how Alpha34 was figuring out the mazes. Collins was irritated, but also curious, so he asked to be enlightened. Tagore pointed to the heat pipes on the ceiling, explaining that the rat was just a good mariner, reading the sky for clues to his whereabouts; most likely Collins also oriented the mazes in the same way, from start to finish. Everyone had a good chuckle; it seemed the rat was actually as smart as Collins had thought, using every available clue to run mazes. That night Collins hung a sheet from the pipes. Alpha34 failed to run the fifth maze on the first attempt.

"Well, what happened to the 34 series?" Walker was curious.

"Collins had them destroyed, and started a new project on aggression." Benny answered seriously.

"But why?"

"That's usually what happens to sophisticated rats, unless they're used for teaching labs, like yours."

Walker was quiet, burning slowly internally at the idea of more wasted lives.

Another of Benny's stories was equally enlightening. For a graduate lab, one professor decided to repeat the infamous 'experiment on the experimenters.' In this lab, one equal generation of rats was divided into three groups: a control group, one group labeled, at random, smart, and the other, labeled stupid. The rats went through preliminary testing to verify that they were equal in intelligence. Each group of rats was given to a set of students and identified as smart, stupid, or control. Each lab produced results that were significantly different. As they expected to see smart or stupid rats, they saw and even measured smart or stupid rats. The times for mazes and responses was actually recorded differently.

For his second full quarter, Walker took Methodology, hoping that he wouldn't have to face too many experimenter effects or errors of measurement, also a seminar on the Psychology of Love, Child Psychology, Language, and Physiological Psychology. He became interested in nonverbal communication, adding a directed study in that area. His journal started reflecting his interest in the processing of all information during communication, including, gestures, postures, positions, and expressions.

> Expectations influence the results in schools, also Rosenthal selected students at random and identified them as high potential; at the end of the school year, those same students increased scores significantly. .
>
> Tone of voice can change meaning from content. Example: Saying 'I'm fine' despondently. .
>
> Factory experiment (Find out who?): Workers in a factory were asked how conditions could be made better. They talked with psychologist, who was trying to improve   productivity. First they asked for better lighting and   colorful walls;

productivity went up. Then they asked for longer breaks and flexible hours; productivity went up. Then they asked for meetings with management; productivity went up. Before the psychologist reported his success to management, he decided to reverse the conditions. He took away the improved lighting; productivity went up. He cut breaks, flexible hours, and management interface; production went up, not down as expected. His conclusion was that attention of others to their work let people increase productivity, and this was the most important factor; only his interest was constant.

Don and Roberta team teaching psych of love. Must be having affair. Class is superficially interesting, but lacking substance. Perhaps love is too ambiguous. The reward of love is other's welfare. The variables are proximity and similarity. The emotional feelings are a mystery, even to D. and R. Cervantes: love is influenced by no consideration, recognizes no restraints of reason Logically, I have never been in love.

He started drawing and putting poems in the journal, but they always remained unfinished.

The spring quarter seemed much longer. Perhaps because he was taking the courses he needed for graduation and not the ones he wanted to. Gerber had another undergraduate course to force on him, by way of preparation and discipline. He read that textbook in a week, and finished the paper the second week. As long as he remembered to get to the exam, he would pass it easily. He was taking seminars on Phenomenology and the Anthropology of Space. Next year, he would start on the doctorate.

In April, Benny came to him with a horror story of research in the monkey labs. They walked in the evening to Guthrie Hall. The lights by the front doors had halos from the fog, radiating away. Walker noted how beautiful they looked.

The rat labs and the monkey labs shared the fourth floor of 'rat hall;' the second and third had offices; the first classrooms; and the basement, labs. Benny took him up to the fourth floor, to the Primate research, funded by the National Institute of Health. The researcher, Sherman Booth, had 17 macaques, 16 crab-eating, and 14 rhesus monkeys. Ten had the afferent nerves leading to one or both forelimbs severed surgically in order to eliminate sensation in the limb. This procedure, deafferentation, was supposed to have application in the treatment of human stroke victims. After a short recovery time, these ten and the others were subjected to tests to determine to what extent they could recover the use of deafferented limbs.

There were small wire cages, all with chipped paint, most with broken and rusted wires. The nearest macaque had a ragged bandage on one arm, several small open wounds on another. He reached down to retrieve a bit of food from a foul, overflowing fecal pan. The bit slipped to the floor, which had scatterings of rodent feces. In the corner, a refrigerator filled with discarded medicine bottles and rotten food in lumps. There were anonymous shapes in paper bags. A plastic sack hung next to the small freezer section coils. Next to it, a freezer, blocked with defrosted, refrozen ice, containing blocks of ice and a monkey carcass wrapped in plastic, older than four months. The director's desk had a pile of papers weighted with a monkey hand severed at the wrist.

"Have you reported this, yet? To anyone? To the SPCA or Humane Society? This is in gross violation of any anti-cruelty code. Have you reported it?" Walker repeated.

"Yes," Benny admitted, "But nothing happened. We reported it and even took some of the monkeys in for veterinary care. We tried to— " Benny stopped, defeated by his position, by the legal process, and by the nature of humanity. "We lost. We were ordered to return the animals. Booth was ordered to clean up the cages, which he did nine months ago. He got another grant from NIH." Benny paused. "I know that you have been stealing rats. Are you going to try to do anything about this?"

Walker shrugged, looking downcast. "What can we do. I need the job, how about you?"

"I've been sneaking antibiotics to some of them. That's all. We shouldn't even be here. Booth's sensitive, like a bear with cubs, or jealous anyway."

Walker winced at the slander against bears. "Have you told anyone else?" he asked.

Benny replied, "Just Mark and Sandy. They were upset, but didn't know what to do either."

"Let's get out of here. I feel sick." Walker exclaimed, blowing air through his nose, trying to ignore the stink. 'Prison,' he thought, looking at a monkey spread-eagled in the restraint chair. Untreated wounds ignored. The restraint chair was a stand of thick pipe. A metal table bisected the monkey and restrained him. Both legs were spread at 45-degree angles and wrapped in surgical tape to the vertical posts. The normal limb was taped to a post also; the surgically altered limb was stretched up higher and double wrapped. On the bottom of the 'chair' was a motor. The purpose of this apparatus was to study self-directing behavior toward the altered limb. Apparently, the monkey had been strapped in all day. Many monkeys subjected to deafferentation mutilated the limb. A short inspection of all the monkeys revealed that 39 of 55 fingers on affected limbs were missing or malformed; this was not part of the experiment. The one monkey with both limbs deafferented seemed to have a fractured forearm. They saw open lesions and old-bandage trauma. They left quietly.

"Dr. Booth considers each of these monkeys worth $60-100,000 dollars apiece." Benny mentioned.

"Strange way to treat a million-dollar investment," Walker replied, taking the stairs two at a time.

Chapter 11 Unnecessary Experiments

The next evening, Booth was startled as he unlocked the lab.

"I don't like what you've done here," came a voice from behind the cages.

"Shit, who are you?" Booth countered. "You gave me a fright." Booth tried to see who it was. "If you're not authorized to be here, I'm going to have you arrested. Well, who are you?"

"Just a concerned citizen," the voice stated. "Concerned that your irresponsible activities cause suffering."

"I am responsible! A responsible scientists. All animal research scientists are responsible people or they wouldn't be scientists. Of course, there are some violations of the Animal Welfare Act, but these are usually trivial. All right, all right, maybe there has been a failure to comply with the NIH Guide for the Care and Use of Laboratory Animals, but I can correct it immediately. Immediately." Booth backed towards the door.

"You are not qualified to judge me, you are no scientist," Booth charged. "No one except another researcher is qualified to set standards for the care of these monkeys. Sanitary conditions are not possible under research conditions. You can't attack research like this. This is viable research, that's benefited and will continue to benefit humanity. It would be inhuman to try to carry out procedures on humans that have not been tested in humans. Wait, I have rights."

Booth's protest was left hanging as he struggled against his attacker, who pressed Booth's hands behind his back and dragged him over to the restraint chair. He pushed him back through the table, which pinched the generous waist painfully. When Booth's hands broke free of the grip, the attacker hit Booth on the jaw and grabbed one hand and stretched it forward and slightly down. Pulling surgical tape from the edge of the table he wrapped the wrist tightly. Ripping the tape, he secured the other hand to the other side. Booth groaned and tried to kick, but his position was too awkward. The attacker restrained the feet next, each leg bent slightly to accommodate the relatively larger size of a human subject to the chair. His head was left free. Booth could feel his fastened body pinched at the waist. It was hard to breathe. What was happening? "Wait, that hurts. Please let me go. It hurts."

"What is happening you're thinking? I am doing an experiment. No don't talk; you are not a researcher. You are not a doctor or veterinarian; you are not even a good psychologist. Your research was derivative, designed solely for personal aggrandizement and the procurement of trendy federal dollars. You are a subject, now. If your research is valid, you can be rehabilitated, just like those who have had strokes. See, if you wanted, you could bite the fleshy upper part of your arms, if you get frustrated."

As he was talking, the attacker loosened Booth's red, black and green striped tie. The arms of the laboratory coat were ripped off. Booth wore only a short sleeved shirt. The brown trouser legs were ripped down from the groin and fell into a huddle around the ankles. Booth's blue boxer shorts stuck out a bit from the hastily modified trousers. Booth urinated; a faint-pungy, warm-damp, smell. He started to speak, but was silenced by a glare.

"I am going to deafferentate your limbs. No, don't complain, I don't want the scalpel to slip. Yes, I am highly educated. I am going to sever the brachial plexus just below the branches by the humerus. I don't want to risk hitting the artery. You will, of course, feel no pain after a sharp sting."

The scalpel made a crescent cut under the left arm.

"Must begin with the left you know, standard procedure." Then under the right. Blood began a regular drip down the arm to the elbow, where it dripped onto the table. Two small pools were forming as the attacker started to cut through the upper thigh, near the sciatic nerve.

Booth screamed in panic, a high, piercing noise. Struggling violently. The blade was removed.

"Please, I know you're upset, but this is for science." The right thigh was cut, with an acknowledging whimper from Booth. Blood started trickling down the inner thighs to the collapsed trouser legs, staining the fabric; even artificial fabrics seem to be stained by blood.

Booth started screaming and shouting for help, long drawn out words, "aaaoooooowwwwhhhhh, heeeelllllllpp. nnooooooo, heeellllllllp" that ended with a mild plea, "help."

"And you shall have it," assured the attacker seriously. "Think about what you have told the NIH about your laboratory about the monkeys being fed regularly, about care being given, about adequate veterinary care being given to lesions and cuts and bites. Since you must have told the truth, someone will come to check on the monkeys in about two hours. Your loss of blood will not be critical. Of course, those are open wounds, and there seems to be bacterial growth on that pile of shit on the floor, but this research doesn't need perfect sanitary conditions. When your help comes for the midnight check, they can give you penicillin, also. Of course, if you haven't arranged for someone to check ... well, I'm sure someone will."

The attacker followed Booth's eyes to the refrigerator. He went over and opened it, finding the penicillin next to a pile of rotten undifferentiated fruit, vaguely bananas. The penicillin had expired a year earlier. He tossed it back in and closed the door. Booth screamed and flopped his arms and legs. He could only feel the pain in his waist and jaw, however, and the panic of not feeling his arms and legs made him cry and bite his lips. Little pearls of blood appeared on the torn lips.

"I guess I'll be taking the monkeys, now. No, don't worry, I know where to find good homes for them. People who respect animals and will care for them for the next twenty years, who will give them grass and flies, light and toys. What?"

183

Booth was panting and vocalizing, trying to communicate something important, but not knowing what or how. "Oh, don't, worry, the monkeys stayed in that chair for up to six hours, didn't they? And if you get stressed or bored, you can use your deafferentated limbs as toys, as you once joked about the monkeys. I'm going on vacation, now. I'm sure that your assistants will be scrupulous about taking care of the project and find you soon."

He glanced once more at Booth, restrained into the pipe chair, an eager gleam escaping the mean little eyes in the curly, chubby little head, then closed and locked the door. Booth emitted a strangled gurgle and shook the chair. The attacker remembered that he had forgotten to put out water or food, but smiled and hoped one of the assistants would remember.

After his experiment with Booth, he was still tense and hungry. Hungry for what? He realized that he needed a release. He was excited. He couldn't just go through the campus grabbing someone.

He ran back down dark streets to the house, and up the stairs. On the second floor, he stopped at Deirdre's room, pushing open the door. The chubby little education major wasn't there. Leaving the door open, he ran up the next flight and down the hall to Lisa's room, pushing through the door. She was curled up on a cushion under a light, reading. She started to rise, questioningly, as he grabbed her. He lowered her back down, searching through her lips with his tongue, his hand in a knot of blonde hair guiding her head. He pressed with his chest and loins, as she gasped and tried to speak. His left hand slid down until it grasped a buttock; his right hand slide around her side and cupped a clothed breast. Her hands, at first pushed against his chest, twisted into claws and gripped his side. His rubbing became more frantic. He lifted slightly, gazed at her with the intensity of a nova. Then rolled her on her stomach on the floor pillow. He pushed her skirt up, his knees on the backs of her legs. Using both hands, he unzipped his trousers, and tore her panties down from the back. He forced himself in, shifting his legs slightly. The first penetration released a flood of nervous explosions starting at the center and reaching his shoulders and ears. She arched slightly, cursing. He moved both hands to hold her buttocks just above the curve. Thrusting inward, pulling back. He imagined her breasts, still bound, but pushing against the pillow. His eyes moved down to his own rigid member, moving with atomic precision along a path as ancient as human life, until a critical mass was reached; he could not contain himself any more. He cried out and rolled his eyes upward. He kept thrusting as the spasms subsided.

He gazed down past the curve of her buttocks, to the thighs, knees and calves, rubbing her leg with his left hand. He noticed little blonde hairs on the small of her back and top of her buttocks. Lisa lowered her hips slightly, and rotated them upward from the legs. She shifted back and forth until he heard a little sigh and a break in tension. He pulled back until he dropped free, then rolled her over on her back. As her bent leg met his chest she straightened it. He rolled backward, his zipper pinching his balls, left hand pulling them up and protecting them from her fists, which sought his face, in retaliation.

Her words came in ragged gasps, "You" punch "bastard" punch "not" punch "like" "that" punch punch. Her first punches had been direct and fisted, but now her hands were looser and she was swinging her arms sideways. He felt blood trickle down his nose. He rolled her on her side, as she weakly slapped an ear. He bit his lip in anger, then felt the blood drop on his chin. He pulled his balls and pushed them back into his trousers, leaving the zipper down. He stroked her hair, noticing that her skirt was still around her waist and her panties were a loose flap in front. He ripped the buttons off her blouse, and pulled her bra up, while cupping a breast and pushing it up toward her shoulder. She brought her knee up swiftly, hitting the upper thigh and penis. His body snapped forward, forehead hitting her shoulder. With an effort, he brought his hands to her shoulders, and pushed her over, his anger evaporating as

185

he saw the concern and hurt in her eyes. He bent her back, tried kissing her jaw, then eyes, whose lids fluttered like nervous moths, then her forehead, down to her nose, then her lips. He kissed as gently as he could, feeling his passion start to swell again. He ripped his own shirt open, scattering buttons to the left.

He became detached. He could feel his own sperm cells forming in the testes, softly folded in the scrotum. The cells were formed in seminiferous tubules, which were long, thin canals coiled into lobules. They had been producing millions of sperm daily, since puberty. During arousal, the mature sperm cells left the ducts and passed through the seminal vesicles and the prostrate gland, where other secretions were added. The erection of his penis was due to the engorgement of spongy tissue with blood. The veins that normally drained the blood had constricted as the result of a combination of friction and impulses from the brain, blocking the outflow of blood. The rigid penis penetrated the vagina, rubbing against the clitoris and labia. As the glans was stimulated, the pelvic muscles contracted rhythmically, causing ejaculation. The muscles in the wall of the urethra contracted, expelling the sperm through the opening.

A combination of her juices and his appeared as a white froth on his hairs at the root of the penis. He looked at her flanks still moving slowly; her breasts rolling gently, nipples erect.

She started to say "Get off," but stopped. Her well aimed fist broke through his detachment and his lower lip.

He stood up suddenly. He smashed his fist through the plaster stair wall, ran out of the house and slowed to a walk as he neared the park. Doubly damned and really stupid. He knew what rape was like; now he was no better, as ugly and defeated by life as any loser. What now, he wondered? What can I say? Or do?

Lisa lay still for a moment, in shock. She got up and hurried to the bathroom. She took off her clothes and showered, first hot, then cold.

She cleaned herself, asking herself: How could he? I like him, what is wrong? Why me? After she had dried off and put on clean clothes, she went downstairs to Casey's room; she knew that the nursing student had been raped last year—she would know what to do. A curse on this town, with its ugly rampant males, too stupid to know what to do but too aggressive to stop. A curse on him!

After absently scrapping a spot of cow manure off his shoe, Mack addressed his only daughter, "Listen Belle, this is ridiculous. I want you to date, you're over 30 now, godammit. You think any other father has to force his daughter to date, Hell, I should be trying to save you from 'em boys!"

Belle Jenny was over 30, but didn't look much over 20. She was tapping her foot, staring at her father's feet.

"Oh, I know, I'm 'sposed to take 'em off in the house. Takes so long to tie 'em. Oh, all right, I'm going!" He stomped off, not happy with the rules or his obstinate daughter; at least she was an excellent businesswoman and ran the business side of things. He smiled, then frowned as he remembered that he would eventually need an heir to take over.

Belle loved her father; he was a successful farmer, but just never got used to any luxury that required changing boots or clothes before coming into the house. And, she knew he was right, that she should be dating or thinking about marriage. Her faithful biological clock was counting down the years of fertility; her body felt gravid with need, but no one she knew felt right. She decided to keep him happy by giving the "professor" a date. She remembered him when he played in mud, and no university appointment could ever supersede that image.

The death of Dr. Booth sparked a series of debates on animal experimentation that petered out before the outrage of the mutilation, and long before the investigation was shelved. Walker watched an entertaining confrontation on the Merv Griffith show, between Dr. Herman Mantle and Todd Austin.

Dr. Mantle: "If all sensation is eliminated from a limb, how can the animal suffer physical pain? Broken bones, open wounds, chewed-off fingers, are the inevitable result of research like this. But it is justifiable, if it would relieve human suffering."

Mr. Austin: "This is cruelty. If we exploit animals for the good of humanity, we must do it humanely. Only humane research can be valid anyway. Besides, if that is justifiable, then how can you be outraged at Professor Booth's death? He didn't suffer any pain, I heard."

Dr. Mantle: "He had to, he had to—humans can anticipate and imagine their death. I'm sure Dr. Booth suffered terribly."

Mr. Austin: "But if he did, then surely his research animals did."

Dr. Mantle: "No, they could never imagine dying ... Listen, let's get back to the debate: All knowledge is of potential use to humanity. Its pursuit cannot be questioned or obstructed. Not only would it be a violation of freedom, but against the best interests of society. The ends justify the means, if there is benefit to society, and there is."

Mr. Austin: "Ridiculous! Ends are infected with means. Many of these experiments do not contribute to scientific knowledge. They are in compliance to federal law that states, essentially, if human beings want to put dangerous chemicals in or on their bodies, thousands of animals must be mutilated to make sure that it isn't too dangerous. What woman, no matter how vain, would put cosmetics in her eyes until her eyes melted? It is a cheap public relations gimmick."

Dr. Mantle: "Well, animal models are different. Surely you can see that. Animal models find cures for human diseases. Drugs and vaccines are developed. Right this very moment, we are working to find a cure for malaria."

Mr. Austin: "In an artificial laboratory? In total isolation? Not likely. An owl monkey in a two-foot steel cage is not likely to be a good model for malaria, which interacts with many social and environmental factors.

Sure, a vaccine may be developed, that might work to alleviate the disease, but why not learn how to prevent it? Why not use that expertise to give clean air, food, and water to the people who contract malaria because they are hungry and stressed?"

Dr. Mantle: "Some models mimic human disorders so closely that there are no alternatives. For instance, chemicals can cause emotional disturbance in monkeys that is parallel to that in humans."

Mr. Austin: "But if the studies are relevant to human disorders, then the animals must be subjected to great suffering. If the pain is so analogical, why not use humans?"

Dr. Mantle: "But that is not acceptable."

Mr. Austin: "Why not? The people are in pain, anyway, and surely would appreciate the attention to their disorder that is so lavished on artificially sickened laboratory animals. In fact, some psychological studies show that people improve with attention."

Walker watched the talking heads. It is good to talk, but better to act, he thought.

He looked for and found an apartment later that week. Neither Lisa, nor Deirdre or Nathan had spoken too him. He wondered what she had told them. He felt ugly and sick, but couldn't summon the courage to talk to any of them. He knew it had been rape. Some part of his soul had withered. He wanted to say to her—but what would he say? 'I was too excited?' The new apartment was on Brooklyn, in a four-story brick building, well maintained. It was a studio, with a collapsing bed, kitchen and bathroom. He didn't notice much of it. He cooked a batch of chocolate chip cookies. He ate them alone.

The quarter ended uneventfully. Walker asked to quit the program early for personal reasons. He had enough credits for the Master's degree, however. All the lab assistants had been interviewed. He said that he had never been in the Primate lab. Presumably, Benny had not mentioned it. Benny had turned the monkeys over to a radical group from Eugene, Oregon—Animals First. They had agreed to find homes and apparently did.

He was talking to a young veterinarian hired to provide care for experimental animals.

"I know someone you'd really like," Jerry Swenson was saying. "This big, bad-breathed, saxophone player of a veterinarian up the highway founded his own wildlife clinic. He treats blue heron, bittern, snowy owls, trumpeter swans, hawks, eagles, falcons— "

"Eagles?" Walker interrupted.

"Yea, he has a real bash when he releases one. I went to one last year. He had received a young golden eagle from a state game biologist who had found her in a coyote trap— or two kids found her and called the biologist— something like that; but Brad tried to care for her. She wouldn't eat. He examined her mouth and found ulcerating sores— that's common in starving eagles, which explains why she didn't eat for the biologist. They like to keep eagles themselves. Normally, vets don't have permits to treat wild animals, but Brad— "

"Jerry! Finish."

"Oh, yea. Brad finally fed her by forcing hamburger down her throat with forceps. When she got better, he gave her frozen mice. After two weeks, he released "Golden" at a champagne and cake party, in which she did not participate. Brad was dressed up in top hat and tails. Think you'd like to meet him?"

"Think you could introduce us in less than ten minutes?"

Walker and Jerry laughed. Jerry liked to talk. Dr. Brad Healy was impressive in physical girth as well as in breadth of interests. He was a partner in a clinic; designed his own research on fertility in mares and elephants, and operated a wildlife retreat dedicated to restoring incapacitated animals to their natural state. He also forced both of them to attend his Dixieland jazz band session that night. Everyone ate and drank too much.

They stayed outside his house in sleeping bags. Brad was up early to feed his charges. Walker accompanied him. He felt a kinship with animals. Brad introduced each animal, with a short story about how she or he came to him.

In a little house by itself was a red-tailed hawk. When the door was opened the hawk launched himself directly toward the opening. Brad raised his hands with spread fingers, and the hawk veered upward, wings spread. "I'm going to release him today. Wanta watch?"

"Sure," Walker replied, eyes never leaving the hawk, whose eyes never left him. Brad put on a leather glove from a white cardboard carton in the corner. The bird refused to hop on the glove. "Open that box in the corner, quickly."

Walker folded the box open, noticing the breathing holes and the handles. Brad came carrying the bird by the feet, wings spread and drubbing his shoulders. He flipped the bird around and into the box, careful not to hurt the wings.

When the lids were closed, he said, "Let's go."

"Just like that? Now?"

"Sure, why not? I'm going to release him over the hill." Over the hill turned out to be a three mile walk, taking stretches carrying the container. Beneath a fence post, Brad set the box down.

"You let him go."

Walker shrugged, but took the glove.

"Hold him away from your face. Reach under the wings. He won't bite."

Walker opened the box quickly, noticed which way the bird was facing, and reached in the other way. The hawk bit his arm just above the glove before he got him out of the box. As he lifted out, he felt the wings thud against his head. He kept lifting his hand higher. Then the hawk glided to a fence post.

"Well done," Brad commented. "Did he get you?"

"Yes, a little. Another kind of virginity lost," Walker was surprised that he was not angry at being cut—perhaps because he understood being trapped.

They both watched the bird preen on the fence post. He seemed much smaller with his wings folded.

"What happens, now?" Walker asked.

"Whatever he wants."

Walker approached the post slowly, stopping every foot. When he was three feet away the hawk lifted to the side, flapped his wings twice and glided up into a pine, forty feet above the ground.

"Will he be back?"

"Maybe, if the wing isn't well. He may hang around for a couple of weeks, then go. Hawks are territorial only over part of the year. This one—"

Walker was watching the hawk, who was now sitting in the tree a hundred yards away. He started moving toward the tree. There was a gulch halfway there. He leapt across, rolling with the impact. When he got to the tree he stood under it. What was he expecting, he wondered, conversation? the secrets of flight? He turned at a noise and saw Brad climbing the sides of the gulch.

They sat under the tree for several hours talking about wild birds.

Finally, Brad said, "You ought to go into veterinary medicine. I could recommend you at wazoo."

"Wazoo?"

"Washington State University, in Pullman. I know the dean there real well."

"I don't think I could survive any more school. Besides, I have a good offer here, in Seattle."

"Why don't you go over for a few days. Come with me. I'm going over for a meeting on people and pets, pet therapy, aging pets, people something, I think."

Brad trailed off trying to remember the name of the meeting.

I could, Walker considered, I was going to Couer d'Alene for another interview the week after anyway.

The drive across Washington was a lesson in geology. Neither of them drove, so they were riding with a geology student going back to Pullman. They were treated to the history of plate tectonics, the Pacific plate in particular, rock formation, mountain building, erosion, and human influences. Brad watched for birds, Walker scanned the horizon for signs of deer or coyotes. Fortunately, driving must be a habit, Walker mused, or we all would be dead several times. During the long drive through the scablands, created by the rupture of a dam in the Pleistocene holding back lake Missoula, Brad and Walker dozed. They stopped for cokes and sandwiches in Washtucna. There was a drive-in next to the two-lane highway. The approach to the Inland Empire was decked with wheat fields and complicated by roads that lead in every direction, except to Pullman. Finally, a sign welcomed them to the home of the 'Cougars.'

"When was the last time a cougar lived around here, Brad?" Walker wondered.

"Probably 1910, earlier, later, around then."

"Why don't we start naming our teams after mechanical equipment, instead of vanished species?"

Andy got into the game, "You mean like Harvesters or Combines?"

"Or backhoes or fertilizers."

"Or steamrollers or bulldozers." Brad added.

"Or vacuum cleaners or toasters," Andy suggested.

"What would you call them, then, for nicknames, 'Go Suckers!' Yea Breadburners?" Walker asked.

Brad started giving directions to let them off at the Vet School.

They paid Andy for the gas and thanked him.

"Well, I'm going to stay with Lansing, the pharmacist at the school. There's a good barn over there for you to sleep in, plenty of cows if you get horny," Brad clapped him on the back and breathed on him. "Just kidding. I made arrangements for you to stay in a dormitory room. It's five dollars a night, clean sheets, and there's plenty of cows in ca—"

Walker elbowed him in the ribs, which started Brad coughing.

They were already late for the opening dinner. Brad had already paid in advance. "My treat, my only treat."

About fifty people were seated in the Scandinavian room at the Student Union Building. White table cloths, catered; it still tasted like institutional food. Walker gave his chicken Kiev to Brad and had more salad. How could anyone eat something that flew. The dinner featured a series of anecdotes by the dean, Dwight Paxton. The rest of the conversations dealt with the medical aspects of pets.

Sometime during the meal, Walker became offended by some of the assumptions of veterinarians.

"Why have pets at all?" he asked Dr. Beltran, who was seated on the other side from Brad. "It's bad for the pets certainly, and worse for wildlife, which is displaced."

"Well, no, it's not necessarily bad for the pets. Many people care for them properly."

"But they use them for child surrogates, for friends, for therapists."

"Why is that bad? People sometimes need to relate to animals."

"It's bad because the animals are not children, friends, or therapists. Treating them as such puts an unfair burden on them. And when they can't carry it, they're abandoned, beaten or killed."

"Surely your views are too extreme," Beltran judged smoothly. "It is healthy for animals to be petted, to be fed regularly, and have warm quarters."

Parts of the argument were interrupted by the serving of desert.

Brad interrupted, "Go get him, George."

"Most pets," Walker began again, "are domesticated at a neotonous stage. They depend on us as alpha animals, and never develop beyond the young puppy stage—"

"But that's not true of the horse or cat," Beltran interrupted.

The argument went on through dinner and into the evening symposium. Brad spent much of his time crunching his cough drops and rattling the paper. Somehow the symposium went on.

The next day Walker went on a tour of the Veterinary School. The tour was given by a thick, balding editor in the school, Alan Merchant, who gave a brisk tour and obviously glossed over the information he wasn't sure of. Two ten-year old girls, with their parents, and one other couple also took the tour. After a short film, narrated by some other aspiring editor, the tour began in the Necropsy Laboratory.

"Dead animals are brought into this laboratory so that the cause of death may be determined," Merchant began.

A white horse was laid out on the floor, below a large track for carrying heavy loads. Walker wondered how the horse had lived; pet, farm animal, wild? He could visualize it running, and snorting.

"— over 100 diseases that people can contract from animals or their parasites. Are there any questions?"

One of the fathers wanted to know about the ratio of women students to men; then about admissions requirements, as if they wouldn't change in ten years.

The pathology museum was a set of monsters behind glass. A hydrocephalic lamb. Cephalothoracophagus, two lambs fused from the head to the abdomen. Dicephalus Dibrachius Dipus, one calf with two heads. And more.

One little girl asked what a 'moster' was.

Merchanter replied that the word came from a Latin word, meaning 'to point out.' Monsters were unfortunate creatures that pointed out the errors of life.

Humanity is such a monster, Walker suspected.

The rest of the tour was taken up with visits to a surgery room, radiology, the anatomy museum, with its formaldehyde atmosphere, and the large animal barns. "72,186 large animals, mostly pigs, were treated here last year," Merchant was saying. "Each animal is weighed, before it enters and before it leaves."

Walker stayed behind and petted some of the horses. Two students were preparing a mare for some procedure. He was surprised at how careful and gentle they were.

Brad left the next day, after arranging an interview for him with the Dean. The interview went well. Walker expressed surprise that the school would consider a psychologist for admission or staff.

"Brad said that you had courses in zoology and ecology. We actually prefer people with a broad, diverse background," the dean commented.

Walker maneuvered Paxton into talking about his own career, which began in dairy herd health. He looked around as Paxton spoke, noticing the cow emblems everywhere. The dean also spoke of the importance of veterinary medicine in the contemporary world, showing how veterinarians were carving their own niches in industry. Walker noticed that almost everything having to do with animals was already an industry, meat-packing, chicken farming; even the pet care industry and the horse racing industry. All this immense industry from grains of thought.

"Here's a little folder for you, on 'Research at Washington State University.' It describes all of the projects being pursued. Excuse me," Paxton leaned toward the intercom. "Daisy, I need to call Horvath; get me that number, would you."

Walker got up, just as a bald man in a white coat came in, brandishing a piece of paper. Paxton looked at it and signed it.

"I hope you will consider applying here in the fall. In the mean time, take the tour, walk around and get to know the place. We're growing real fast," the dean boasted.

"Thank you, I will," Walker agreed, shaking hands.

As he left, he heard the phone ring.

He stopped up at the Compton Union Building, CUB it was called, for a cheese sandwich and coke. He thumbed through the research report as he ate. There was something that caught his attention. He bused his plate and left to return to the Vet school.

The ebb of students indicated that classes had changed. He dropped into the flow, trying to read the cards on the doors as he passed them. The students ahead were talking.

"Sure, we're going up to Longacres tonight with John."

"John's the track veterinarian?"

"No, Harry Milgram. Harry's put his whole life in the industry."

Walker saw the Veterinary Pharmacology office and turned in. "I'm looking for Dr. Rand?" he addressed the phalanx of secretaries far behind the counter.

After a few moments of chatter, one of them volunteered, "He's in Spillman. This is McCoy. He may be in class."

Back out in the hall he asked a student where Spillman was. And received directions. He followed two female students in white jackets.

"— taking Practice Management. God, it's a travelogue of clinics, tax accounting, bookkeeping, insurance, organization. I didn't think it would be so material."

"Try taking the ethics seminar. Did you here what Paxton said in his intro? The most ethical question he had to face was, 'How large should the sign be?'"

"No, but I'd believe—"

Walker was going off course so he crossed the parking lot. He was going to miss getting to Rand before class. He supposed that it wouldn't be too painful to see part of the lecture.

The classroom held thirty; almost that many were present. Rand, if it was Rand, glanced up as he entered, but continued lecturing.

"— physiological responses to physiological cues; the responses are observable and the cues are identifiable. The connection between physiology and behavior is strongest with ingestive behaviors."

Walker sat in back and looked around the room. The desks were old wooden ones, with permanent writing pads. Most of the students had their heads buried in paper, notes to the right, printed handout to the left.

"—endocrine influence on energy-storing tissues is important for providing nutrient availability to body tissues," Rand was saying, "it only palliates the animal's need for external calories."

He paused to let some of the writers catch up. Walker noted that he had typed notes of his own.

"There is evidence in the literature and in experience—say when a lactating goat doubles her food intake to compensate for glandular loss—that animals increase their caloric intake in response to increased metabolic demand. The expenditure of thermo-regulatory calories under cold ambient temperatures, the condition involuntary of an inadequate dietary situation, these energy-balancing behavioral responses demonstrate that feeding is controlled by the animal, but offer few clues to the specific metabolic events going on. In fact, under laboratory conditions, only one metabolic change can be shown to increase food intake, and that is glucose utilization. This phenomenon was first noticed when hypoglycemic rats—made that way by insulin injection—increased their food intake. Jean Meyer proposed a glucostatic theory on the control of feeding based on this observation. This theory, however, is not supported by experimental data."

As Rand paused, Walker translated the lecture into commonsense English, 'mothers and cold animals eat more; animals can be forced to eat more, but we don't know why.'

"Yet evidence continues to mount that pharmacological interference with glucose utilization results in increased feeding. There is direct evidence—work with antimetabolic glucose analogues that inhibit glucose utilization—that glucose utilization is monitored in the brain. 2-deoxy-D-glucose—2-DG—blocks phosphohexose isomerase in rats and increases feeding. 2-DG prevents glucose-6-phosphate from being metabolized through the glycolytic path. It is now believed that brain receptors cause hunger when depletion of their own energy stores is detected. Any alteration of these receptor energy stores causes increased feeding."

Walker looked up at the clock, then at the water-stained ceiling.

Rand continued, "Our understanding of the physiological controls of ingestion is sketchy. Yet feed efficiency is of obvious importance in animal production. Disorders of feeding are costly to the food animal industry. Before any of us can successfully manipulate the intake of food by animals or man, the constraining factors on spontaneous ingestion must be investigated and analyzed.

"Dietary variety and the availability of excesses of highly palatable calorically dense foodstuffs had led to the failure of controls in men and to disorders such as obesity. Nutritionists have calculated that the average woman gains eleven kilograms after the age of 25 and before 65. In fact, such a gain for a woman represents only one fortieth of one percent error of control per day—an excess of only 350 milligrams per day. Bodily fat stores in mammals are regulated within fairly narrow limits. There are contributing factors to the failure of precise control: age, genetic predisposition, emotion, exposure to variety, the ability to afford quantity. Our own failure as scientists to deal with obesity and other eating syndromes, such as anorexia nervosa, results from an ignorance of the ways in which adipose tissue participates in the control of food intake."

Walker shifted uncomfortably, then noticed that everyone was shifting and changing gears; pencils were put down, papers were shuffled. Even Rand leaned against the podium.

"Fat cells are capable of either stimulating or inhibiting food intake. Your laboratory sessions this summer will deal with fat-inhibited feeding. Each investigating group will be assigned twenty rats, which will be force-fed by stomach tube. These animals will gain weight much more rapidly than the single control group. When tube feeding is terminated, some of the rats will be sacrificed to determine the percentage of fat. All animals will be weighed. The remainder of artificially-obesified rats will be permitted to feed normally. You will record their feeding patterns. The hypothesis to be tested is, do fat cells inhibit feeding? See you tomorrow."

Walker waited until after the troops had filed out. He introduced himself and began to ask questions about Rand's research.

"It's quite important. We are trying to prove that elevated fat cells may stimulate food intake, while a normal number of normal fat cells that are temporarily distended may exert an inhibitory effect on feeding."

"And how do you go about proving it?" Walker asked.

"We are causing rats to become obese by exposing them to high caloric diets. Different groups are exposed for different lengths of time, by thirty day periods. Rats are sacrificed after each period and the number of fat cells counted."

"What about age-specificity?" Walker asked, feeling vaguely disturbed.

"Oh, yes, of course."

Walker couldn't listen anymore. "What about the rats?" he asked.

"Well, what about them?" Rand answered in irritation. "They're treated well; they're cared for."

"You feed them what?"

"Chocolate chip cookies."

"And that's a balanced diet?"

"No, it can't be and get results."

"But the rats would eat a balanced diet, if they had fruits and grains to choose from?"

"Well, technically, yes, but—"

"So, you're feeding them, forcing them to eat junk food against their will?"

Rand smiled condescendingly, "I don't know that they have a will? Do you?"

"Yes, they do. Try turning them loose," Walker suggested.

"I don't think I have to justify this to you. If you don't mind I'm quite busy." Rand tried to terminate the discussion.

"Why not just observe humans. Good observations will do just as much for your hypothesis as this unnecessary experimentation."

"This is for the betterment of humanity," Rand affirmed.

"No, it's for idle curiosity, limited by laziness, and encouraged by trends in government financing. No more." Walker was going the same way as Rand. There was an embarrassed silence until Rand turned off alone at the next junction of halls.

Walker was depressed. He walked by other classrooms. Drifts of scholarly endeavor teased his ears as he walked.

"— hypothalamic control of integrative processes— "

Then from the next room, "— mechanisms for the dissemination of viral—"

Then the sounds of engines being started in the parking lot.

He had a salad at the CUB, took in a free movie, and went to bed.

Rand was back in Spillman, shutting down for the night. Spillman was a single-story world-war-II, temporary building; it would probably last another thirty years, Rand thought. Once the fluorescent lights were off, it was positively spooky. He knew some of it was his imagination. Some of the sounds were recognizable. Another wild cat, probably abandoned by its student owner in the spring, had had a litter of kittens under the building. There was no way to keep them out. Occasionally, a crew from physical plant would come to capture the cats and distribute them to outlying barns, but Rand hated living above them; dirty, scruffy little pests. He had tried to catch one last month, using milk as bait, but the little bitch had bitten the shit out of his hand. It was still tender. Still clutching his hand in memory, he checked to make sure his charges had water. He hoped that new fellow wouldn't matriculate here. He would be trouble; another bleeding heart. Too many bleeding hearts and nothing would ever get done.

He locked the door and walked down the dark hall. Going down the outside steps, he glanced back at the windows. A red dot. What was a red dot doing on? Warning light. Must be for a pump or something. He tried to remember what he had that had a warning light and would be left on all night, but he couldn't. Cursing, he turned back. If only he weren't so damned conscientious, he thought, he could spend more time at home.

He had to unlock the front door. Then walk back to the office and open that door. Then go through the office and unlock the lab door. He didn't bother turning on the lights. When he walked over to the wall where he saw the light there was nothing on the shelf. He went to the window and looked out. And looked back inward. Then he heard it, a pittering of feet. Mice, he thought, the building's got mice, too; why can't the cats catch the mice.

Going back out, he tripped over the fifty-pound feed bag, now filled with cookies.

"Damn!" he said out loud, "Who moved that?" He bent over and lifted the bag against the wall, hurting his back a little. Maybe I'll have one, he thought. He reached in the bag.

"Oh!" he felt himself being pushed into the bag.

He struggled but couldn't force his way out. So much sugar made him feel slightly nauseous. He was going to ream out the bastard who was holding him in here. He moved his right arm around and pinched the arm of his assailant. He dug into the coat as viciously as he could. His head was rammed into the cookies. He could feel them crumbling from the pressure. Then the pressure was eased and he turned around angrily. He saw two red dots looking into his. He opened his mouth to scream, but felt a mound of sand, cookies? he wondered, rammed into it. He tried to scream, then breathe, feeling crumbs enter his lungs. He tried swallowing.

"I won't get to drive my Z again," he thought.

The assailant whispered, "Eat your way out."

Walker woke up. Today he had to get to Coeur d'Alene for his interview at North Idaho College. Taking main street downtown, toward the bus station, he noticed several police cars headed towards campus.

"You don't want to see this." Detective Daugherty advised.

"Why not, he was my husband for ten years, the father of our sons."

"You don't want to see this because he did not die a dignified death."

"No death is dignified," she insisted, pushing past him.

He addressed her back, "If you could give us a positive identification, then."

She opened her mouth to gasp when she saw him, but nothing happened. She could see his hair and forehead sticking out of a feed bag. Sand in his hair. As she came closer, she saw more of his features. His eyes were closed, but their were brown crumbs under them. Crumbs not sand. Cookie crumbs.

She started to laugh, then felt the policeman beside her. "What happened?" she asked.

"Someone choked him with cookies, we think. We'll know more after the coroner reports. There are cookies in his nose and throat." Stuffed like a turkey, Daugherty thought.

"Coroner?"

"Yes, mandatory in murder."

"Oh? Who?"

"We don't know, yet. He won't get away with it. Too many clues, fur, from a coat, blood under his fingernails, we think. Possibly witnesses."

She gasped suddenly, "You can't report this, choked with cookies. It would be—it would—it—" she couldn't finish.

"No ma'm, suffocation, the report will read," he assured her. She walked back out, less steadily.

"I'll need to ask you some questions, if you feel up to answering them," the detective offered.

She wondered if he had thought of her last, or of the kids. How selfish of me she thought.

Reporters love murders, unofficially, of course. From a distance, too,

Brian Tanner corrected. People were interested in them and bought papers that reported them. Murders sold paper. And lasted a long time. Much longer than scientific discoveries or good works. Brian set out to interview the detective in charge.

Chapter 12. Regions of the Mind

Just two months ago he had interviewed. Now he was living here and teaching here. He taught two classes per semester at North Idaho College. NIC, as it was known, was small, 600 students. The college was in Coeur d'Alene, beside the lake of the same name. He had come here because of the name. It was refreshing to see some Indian names kept for cities and counties, even if the settlers did make sure that the Indians were never kept. He expected that most of the Coeur d'Alenes had been pushed into Alberta long ago.

The college comprised several one or two story brick buildings. He taught in Seiter Hall, in the life sciences. The college was nonresidential, although there was one dormitory, Sherman Hall. It used to be a Junior College. It didn't grow up but it did grow older, and Junior was dropped from the name, for increased dignity. This fall he was teaching Introduction to Psychology 100 and some vagary called the Philosophy of Mind, a 250 number. Actually, he was rather happy to be allowed the freedom to explore outside of a discipline. He was sure it would only happen once.

Drinking his orange juice for breakfast, he meditated on his summer. Another once in a lifetime experience, knowing he had a job in the fall and enough money to enjoy the summer. He had gone back to Seattle for a month to conclude his affairs (nothing from Lisa—he hoped her dreams were not as bad as his; he wished to say something, but could not). Then he had come to Coeur d'Alene two months early to find a house. He roamed around Montana and Idaho for a couple weeks, after renting a one-bedroom house on Cedar Street that wouldn't be available until September. Coeur d'Alene was still a tourist town in the summer, and he couldn't afford it. Now in the fall he rented a canoe and paddled around every weekend. He had been sunburned early. But he had seen fish, and deer, and bear, and eagles from the river.

Seen so much. Seeing was the subject of this morning's lecture, on the sense organs. He still had to prepare. The children looked younger, now. He wondered how he looked to them. Probably not much different. He knew that Sharon had a crush on him. She was waiting on the sidewalk in front of the Hall; they walked in together.

Walker started immediately: "Today, the eyes, often referred to as 'windows to the soul.' The human eye is an organ ..." Once he wrote down the lecture it seemed almost anticlimactic to read it. He wondered if he should xerox copies to hand out. No, taking notes cemented the subject matter more firmly in the memory.

"The eyelids are thin folds of connective tissue covered by a thin layer of skin. Each eye has a tear gland, lachrymal gland, located in the upper anterior portion of the orbit. The surface of the eye is kept moistened by tears. The salty fluid empties into small ducts in the nasal cavity. Sadness increases tears so fast that they overflow; that overflow is crying."

"George, Just sadness? I mean, what else causes them to flow?" asked Sandy.

"Well, any strong emotion, or any strong irritant, like onions." he answered. He liked questions. They were a sure sign someone was awake.

"—one tenth of the cerebral cortex is reserved for vision. Visual stimuli are converted to electrical pulses in the retina, by the chemical activation by light, then conducted through the optical nerves. Complex processes—yes?"

Bill started moving his lips before speaking, "What happens, don't they all fire at once, don't, well, vision is constant, how does it work?"

Someone snickered.

"Good question. In fact, the eye is vibrating all the time. When this constant tremor, called nystagmus, was first discovered, it was thought to interfere with vision. Now, it is known to be essential to it. The eye cannot remain stationery—"

"What happens?"

Walker raised his hand, palm out, and continued, "In an experiment that compensated for the tremor, using mirrors timed to the eyes movements, Ratliffe and Riggs were able to freeze an image on the retina. When that happened, the image disappeared after a few seconds. The visual field became gray."

"But how did they time it?" Sharon asked.

"By using a mirrored contact lenses on the eye, reflecting light off it and back through the pupil. Please look in your books, page 229, at the diagram." Walker paused to check the page.

"Now, where were we? Hmmm. Furthermore, vision is a figure-ground phenomenon. The sky, for example, is an excellent ground. It is a nearly uniformly colored visual field, a gansfield. It may be 80 or 90 percent of our field of vision, but it isn't seen; whatever figure is being focused on reduces awareness of the ground." Walker meditated on the sky as he lectured. Once, that was all he could see from prison. It became his 'mandala.' He started to lose his place speaking.

"Complex, uhmm, processes uhh operate in the eye and brain to perceive patterns, in color and in depth. The interpretation of this information is aided by memory. Which compares the images of things seen before. Only ten percent of the light that enters the eyes reaches receptor cells; the rest is absorbed in the eye. Cats and some other mammals can see at night because the inside periphery of the retina is reflective; light is bounced around until it reaches a receptor. And it takes less light to form an image. That is also why light seems to come from cats eyes; it reflects out. The eyes appear red because that wavelength is reflected out."

"Bats?" tried Sharon.

"No, echolocation, not sight," Walker replied, expecting some challenges. "And that brings us to another sense. Hearing. Pressure waves vibrating the air are picked up by the ears. The eardrum vibrates sympathetically; the sound wave passes to the three auditory bones in the middle ear—name them later—and to the fluid-filled cochlea in the inner ear, where they are converted to nerve impulses. The 24,000 receptor cells in each ear send signals to the brain—"

The bell rang. Walker concluded, "And if anybody's home, they answer the phone. Time's up. Thursday, the anatomy of the ear, see you then."

He ignored everyone, especially Sharon, as he walked back to his house to eat and write. Love is fifty percent proximity, forty percent opportunity, seven percent sexuality, and three percent mystery, he analyzed; let's hold out for the mystery. Too bad, the other ninety-seven percent were ready and waiting. His house had been built by a local craftsman in the fifties. It was simple, but well-made. Besides the bedroom, it had a living room, dining area, full kitchen, and full bath. It was in the center of a quiet residential area, two blocks from the main road, and four from down-town; five from the lake, and six from the college.

Water was probably the rarest substance in the universe, probably the most valuable. It was a perfect solvent, picking up something from everywhere it flowed. Walker knew that if his senses were sensitive enough, he could probably identify the sources from which most of the lake had come. He felt at peace watching the lake, with its wind-driven waves and bottle-green depths. Even a shallow lake had secrets, hidden treasures or, especially with this lake, poisons like lead.

He melted cheese over cauliflower and broccoli. Then had lemonade, an apple, and part of a chocolate brownie. A chocolate addict always has chocolate. Probably everyone was addicted to something, he mused, at least one thing, always one thing, minimum. As long as his was chocolate, little else should tempt him. He put his notes in an old transmitter carrier, which he had found in the Spokane St. Vincent de Paul shop, which reminded him of the Air Force, and which had more personality than a backpack. This afternoon's class would be good, he hoped.

"Today, let's concentrate on what is not known about the mind. You all do most of the work today, I'm weak from thinking. How about hypnosis. Anyone know anything about hypnosis?"

"Uhhmm, not everyone can be hypnotized," Mike offered.

"Fine, more?" he looked around at the disgruntled expressions. Lazy sods, he thought, it won't hurt you to try and fail here, or succeed.

"It can be used to control or cure smoking," Mary said.

"True, but how?" One minute of silence was about the limit he had found, before the class resembled a funeral.

"Let's consider this. If a hypnotized subject is told that the pencil that has touched her skin," he looked at Mary, "is red-hot, and then awakened, burn blisters will form on the skin. Why? Has the body been fooled by the mind? Are burns in the mind, just in the mind, primarily in the mind, or also in the mind? Let's examine each of these," he urged. He knew that he was going to do most of the talking, even if half of it was Socratic suggestion. He was still asking half an hour later.

"How strong is the mind? Consider G. Walter's experiment. Electrodes, attached to the subject's scalp over the frontal cortex, transmit electrical activity in the brain to an amplifier. In front of the subject is a button which turns on an interesting television scene. One second before she presses the button, a surge of about 20 micro-volts occurs in the cortex. When this readiness wave is amplified, it can trigger the button to make the teevee turn on before she presses the button. The intended action produces the result."

"What about bending spoons?" Alice asked, hoping to talk about Yuri Geller.

"Most experiments of that nature are usually faked. No, no," he waived his hands, "I'm not saying that all such acts are. It's just that they have not been observed and repeated under clinical conditions."

"But what if clinical conditions," Harvey spate with distaste, "are inimical to mental phenomena? Science is a basilisk that kills what it looks at, and only sees by killing," he added.

"Indeed, much science is—good simile by the way, Harvey—," Walker admitted, "which is why we need a more Goethean science—contemplative nonintervention." That was what he really wanted to talk about, an organic approach to nature. Then he added, "if magic is real, I'll believe it when I see Geller or someone in orbit around the moon without a spacesuit bending spoons in a ring around the moon—not before."

He continued: "Let's think of some answers for next week. The mind is bewitching and bewildering. Intention is magic, images are magic. How much of the brain do we really use? How much of it could we really use? 20 percent? More? How much of that is necessary for the basic operations of sleep, memory, food searches, building shelter, sex—"

Giggles came from some in the class.

"In your case, probably 60 percent. Why is the operation of speech so ambiguous? How can it be ambiguous and work? Is memory like a hologram? Think about those for next Monday," he concluded.

He hurried home. Ms. Crofts, a librarian, was coming over for dinner. And he hadn't started preparing it. He sighed—no way to rush lasagna.

As soon as he came through the door, he threw his papers on the desk and put on a recording of Pictures at an Exhibition, by Modeste Moussorgsky; an old piano version by Brendel. He opened two cans of S&W Italian tomatoes and dumped them in a four-quart pan. Then he added oregano, basil, rosemary, marjoram, savory, and thyme. A can of tomato paste. He filled the empty paste can with a French red Bordeaux, LaRose Trintandon, and poured it into the tomatoes. He threw in a little of the cheeses, Romano, Parmesan, and Mozzarella. And turned the burner on low. The stove was classic thirties; it stood off the floor by two feet on four shaped steel legs, black. He sautéed onions, mushrooms, and celery in a nine-inch iron pan, then dumped them into the sauce. In a large bowl, he mixed two cups of dry curd cottage cheese with two cups of ricotta cheese, adding one half cup of parsley. Seven cloves of garlic were squeezed into the sauce. One into the cheese. Then he added four whole eggs and one cup of mozzarella cheese. Still not satisfied, he sprinkled Romano on it until he couldn't see any of the others. He mixed it all together, the cheese and eggs formed a yellowed white, highlighted by green parsley. One a third burner, in an eight-quart pot, he boiled one package of wheat/spinach lasagna noodles for fifteen minutes, al dente, putting a teaspoon of olive oil and a pinch of salt in the water so the noodles wouldn't stick together. He cut up the tomatoes in the sauce a little more while the noodles were boiling. The dishes in the sink were too intimidating, yet. When the noodles were done, he cooled them in tap water to stop the cooking. Splashing a little sauce in the bottom of two 'nine by nine by two' glass dishes, he began building the lasagna in both dishes simultaneously: layer of noodles, layer of cheese, layer of sauce; repeat once, until dish was full. He grated mozzarella over the top of both and put them in the medium oven for forty minutes.

The record ended. He put on Islamey, by Balakirev, for the dishes. Balakirev, whose music was not widely heard now, had called Moussorgsky "almost an idiot" in exasperation. After Moussorgsky had written Pictures, Tchaikovsky had expressed the popular opinion that it was vile and cheap, raging that he would send it "to the Devil!" For cooking he put on Moussorgsky. Walker was happy that he had timed it right, so that the 'Great Gate of Kiev' would open just as he was putting dinner in the oven. The oven even resembled the hut on fowl's legs of the witch Baba-Yaga.

The library was quiet after five. It was quiet almost every night. She could hear the low hum of a fan somewhere in the basement. The fluorescent lights had a higher, thinner, hum of their own. She heard a set of footsteps going toward the copy machine. With an effort, she turned back to her computer terminal.

Helen had not been interested in computers in the library. What she liked about libraries were their medieval atmospheres—the silence, the traditions, even the smell of old paper. But she had become an expert on computers by default, just as she had with microforms when they had made an appearance years before. After she had learned the acquisition and search programs, and worked with them for several months, she realized that she had twice as much free time. The computer also offered her access to a national network. Now, she put all of her correspondence and articles on-line.

She pressed the "break" key and received a command prompt. She entered a "t" and the time appeared on the screen. Forty more minutes until closing. She finished the book review for the New York Book Review, typing in the last paragraph.

'The blurb on his book asks if it is quackery, stupidity, or diabolical propaganda, to which an informed reader can only answer: YES! His ideas may be accepted by economists, but not by rational scientists. Economists have become the priests of the new hunger, the industrial peoples' hunger for money and convenience, gadgets and fame, that isolates mere hunger for food and life behind the glass wall of television. From his comfortable chair in vitro, Mr. Cayman confuses the prophets of doom with the Cassandras of caution, which is a truer description of alarmist ecologists. Only by ignoring the overwhelming facts from varied sources, from the United Nations to Bell Telephone, can Cayman pretend that Hardin, Ehrlich, the Club of Rome, and others appear to suffer an unfounded hysteria. His own opinions are founded on a solid rock of ignorance—ignorance of economics, ecology and history.

The function of a Cassandra is to be wrong. If we heed the warning, Cassandra will always be wrong—and suffer twice for it. One of the goals of Mankind at the Turning Point, another Club of Rome study, was to force us to act to create the future as "self-fulfilling prophecy." We can do that only by being aware of the ecology and economics of the earth, not by lying to ourselves and trusting blindly in technology, as Mr. Cayman has done.'

She entered a print command to get a hardcopy. She saved a copy on a disk dataset. Then she pulled up a schedule of meetings. There weren't very many, a college ad hoc committee on appeals, the faculty council next Monday, a dinner invitation, and the monthly meeting of the President's Task Force on the Long-Range Economic Future, in Chicago. She hoped she could avoid another confrontation with that jerk, John Franks. Franks had been quiet as mouse at a cat convention during the first year, but now that they were considering the effects of macro-engineering projects on employment, he had an opinion on everything, an expert opinion in his own words, and he presented it forcefully. While she thought transatlantic tunnels and transcontinental bicycle paths were reasonable projects, she regarded a dam across Hudson Bay or a dam across the Amazon river as insane. Technological feasibility was never a sufficient reason to create more destruction than benefits. Franks never understood the effects of some macro-engineering projects. The Aswan dam provided some irrigation and electricity, but not enough to offset damage to fisheries, soil, the archaeological heritage, and human health. People like Franks were inherently stupid. They never learned from their mistakes. Each of their projects had the effect of increasing human suffering in the long-run, while increasing their own prestige and wealth immediately. She sighed, it was the way of the world. She could only fight it. She printed a copy of the schedule, just to be sure, and hurried downstairs to supervise the students closing up.

He set the table in the kitchen. It was warmer, and handier. He set out the plates. Lit a candle. He put out a cold plate, with marinated artichoke hearts, baby corn, sliced carrots, and lavosh, unleavened cracker. He put frozen green beans in a pan with water, to wait until the lasagna came out. Helen Crofts looked plain from a distance, but less and less plain as she came closer up the walk. Helen, daughter of Leda and the swan. Her legs spoke to him first, advertising their willingness to be caressed. Her neck called to him; then her lips. Then the doorbell. He straightened up, left the window and went to the door.

"Please come in," he invited.

"Thank you."

"Did you have trouble finding it?"

"No, I walked, thank you. It is so nice to walk in the evening."

He took her light cotton jacket and hung it by the door. "Dinner won't be ready for fifteen minutes, yet. Would you like some wine?"

"Yes, thank you. This is a nice house. I have never been in here before."

"You've lived here long?"

"Young man, I was born here," she snooted. "I even remember the man who built this house." Little repetitions of life had left their mark on her attitudes and face.

"You aren't much older than I am," he assured her.

"Why, why," she appraised him humorously, "I'm old enough to be your," she paused, looking oddly at his ears, "older sister."

"All right, maybe a year" he laughed. "Where did you go to library school, then?"

"Seattle, UW."

"Really? So did I!" he exclaimed. Somehow the kinship of school was stronger than of city or family. They talked of the libraries there. She hadn't seen the new undergraduate library, yet, although she had heard of it.

"Is Herman Reinmuller still head of it?" she asked.

He said he didn't know.

Clothes usually make a woman look better than she looks naked, or worse. Rarely did they express the body well. Helen was no exception. She choose conservative styles that set trends in the lack of imagination. Her skirt came below mid-calf; her blouse had a high collar. Walker thought that she was advertising that she was off-limits. Maybe just friends then. With sex, unlike food, there was no hurry. They had a dinner, and explored the ranges of each other's reading. She was interested in anthropology, archaeology, 17th-century literature, and flora of the Amazon. The only thing she liked about psychology was the study of dreams.

"I think that dreams do presage the future. The mind puts together its clues and presents them in a story. Most of the themes are symbols for needs and desires."

He yawned dramatically, symbolizing his boredom with dreams.

She feigned to ignore him, telling him about a recent dream to prove her point. "I dreamed that my brother and I pushed a cement truck down-hill, watching it mash the neighbor's cars. Then we hid in the house, but were found by the driver. Who told us that my daughter was in the cab. I raced down to the bottom of the hill, where the truck was lying on its side, one huge tire still spinning. When I looked in, there was a dog standing down on the other door. We took it to a hospital, where I was shot as a spy. But I was reborn to search for something—I forget what—but it was important. Anyway, I couldn't find it. Then my mother returned from shopping. Now, how would you interpret that, huh?" she challenged.

"Well, well," he said, trying to think faster than he could speak. "Your mind was probably trying to resolve some difficulty with your mother, drawing on experiences with trucks, pets, and your brother," he sighed in relief, it sounded so rational.

"But I don't have a brother, or a daughter," she announced

innocently.

"What do you think it means?" he said to transfer responsibility for interpretation.

"I think it symbolizes needs. It may predict an accident when I do have a daughter," she related seriously. "The truck stands for the implacable workings of fate—"

He threw a pillow at her hand. "The pillow stands for the judgment of God."

She placed the pillow in back of her chair. "What do you dream?" she asked, ignoring his childish behavior.

Walker couldn't answer. He didn't remember any of his dreams, if he dreamed at all. "I don't remember any of mine."

"I'll bet you do; they're just stranger than mine."

He decided to try a technical diversion. "Maybe dreams are just pieces of shuffled holograms, if memory is hologrammatic. Then, if—"

"Excuse me," she interrupted, "But I see a problem already. I've read Arbib's presentation of that. Here is the problem I see. If a hologram is a metaphor for memory. If the universe is a hologram, as David Bohm, says, then how can there be free will? It may explain precognition, how it's possible, but it means then that the universe is predetermined. Yes?"

He scratched his head, which suddenly itched. Then looked at the magazines piled on the desk. "More tea?" he asked. "I'm thinking," he added.

"Yes, thank you." She watched him pick his nose unself-consciously.

While he brewed the tea, he answered. "Precognition. Yes, it could be an explanation, but it wouldn't rule out free will. After all, there is no law that says all experiences of precognition will occur. Example: what if you saw someone killed in a truck in a dream. Then the next day warned them not to be in the truck. Then what if they believed you and never rode in a cement truck? More," he said, ideas skidding in to each other in back of the turtle's slow voice, "a holographic universe would not

215

contradict Christian or oriental teachings, which would be metaphorical. The serpent, Eve, and Adam go against the highest will and are free. Afterwards life unfolds, and its unfolding is not pre-determined. Each being is separate, restless—"

"Physical events would determine—" she interrupted.

"No, they may seem pre-determined, in one, or even three, dimensions, but with another dimension added, be free to miss or collide. Furthermore, the future is shaped as much by curiosity and desire as by physical events, even holographic events."

"Yes," he was saying again, "psychic events can shape physical ones. With language, the shape of the brain changed. Dolphins noticed the difference in humans 30,000 years ago. In right-handed people, the right brain hemisphere is wider in the front than the left half; but in the back, the left half is wider. And the skull actually bulges to accommodate the swelling."

"How do you know what dolphins noticed?" she asked strangely.

"I know them," he said simply. Then he told her about dolphins.

After midnight, he walked her home. He kissed her on the lips, and turned to go back. When she touched his hand, he kissed it, too, flowing into a deep bow. He jogged back. Friday night was his free night, for writing or painting. Tonight, he wanted to start his article for the 'publish or perish' race. Once settled at his desk, he began the article with a discussion of vagueness.

'According to C. S.. Peirce, logicians neglected the study of vagueness, not realizing the important part it plays in mathematical thought. Vagueness is the antithetical analog of generality; generality is the indeterminate character of a sign; the human mind completes the determination. A sign is vague when determination is left to some other sign to complete (as in almanacs). The principle of contradiction does not apply to vagueness. Things are vague intrinsically. The order of nature is vague. Over five decades later, Max Black wrote an article on vagueness that became the inspiration for a general (fuzzy) set theory.

Fuzziness is what Black called vagueness...' He started other paragraphs with thoughts unfinished.

'The theory of sets is a basic tool in mathematics. In fact, every branch of mathematics can be considered a study of sets of objects, as geometry is the study of sets of points. A collection of objects is called a set. But most classes of objects encountered in the physical world are not sharply defined. They do not have a precisely defined criterion of membership. As Peirce explained, they are vague. This is also the concept of fuzzy sets. A fuzzy set is a class with intermediate grades of membership. Grades of membership reflect an ordering of objects in a universe (set).

'Mountains are prominent features. Let us take a universe of mountains and abstract a set of high mountains. Many mountains in Northern India will be in the set, but not all of them. Mountains in Greece, Borneo, and Australia will be in the set. But many mountains from India that are not in the set are actually higher than many of those from other places. The word high is not precise...

Set theory can describe nonhierarchical orders, also. Lorenz has example of cyclical pecking order in geese, where B submits to A, A submits to C, but C submits to B. Not all the relationships can be realized at the same time. The relationships can be represented through interlocking sets, where hierarchical ordering breaks down.'

Here he added a discussion on the dialectic of Plato. He paused to listen to an owl outside. The wind whistled through the pine needles. Then he finished excavating the conversational field.

'Since there are always any number of relations in a situation, the use of dyads and triads can become complex and unwieldy. Therefore, the idea of a conversation must be extended. Conversation depends on participation. All events are subjective. The conversation indicates inner events...

'Conversation is direct. Each side has a perspective and this is the heart of the process. When conversation is considered as a totality, there is no distinction about what is contributed by whom. The process is a coherent event shared by the participants, not a simple information exchange. Communication is presentation of one's self, of one's life; that may evoke correspondence in others—even entrainment. The activities of two communicators combine to make the universe of the observer more ordered and redundant. The nature of meaning depends on the frame of the observer ...

'Given the indeterminacy of relations between subjects, a theory of conversation is justified. Conversation replaces the idea of duality and triadicity. The word conversation is derived from the French meaning to live with, from the Latin, meaning to turn with. Since all things are in some sense subjective and unique, there is further—'

He couldn't write anymore. He went to sleep. Sunday, he asked Helen if she would got canoeing. She agreed if he would accompany her to church. She wore sweatshirt and jeans.

"You look young enough to be," he started, "my younger sister."

She laughed and told him a good place for lunch. They talked about eagles.

That afternoon, he went with her to a local service. He saw the sign first: "God, guns, and guts made America great" in hand-carved, foot-high letters. The fundamentalist preacher of the Idaho Bible Church was waiting outside to greet his congregation. When he smiled at them, his teeth showed little gaps, as if each one had been driven with a hammer. The preacher, Bob Gains, wore a cowboy hat and Pendleton shirt; jeans and a belt buckle that said 'Mac' in bronze. A rifle was leaning against the wall. Walker wondered if it was loaded.

"Howdy, Mrs. Helen," he greeted her, reaching for her hand and nodding at Walker, eyes narrowed slightly.

"Hi, Bob," she replied, "This is George Walker. He teaches at the college."

Bob looked at her softly, "Not a commie, is he? Like 'em others?"

"Hell, no, Bob, let's get this show on the road." Walker replied

Bob smiled and looked up the road for more congregation.

When they got inside the log cabin, Walker noticed that there were only eight other people on the benches.

Reading his expression, Helen said, "Bob doesn't have a very big congregation."

Walker opened his mouth, but couldn't think of anything to say.

"He was a good friend of my father's; that's why I come. They worked at the mill in the forties. Probably the best time in their lives that either of them ever had," she explained, anticipating his questions.

Walker was quiet, looking around the cabin, first at the carved cross facing them, then out the two small windows on each side; the cabin was on the side of a hill, downhill was a small stream.

"Why Am I here, talking to you!?" Bob thundered as he walked in, pleased that the group was larger this week. "Because of the fear of going to hell! That's why. I went down the aisle to give myself to God. Why don't you do the same."

Nobody moved, so Bob continued. "Something is wrong with this country, mighty wrong. When I fought the Japanese, we depended on our guns. Now we talk to them and buy their tinny little cars. When I fought the Hun, we depended on our guns. Now we drink their beer and eat their stale little sausage. Now, I still live by my gun. What it brings down I eat. But I can't be set. Cause I know that God is going to judge this country again. Those Chinese and Russians are going to invade us. I know this. And unless every able-bodied man and woman has a rifle and a hundred rounds, those slavs and slants are gonna roll over us. I can tell. The queers, the pornographers, the abortionists, the nigger-lovers, the atheists are eating away at the foundation of this great nation. And we have to stop it. We have to protect our flag. We have to be ready." Bob had taken off his hat and now hunched his shoulders awkwardly. "Now let us pray. God, give us the wisdom to buy our guns, and the strength to use them. To protect your country, America, God Bless Her. We must have faith. That we can save our country. We must not let God's country go the way of the dinosaurs, its predecessors. My own faith is renewed, seeing you praying today. Amen." He concluded with a moment of silence.

Helen nudged Walker to let him know Bob was finished and they should go.

On the way out, Walker asked, "Don't you think we should reason with these people, first, Bob?"

"When people talk to me of reason, George, I go for my gun. That's a sure sign they measuring your weakness."

"Right you are, Bob, but that doesn't mean we can't reason after drawing down on 'em."

"Well, maybe, as long as they see we mean bizness" Bob conceded. "You have a nice day, Mrs. Helen."

They walked back toward town. Walker asked about her husband.

"I married in school," she said, not naming her husband by name, "and he left me after he graduated. I finished putting myself through and came home. By then, my parents had told everyone I was married. I told them all he died in a motorcycle accident."

"Any more like Bob around?" Walker mentioned sarcastically.

"Yes, but Bob is harmless. He wouldn't hurt anyone."

"He kills animals, doesn't he?" Walker reminded her.

"Yes, but he eats what he kills."

Walker considered that.

Helen addressed him, "George, Northern Idaho is attracting weirdoes. I mean real weirdoes, not just hunters and hippies."

"Like who?" Walker asked.

"Besides the rogues and misfits?" She paused. "Nazis. Idaho Nazis. They have their own enclave north of here. Witches, there are witches doing animal sacrifices and God knows what else."

Helen had frightened herself. She felt less secure with so much madness around. He hugged her quietly.

They went to her house, a brown bungalow close to the lake, and played with her cat, Athena, who had one gold eye and one blue. They ate dinner, talking about cultural change and security. He undressed her slowly, then lay down beside her and stroked her neck and arms. He discovered that her clothes were not an adequate a showcase for her body. When she complained that he was still dressed, he let her take of his clothes. He lay down beside her and held her. When she reached up, he kissed her. They held tightly, each content just to hold.

Chapter 13. Lord of Animals

Then another week of classes. This week, no one seemed interested in doing more than taking and storing their quantum bits of knowledge, for later retrieval and evaluation.

In the Friday class he tried to startle them again.

"Psychology isn't really a science, yet. It has no workable concept of the mind—that thing it's supposed to be studying. The psychology you are learning offers explanations, and even treatments, but not understandings, not cures. The mental health professions are all mental disease professions. Most of them, especially psychology, are trivial barbaric practices that distort laboratory animals to reach irrelevant and inappropriate conclusions about humans.

"No, sadly, psychology isn't a science, it's a ritual of control. Drug addiction, insanity, suicide—these problems aren't cured; they are controlled, barely, if at all."

Having their attention, he continued, ending on a less negative note.

"Yes, psychology is a failure. But science is an occupation where failure is expected. Constant failure, which plagues psychologists, isn't healthy, they can't even improve on the natural recovery rate, but mixed failure and success provides for learning, and constant growth. That is what we should strive for—some small step of understanding. My advice is start with yourself. Make yourself healthy." He was the first one out of class. He had detective work to do. He was curious about the Nazis.

He went to Spokane on Friday for supplies. He stopped by Goodwill and all of the other resale stores. He walked up and down second and third streets asking questions, stopping in the bars. He didn't bother to eat. He spent three hours in the city library. By that evening, he had all he thought he needed. So, he made two telephone calls.

He met Henry in Spokane on the following Saturday afternoon. Saturday, the day of Saturn. They drove past Priest Lake to the farm. He saw a very small farmhouse, white, with a very large barn, red, in back. They got out of the Rabbit and walked toward the barn. A young blonde man, dressed in black, greeted them with a 'Heil!' They waved back. The barn was a shell, concealing a large meeting room in the form of a baronial hall, 80 by 140 feet, Walker guessed, with 30-foot ceilings. They waited with ten other men.

Henry leaned over and whispered to Walker, "Last month, Fritz Guinken was beheaded on that altar; his head was the vehicle for communion with the Masters of the Caucasus." Henry watched Walker for any inappropriate reaction or weakness.

Walker smiled slightly, "Will another be honored today?"

"No," replied Henry, satisfied that he had not made an error in judgment. He was not ready to be honored himself. And a mistake in sponsorship would draw attention to him.

An SS 'Black Knight' Officer stood at the altar. "There is no going back, only forward, to fight the Jew. I swear to you to be loyal by the holy sign. Our God is Walvater, the self-born power; he whose rune was the Aarune and whose trinity was Wodan, Wili, and We."

My, God, thought Walker, the three stooges; was this real?

"The low-class brain of the jew will never comprehend the unity of a trinity. The jews know very well they have to fear."

Walker was surprised, Christ was a German, then?

"It is written in Moses 5.28.49: 'and the Lord will awaken unto you a people from far away, from the end of the earth, which flies like an eagle, a people whose language you do not understand.' Adolf Hitler was the voice of Jesus Christ, who desired to become the flesh and blood of the German people. The jew is the embodiment of evil. His qualities are evil, his intellect, conscience and truth. A new biological species shall arise from German blut, a true aristocracy. The masses will be liberated from the burden of will.

"Let us pray: Fuhrer, my fuhrer, by God given me

Defend your state as long as may be.

Thou rescued Germany from deepest need.

I render thee thanks for my daily feed.

Stay by me forever, however low my plight

Fuhrer, my fuhrer, my faith and my light. Hail my fuhrer!"

Walker started laughing. Eagles? These people should be worshipping mosquitoes. Bad timing though. He was grabbed and punched in the mouth. He was still giggling, spitting red foam. Someone ripped his shirt off. The bottle of natural gas taped to his side was exposed. He lost some hairs as it was ripped off.

He saw Henry jabbing at him, shouting, "Spy! Jew! Spy!"

He was dragged to a series of rooms in back of the altar. Past a library, rooms with beds and tables, and a cloister. To a test arena.

"Rudolf, get the dogs!" He was thrown into a small arena. Sand got under his socks. He looked at the faces looking over the wood stockade. It had been only four feet high, when he went by it, so the arena had been sunken.

"The world conspiracy of freemasons and jews must be combated. You are a parasite, jew, incapable of change; a parasite who would drag those of us of pure blood down to your semi-human dross." The black night officer stood proudly, as doubtless he had before.

"What is this room for?" Walker asked, wondering if the Romans were being revived at the same time.

"It is a tempering room, jew," came the half bellow. "It is where supermen learn to think with their blood. It is where we harden ourselves to any ordeal," he boasted. "It is where we learn blind obedience, Kadavergehorsam—cadaver obedience, to you, jew!"

But Walker had recognized the Arab formula: 'Be between the hands of your sheikh like a cadaver in the hands of him who washes you.' He looked at the patterns in the wood.

"Here we drill and march to exhaustion. To destroy pity, we tear the eyes from three cats."

Walker felt his lips curl.

"Here, you will learn liberation from your burden of flesh."

Walker never would understand why simple threats required such long explanations.

"To be hardened to any ordeal, each of us has been in this arena stripped to the waist; for 12 minutes we had to fight off 3 attack dogs. If the dogs hesitated, then they were choked. You are shirtless. You will be honored with six dogs. Rudolf!"

Walker turned to the other end of the arena, praying that he would not have to hurt an animal or be hurt. Six German Shepherds, black, white and tan, were hurtling towards him. He straightened and bared his teeth, staring at the dogs. The dogs stopped short. No dogs attack a healthy alpha male, especially one much taller and stronger.

"I have thought with my blood," Walker said, recovering first. Then leapt the wall and rammed two startled heads together. The dogs followed.

"I am Wodin! Loki! I will liberate you from your burden of lies!" he exclaimed, punching Henry's heart into his spine. He felt a large powerful hand on his left shoulder; he turned left and rammed stiff fingers into the throat of the larger man. The dogs were attacking anyone who moved, slashing and biting furiously. One of the dogs tore out the throat of the black knight; two others worked at his crotch and armpit. Some of the soldiers had gone behind doors; others were cowering still.

Walker ran through the corridor to the altar, knocking over candles and torches. Someone was running towards him, fumbling with his holster. Walker didn't slow and hurdled to strike the sergeant with pointed toe just below the sternum.

Leaving the doors open for the dogs, he ran out and started Henry's Rabbit. He drove it back to Spokane. His thoughts were punctuated by the Rabbit's missing on a cylinder. Their evil could give his evil a bad name. Stupid doctrine, really, that Jews were evil and had to be exterminated. This was the Gnostic position taken to extremes. The position of two worlds, one good and one evil, light and dark, spiritual and material. They thought they were light, good and spiritual. They thought they were Thor and the teutonic Gods, and that the Jews were the children of Satan, responsible for evil, dark, and matter. Well, he was Satan and terminated their power. He was a beast, nature, Loki. They were dead. And they were dead because they were inconsistent. Their cult was racist and preached hatred. They were the illiterate children of Hitler, with their desperate dreams of purity and knighthood. Influenced, like Hess, by arguments of no importance at the very limits of superstition.

Was Hitler the devil as many later identified him? No, just a miserable someone trying to balance himself and failing, and doing immense harm to others. Hitler said that all the great movements of history are volcanic eruptions of passions and spiritual sensations provoked by the goddess of misery or the torch of free speech thrown to the masses. The forces of change are found in hysteria not science, said Hitler, then seemed to prove it.

'And how are you different, Lucifer? Who wipes out those he hates?' the question came into his mind unbidden, unexpected.

'I kill no one who does not wish to kill others in my name. Has ever God done less?'

He sat on a rock by the lake Saturday night. The day of Saturn was almost over. Saturn ate his children to prevent them from succeeding him. And failed. God banished his, and would fail. Was he Lucifer? Why did he remember so little? Were all animals his? So far, he thought, I am just reacting mindlessly.

He walked over to Helen's house. 'Helen, thine eyes' but he forgot the rest, too tired. She was in her robe and looked worried when she saw him. She brushed pine needles from his back.

"Where have you been?"

"Meditating," he answered.

"All night?"

"Yes," he answered abstractly.

"Come on, let's take a shower," she commanded, leading him through the hall. She took off her robe. He watched her. Then she took off her nightgown. When he still hadn't moved to undress, she got in the shower and turned it on. He stuck his head in and looked at her. She was already soaping her hair. From her shoulders to her waist, she was still very girlish, her breasts only slight swellings. The nipples, however, were not girlish. She narrowed at the waist considerably, and curved nicely at the hips. From the front and back, she was nicely hour-glass shaped. Her hips and legs were firm from walking. He noticed tiny blue lines on her thighs, and the water streaming down. He stepped into the shower dressed and hugged her to him, kissing her and her soap.

Keeping her eyes shut, she whispered, "Clothes dirty too, huh?" He dropped his trousers and ripped open his shirt, and pulled her close again. Each gripped the other's buttocks and squeezed. Breathing while they kissed pulled little droplets of water into their mouths. He rotated against her. Then lifted her a few inches, his hands spreading her legs slightly.

"You can't do anything like this," she whispered.

"Yes, you can," she acknowledged as he lowered her a little. Then she pushed back from his shoulders and lifted her feet to the sides of the tub and in back of him. He leaned backwards, holding her waist in both hands. She began to move up and down. He was lying in the tub, with both legs hanging out. She was bending over trying to untie his dripping shoes. His right hand snuck beneath her robe and rubbed her breast. She turned on the hot water and he sat up quickly to add cold to it.

"You already fried me, not need to boil me," he smiled.

She shook her head and carried the wet clothes outside to hang up. He filled the tub and lay back in it, making motorboat noises with his lips. "Let's go to church," he suggested. "Not Uncle Bob's either." She had raised her eyebrows. "You have a regular one, don't you?"

She regarded him quietly.

He smelled the sweatshirt, "This is all I have to choose from, a sweatsuit?"

"You haven't been to church recently have you? Some of the clergy wear sweatsuits."

She looked at the clock in the kitchen, and added, "Okay, St. Mark's Episcopal church. The congregation meets at 9:00."

It was a singing congregation, so they both enjoyed that part of it. Walker was restless afterwards and wanted to talk to the reverend. Helen saw Emily Radner from the college and talked to her for a few minutes. When Emily was talking, she heard snatches of the argument between Walker and Dennis Gant.

"God placed fossils in the rocks to give us history," the reverend affirmed.

"But why trick us," Walker explained. "Why not just give us the real thing, if he is omnipotent?"

"Because He is He. We have not been allowed to penetrate his intention," Gant pronounced smugly.

"Then why did he give us minds to be fooled by fake fossils?"

"Simple, to test our faith. I've had that question asked more persi, uhh, persipaciously by better scholars than you. Doubtless you are a godless atheist."

Helen bid good-bye to Emily and went to stand between the two men.

"No, I believe in a God of some kind, but not perfect."

"Why not perfect?" Helen asked, trying to make sure that the debate became nothing more.

"If a perfect God existed, why go on living or thinking? All the questions answered, all the music played." He looked at the reverend, who was waiting to speak, probably still keying in on the first phrase. "Faith," Walker continued, "is a reason to avoid thinking. Consider," he hurried on, "if God were not perfect, but were being made, in the making, that would explain why the universe is evolving."

"This is foolishness," Gant judged. "We are being tested on earth."

"What if we were making God as we lived, if our actions determined what God would be."

"George, why can't there be both in some sense," Helen struggled to compromise. "God was perfect, and then decided to immerse himself in the world?"

"Why would he do that?" sighed the reverend, looking at his watch.

"Because, God is dull, slow and indifferent, as you imagine him, burdened with being almost human." Walker sneered. "What I'll never understand is why the devil is close, concerned and active, when God is petty and remote. God may be good, but he is anemic. But the devil is good, too. He offers reason and mystery. He has depth."

"Don't you think that's the same mistake—" Helen started.

"No! You are the devil!" Gant overrode.

"No!" Helen exclaimed, looking at Walker.

His eyes burned with a peculiar bluish flame. Were there treasures blooming in the earth this summer's eve? she asked herself.

"I know you are not the devil," spoke Gant, taking back a step from apoplexy. "The devil is black. You are not black."

"No, I am brown, the color of the earth. But you are wrong, surely about the devil being black. There is nothing in your bible about it. Furthermore, among African Christians, the devil is white; and red for many oriental peoples. The English consider him blue; Italians, yellow; and Spanish, green, although that was the sacred color of the Moors. What do you think the devil is like?" he asked, curious about any description of himself.

"Well, he is thin, lean and gaunt, from hunger, perhaps. His skin is hairy. His eyes are red coals. He sports a beard on his chin; his ears are pointed. His back is humped, his left foot is crippled, so that he limps slightly, and he can never rid himself of that limp."

Walker was busy regarding his own hands and feet during this inventory, pleased that they were not black and nobby, overly hairy and clawed. The limp, from the fall from heaven, was more likely a reminder of fear of lightning falling from heaven. All lightning demons—Thoth, Loki, Vulcan—limped.

"That limp was from his fall," Gant stressed.

"But what does he wear? Does he go naked, with an enormous, turgid prick?"

"No, he is gross, as you are, but he dresses as a gentleman. In fact, it is difficult to tell the two apart," he sniggered at his joke.

Helen dragged Walker away, "You are boys," she hissed. "Didn't you get this out of your system in school rap sessions?"

Walker raised his arm, then lowered it smiling, something leaving his eyes.

"Yes," he admitted, "let's try another church next time. That guy was so classic that he ought to be remembered," Walker mused. "Let's say, with his IQ of 50, he is one Gant power. That means you register at three Gants; most of my students at two Gants; Reverend Bob at 1.36 Gants."

"Beware of using more precision than the subject warrants," Helen said, then when she saw his raised eyebrow, explained, "Aristotle—besides this is my church, where my friends come to pray and sing. Don't make it hard for me."

They walked back to her house.

"Helen, I'm tired. I don't remember anything anymore," he confessed to her one day in the library.

"Why don't you see a doctor."

"Because I don't like talking to people who know less than I do," he snapped. "Besides, it's a spiritual problem, I think." She pulled a book off the shelf and then slid it back. Automatically checking the call number against the title.

"I do know someone. But you—" she trailed off.

"Who?"

"Marie LaCarte."

"Who?" he repeated.

"You wouldn't know her. She is a Coeur d'Alene."

"What is she?" Walker asked, thinking a psychiatrist.

"She is a friend of mine. I will introduce you to her, but you will not, not mock her," she emphasized.

"No, if you ask."

"I ask," Helen declared.

"All right. Is she—"

"She is a shaman, a holy woman."

"A woman shaman? I didn't know they existed." Walker confessed. Some of the Plains Indian tribes gave women important roles; he had always assumed that Northwest Indians were more conservative.

That night over fish and rice, she told him all that she knew of the

Coeur d'Alene tribes.

"Their land was rich in fruits and berries, roots, herbs, and mints. The women gathered berries and nuts, and roots for medicines; the men hunted deer, elk, moose, fowl, white fish, rabbits, sometimes bear—"

Walker's lip curled involuntarily, but Helen was talking.

"—chased into the lake and killed from canoes. Normally, they lived in individual family clans. They spoke a Salish language. Every year, in June, large groups gathered to dig Camas root, around Clarkia and Moscow."

"The Coeur d'Alene were centralized and had strong leaders. Each village had a council with male and female members. A large village had a headman or woman who regulated economic and religious affairs. Their only real power was their persuasive abilities and the public esteem they built up. Chiefs were elected or deposed by the council. The band chief regulated basic resources. Next in authority were a war leader, hunting leader, and shaman, chosen for their respective skills. The villages were grouped into three formal bands: Spokane, Coeur d'Alene, and St. Joe. That was before the white man."

"When can I meet this woman?" Walker asked.

"You have classes this week. Wait until next Saturday. Besides, I need to talk to her, and ask her if she is willing to waste time on an ungrateful, irrational, potentially violent white-eyes."

"My eyes aren't white," he protested, digging his toe into her calf.

"No, but your brain is, your heart is," she accused, grabbing his foot and twisting it.

No, it's brown, too, he knew.

Marie lay on her side, indifferent in sleep. Slowly, there was music, and light, dancers around a fire. One held up a metal disk. She woke, gazing at the wall. Its smoothness dissolved as from acid on a copper. An unknown profile. She groaned, and blinked. Redimensioned. The smoothness was scored with scratches as she watched. Scratches outlined figures sharply across a fissure—the code of mystery renewed in red. The deer were running. Bear masks, elk masks traced on the wall of the cave. We put on their skins and faces to learn how they behaved. They were kin. We needed them as they needed wolves and men. We took only the weakest, the sick and old. Their strength was ours, we would not let it diminish or die. Now the elk are silent, photographs show only hide and not the motive. The real face is never seen. Now men kill the strongest for trophies and dismiss our art. The image of the elk is seen on cans in the stream—the image of the bear on boot polish. We saw strangeness and sanctity, not the human stink on every feature. The bear was our father, elk helped us to be human. We changed ourselves to fit the earth We fit ourselves to please the earth. Now, the earth is profaned, her son walks.

She woke, wondering what was coming.

The first meeting was difficult. Marie spoke little English. Her 'Hello' was good thought Walker, but the promising start sputtered with the next words.

"A, his'laqht," she beckoned. She was short and slightly chubby. Black hair.

Helen translated, "That means 'Hello, my friend.' She is assuming you are a friend; unless you do otherwise, you may be."

Walker didn't respond, looking at Marie.

"Kuuqhest hischitsts khwe ehntsetkhw." Marie spoke.

"Guest?" Walker tried.

"Yes, you are a welcome guest in her home," Helen swept her arm toward the log cabin, which was smaller, even than Uncle Bob's.

"Ahh, uhhm, tell her I'm grateful, thank you," he said still looking at Marie.

"Limlemtsh. qha'yqhi't chnlimt." Helen spoke to Marie.

Turning to Walker, Helen added, "Why don't you walk around and identify the trees, while we go inside and talk, George?"

Walker recognized an order and began to scan the pines for mistletoe and lichens.

Half an hour later, George was shredding a piece of cedar bark and smelling it, when Helen came out of the cabin; Marie followed her.

"She says that you may come out on weekends to learn with her. But you must learn her language first." Helen offered.

"What do I have to learn from her?" Walker asked.

"You wanted to find out something about yourself as I recall," Helen reminded him.

"Does she think I'm going to be a student, then?"

"Stoodent, yas!" agreed Marie, who smiled at them both. She had a gap where one of her canine teeth should have been, but the other teeth had moved around, closing part of the space.

Walker shrugged in resignation. "How will I get out here?"

"I'll come back for you later this afternoon. I'm going to look up some other friends. Next week is your problem." Helen walked toward the car.

"How am I going to understand her?" Walker complained.

"Learn the language!" Helen shouted without turning.

"Mirabile dictu." Walker expressed, in Latin.

Helen wondered where he had picked up Latin. "Wonderful to say."

Marie took his arm and steered him back under the pines. She waited, then pointed to a bluejay.

"Qwasq'n" she identified it. Then she turned to him, pointed to his lips, and spoke, "sti'm khukhwi'?" moving her finger back to the bluejay.

"What do you want me to do, try to say that?" Walker wondered.

"Qwasq'n" she said again.

"Kwaskwin?" Walker tried.

"Qwasq'n" she repeated.

"Kwaske en," he pronounced.

233

She nodded. Waited a moment and pointed to a fly, saying, "ch'at'ench."

Walker wished the vocabulary identification were done, but he understood how necessary it was. They couldn't speak until they had something to speak about.

She pointed out a woodpecker, fish, mouse, and hawk: "spowa'lqn, qikhwlsh, k'wit'e'n, sqehqe." She acted out other animals that were not immediately in evidence, deer, coyote, eagle, and bear. The sight of her advancing on him with a rolling gait, arms clawing forward, and growling, made him laugh until he fell down; she dug her fingernails into his sides and dragged him over the needles laughing herself.

She sat by him while he recovered some dignity, then said, "smaqhi'ch'n."

He repeated "smakwhech en" and growled.

She growled louder.

"Oh, big growl, smaqhi'ch'n. What is little growl?" he understood, adding a weak growl. Mother and baby, he thought.

Then she stood up, hunched over a little, and said, "hnLamqe'"
Walker held his knees and made a little growl.

She shook her head.

As he looked at her posture, he thought she must mean black bear was little growl; big growl must be brown bear or grizzly.

She pointed to the low sun, "aldarench." He repeated it.

Then she spoke a sentence, "uup'lkhw khwa'ldarench." He repeated it, not knowing whether the sun was low, yellow, dim, or bright.

She taught him the word for tree, then the word for forest. "Ni'syolalqw," she emphasized.

Soon he was pointing at things and asking "sti'm khukhwu'?" When he thought he saw an eagle he looked at it.

She said "mlqnups" at his shoulder. The female eagle was one of her powers. Walker became lost in another language.

"Well, I'm glad you picked me up a little early. My head is spinning."

"Interesting language, isn't it?" Helen mentioned.

"How long did it take you to learn it?"

"Years, but my parents had a cabin that they built near hers."

"Isn't it tribal land?" Walker inquired.

"No, mostly private around here," she ruminated, playing with the napkin.

They had stopped in a small diner near Harrison for dinner. She had ordered only a salad; he had fish. She wondered what Walker wanted of Marie, what was he trying to find? And Marie seemed just as secretive, just telling Helen that she wanted someone to talk to regularly.

"What does she call you, Helen?" Walker probed curiously.

"ChatteqegweL," Helen answered brightly, "bluebird. What did she call you? Does she have a name for you, yet."

"She called me Ansh, I think."

"That means angel," Helen interpreted, wondering why that name.

Walker was surprised; he knew what it meant, but he didn't know how Marie had decided or known.

"Hey," he said breaking the double reverie, "How am I going to get back next week?"

"You, bud," she replied, gritting her teeth to convey toughness with him, "Mr. mystery hunk, are going to learn how to drive. I presume you are old enough?" she teased him.

"You know, I flew a helicopter several times, but I've never driven a car. Cars are the root of all evil. Think, people who drive are going far too fast to notice anything slower than they. And everything in the world is slower, most everything." He stopped as the waitress brought their plates.

"Helicopter? Where?" she asked ignoring the food.

He took a bite of fish—grease was only really edible when it was warm—and told her.

Getting a driver's license in Idaho was painfully easy. He proved he was over 18; he took a written test, identifying most of the signs correctly—he had seen them from bus windows for years; and he took the road test. As soon as the officer verified that he could start a car and aim it, the license was good as his. The most interest they showed was when he actually paid the $7.00. He took Helen's car, a Mustang, back to the college and walked back down past all the car lots. He figured he could afford $600.00. More than that and he would have to get a loan. He wasn't ready to try that yet. He went to all the new dealers first, expecting that they could give him a better deal. He gave up after two of them. The idea of cars was so attractive to people, that it overcame the disappointment of having them. He wanted a low, fast, two-seater that would be fun to drive and relatively good on gas mileage. Industry offered large, six-seaters that were powered to float over anything. He dreamed of the freedom to move; they dreamed of profits that tied him to a job to finance his dream.

Helen had prepared a little celebration for him. He looked at the cupcake with a candle for a long time.

"You know, I haven't had something like that for years."

Well, don't get all soppy about," she saved him, "or we'll have to clean mucus and wax off the icing." He blew out the candle.

"One year old," he counted.

"Year? No way, big fella, that is a phallic symbol. And if it doesn't have any effect, I'm taking it back to the store tomorrow."

"Which store, grocery or magic?" he asked innocently.

"Who cares?" she threw out, straddling his lap and biting the cupcake. She offered him a bit before she covered his mouth.

Later, he probed, "Have you been reading in the modern literature section, again?"

She smiled and said, "The really modern literature stores are in Spokane, with red and yellow-painted signs and blacked-out windows."

They kissed.

He had somehow remembered to ask her where a good, honest auto dealer was. She had told him that where she bought her car was the only one that was both, E. K. Baker Motors. Now, he was standing among the ten-year old fords and Volkswagens. Trying to decide to buy one. Old Baker had a perpetual half-smile. He was average height with thinning brown hair. He obviously did his own work. The overalls were stained with grease and gas, torn in several places.

"Well, you probably want something that saves gas and looks pretty good." Walker had bidden good-bye to looks when he found the lot.

"No, thank you, sir, if you could just show me your three cheapest cars to start." Unlike a hard-core salesman, E. K. just took him in back of the service station. He pointed to a 1966 chevy, a 64 mercury Comet, and a 68 Cougar, for $250.00, 450.00, and 600.00. Walker would have picked up the cougar right away, but everything about it threatened collapse and expense. He looked closely at the Comet. Both front and back bumpers had earned their name, but everything else was clean.

"That's the best one. 78,000 miles. I own one just like it." Walker knew he did, because he had seen it parked by the building; E. K.'s was in perfect shape, newly painted.

"Those seats can be fixed, or covered," E. K. offered.

"I'll buy it for that price if you tune it and give me a good spare." Walker offered.

"I can't do that and make any profit. But if you buy the points and plugs, I'll provide the labor for free. I can give you a good spare, but it won't be new. How's that?"

Walker hesitated, knowing that it was indeed a good deal. "Okay, deal."

They shook. E. K. offered to have the plates tagged if Walker wanted. He did. He wrote out a check for $476.18, including tax, parts, and fees. And he picked it up after his last class that day.

It was easier to praise the joys of a car when you had one. Too bad he couldn't have afforded a Porsche or Mercedes. He and Helen went to a drive-in movie; something they had never thought of in her car. They explored northern Idaho during the evenings. During the days he taught. And weekends were at the cabin. Helen never went with him, saying that she would be a distraction. He had progressed to bumpy sentences and nonabstract ideas. As soon as summer school was over, he intended to camp there for several weeks.

"How is the lake?" Marie had asked.

And he answered slowly, that it was clear, "unqhel khwa chatq'ele'."

"Mee'liche' khwe tmikhw'lmkhw?" she then asked.

He thought for a moment, where is the earth? It is below, "T'u', techgwent."

They went on like that until dark.

Inside the cabin, he complimented her, still thinking in English, you told me a beautiful story yesterday, "'Mi'y'mi'yshitsekhw anqhqhasa'lqs khwa aspa."

She bowed gracefully, then indicated the table, "Ne'chshepeptsin ne'ch'aaya') ne'chtuu'yiLn."

He knew it meant that they would eat after talking, so he tried to tell her that good food and good friends made his heart happy, "Hnlimn le sdumdumtsn khwe twe qhest he'yiLn."

They would be eating rabbit tonight. He asked her if she had killed it. She indicated that she had.

He thanked her for his food, "Limlemtsh."

He learned that she was a medicine woman, "t'e'kwilsh." But he didn't know how to ask what he wanted to know, yet. She took the rabbit from an earthen oven. He noticed that roots were drying on top. The syringa digging stick was by the oven, curved with a crutched handle. He ate rabbit. He slept outside in his sleeping bag, turning regularly on the uneven ground.

The next morning she woke him with, "CheLchischLip."

He wanted to go hunting, so he came out of his sleeping bag quietly, fully dressed. She carried a new compound bow. He pointed to it. She only smiled, putting her fingers to her lips. He kept pestering her with questions so much that she gave up trying to track anything. Then they talked about the woods and woods people. Going back to the cabin after three or four hours, she stopped suddenly. He followed her stare. Then saw a porcupine slowly climbing a ponderosa pine a hundred yards away. She glanced quickly around to make sure that no one else was stalking this animal. Then she walked to within twenty feet of it and put one arrow into its side. The porcupine fell four feet to the ground with a thud.

"Twi'," Marie said.

Too bad, Walker translated. He asked her if it was edible.

She replied that he was edible, if he was cooked a long time, with the right herbs. Porcupine was a delicacy to coyotes, but doubtless that had to do with the difficulty for them of killing one. She had known of coyotes as well as cougars who died from infected spines trying to kill porcupine.

Walker offered to carry it back, foolishly it turned out; the spines kept poking his arms.

"Most of the murders we have around here are from passion, and easy to solve; guilt and remorse bring in more killers, mostly family or friends of the victim, than we do," Edelman paused. No one was hounding him to solve the Nazi-murder case, since the victims had been preaching hate to all of their neighbors for years, but he was a police detective, and good, and he was unhappy with so few leads. Now the trail would be getting covered with the clutter of unrelated events. He put his head in his hands and sighed loudly. The three junior officers waited patiently.

"Sir, uh, perhaps we could ask for help. Ya know, Packard's retired around here; he may be tired of fishing," Phillip, the most junior, suggested.

Edelman smiled, "tired of living maybe, eating possibly, but fishing never. I'll think about, though, thanks. Let's go on to the Herkat case."

His two classes for fall were no better or worse than he had expected. He got Developmental Psychology 208 and Principles of Scientific Psychology 201. He hoped he could fob off 'Priscy' 201 on Busby. Not likely, since there were only the two of them. He liked teaching new courses and seminars, not the plodding stuff like Priscy. Maybe Busby would take it, if he could present it as important enough. He spent every evening preparing his lectures. Sometimes Helen came over; sometimes they worked together at her house. She had accepted his schedule. In fact, he was startled when he had offered that they live together and she had adamantly refused, saying that she was satisfied with her life and did not wish to orbit his sun like a dim satellite.

"Pintch chsentse'i'wes, ansh," she had said, "we are brothers, angel, we cannot get too close to one another. That does not mean that we cannot be comfortable and loving—just never mates."

He thought he understood, so he didn't argue.

He built a double lean-to house of branches half-mile from Marie's cabin. She made him a buckskin tunic with long, loose sleeves for the winter. It was not as long as hers, coming only to the knees. She said she would make leggings later, after he would kill a deer. He had bought her several thin woolen blankets earlier, not knowing if anything he made would be useful.

"You are ready," she judged.

"Ready, for what?" he questioned.

"Visions," she affirmed.

Then he realized that she was speaking English.

"You know how to speak English?" His voice started to rise.

"Yes, very well. University of Idaho," she anticipated him.

"Then why?—"

"Because, you had to know the forest. English would have blinded you to many beings."

"You are a shaman," he recognized.

"Yes, there are many difficult steps to become one; many difficult decisions to remain one."

He laughed lightly, not hurt, or even questioning any more. "What are the steps?" he asked.

She informed him, "I cannot tell you. You are not one."

"Will I ever be one? A shaman?" he probed.

"No, you do not love human beings enough. But you are a keeper of animal spirits. Kuupipe' e tmikhu'lmkhw."

She had switched back to salish, and he didn't understand exactly what she meant.

"You will understand. You will receive visions from your tutelary spirits," she assured him.

"And what must I do to prepare?"

She took him in the cabin and fixed potatoes for herself.

"You must start by fasting for two days; start now. You may drink nothing but water from the stream." He looked at the sliced potatoes.

"I am going to eat. You are going to watch and listen. My life was different than yours in many ways." She told him of her youth.

"I remember many young men who serenaded me with a flute, who visited me and tried to separate me from my chaperone. There was one who was quieter than the rest, smaller but more—" she searched for the English word, finally shrugging, "—energetic. He was my favorite. I told my mother. One day she told me that he was going to propose. This is how it went: As he approached me, I was standing in the center of the lodge; I turned from him, still standing. He sat down on some straw and

241

talked to my back, finally saying in desperation that he wished to marry me. When I did not answer, he turned over the straw and set it on fire. When I put my foot backward to stamp out the fire, still without looking at him or speaking, he stepped on my foot. Then I asked him very formally, 'Why do you tramp on my foot?' Knowing that I accepted, he left without speaking. While I let the fire burn down, he told his parents of my acceptance, and they negotiated with my parents. When they approved, his parents set a date for the ceremony.

"Many gifts were exchanged during the ceremony, which was supervised by an old man who was no longer chief. His relatives sponsored a feast. We built our own house, not far from here." She was silent.

"Gu'l'olkhwalqw," she whispered.

"Under a log?" Walker asked gently.

"He died," her voiced cracked, her eyes teared suddenly. Then Walker understood the term.

He asked how, thinking she wanted to talk about it. She looked past him, eyes moist, with overflow, he thought.

She continued, "His face was painted; he was bound in his robe, hands over his chest, and carried feet first from the house. He was buried by the river bank. I put a branch over the grave. A feast was held for his soul. I had a chance to be his brother's other wife. I had power."

"You believe human beings have souls?" he asked, after a few minutes.

"Every being has a soul," she related.

"Where do they go? To an afterworld?"

"Perhaps. But souls are more delicate than flesh. They can be lost or thrown away. They can be strengthened by ritual and good."

"Your husband's?" he asked.

"le ch'est!"

"Evil?" he guessed.

"No more! I am weary of memory. You will fast."

He was dismissed.

The next day, she had him run to the lake, swim across and run back. He was dizzy slightly when he collapsed in front of her cabin. Sunday, he thought, there must be a football game on somewhere. How attractive it would be to sit, like dreaming. She led him into the cabin. His arms and legs were naked from his exercise. She took a knife and cut a line on the underside of each arm. Turning them over she made four short cuts on the backs of his hands, where the carpal bones were. He closed his eyes and tried to concentrate on stopping the bleeding. He felt the openings sting as she rubbed some sandy mixture on them.

"There were only three horses in my time. The men used them, for hunting, or carrying loads of roots. Young boys kept the horses. That was something girls didn't do. My father had a bridle made of horsehair, a saddle of fur and leather. One night, I rode one of the horses, afraid that something would happen. When nothing did I was almost disappointed. I had done what I wanted and gotten away with it."

"Did you ever tell anyone?" Walker opened his eyes.

"No, but it would have made no difference. We always resisted authority. Although we had leaders, we were taught to be self-reliant and responsible. You may resist my teachings. That is good. I am not always right. But you must be self-reliant."

She was rubbing leather while she was talking. Walker had a sudden glimpse of a President telling his countrymen that they must be self-reliant, and the sudden outbreak of rebellion. No one wanted to be self-reliant and responsible. Then he could feel the blood coagulating, no longer dripping on his thighs.

Marie began again. "Our beliefs are basic: There is a supernatural side to existence, in all of nature. All the beings of nature—rocks, trees, rivers, fish, birds, deer—influence the destiny of men. Their spirits appear in visions. If you quest is good enough, spirits may confer powers," she explained.

"Can I expect powers?" Walker asked, not feeling quite as uncomfortable.

"No, you may only be prepared. Power is unexpected and un—" she searched again for a word. "unbidden. Many may prepare for the quest, but the power may be in an unintended encounter. Powers are natural abilities that are supported by spirits. The spirits choose who to support."

"How will I know?"

"You may not. The spirit can appear in human form or animal nature. It may explain the nature of the power conferred or it may not; it may instruct a special power song or it may not."

Are there only capricious gods? Walker asked silently.

"The vision cannot ever be discussed publicly. It is private. And as long as the proper rituals and taboos are observed, you are assured of support from the spirit," she explained.

"And if not?" he felt compelled to ask.

"Possibly death, perhaps loss of power, perhaps nothing. Circumstances dictate. But one may keep symbols of one's power in a bundle. That helps."

"The symbols come from the powers?" he spoke redundantly. "How would others tell if a power was present?"

She looked at his hands, and spoke sarcastically, "A European needs to ask that? Success," she proclaimed, answering herself, "Success in hunting, success in healing."

"I was born here," he claimed quietly.

"Sorry," she said in an untypical voice, "Indian forget."

"Can one have more than one power?" he asked, and bent forward to kiss and hold her hand. She withdrew it before he could touch it.

"Sometimes two, rarely more. A shaman may have many," she stood up, withdrawing from him.

"Do you? How many?"

"Seven," she indicated.

He had no scale by which to measure. Seven sounded improbably many.

She explained, "A shaman needs to have more to help others in discovering their power and communicating with it. I also have to locate game and roots, with the eyes of a cougar and the nose of a pig, prophesy the future, give advice on problems."

"Can you tell my future?" he probed.

She looked in his eyes, then got up. She went to a shelve, and pulling two dry leaves from it, crumpled them. She came back and sat in front of him.

"You will, no—no, but you will die in the sun, violently, in great light." An explosion, he thought, wondering when. The tension was tangible, electric. He brought it to ground.

"Should I stay here? Until I receive a vision?"

"No, do you think that spirits are tied to trees? Go home, teach. But fast, and run and swim," she smiled.

He wondered what she had seen, only the sun.

Walker had two rough days in class while his body adjusted to not eating. One hundred seventy pounds; almost a perfect weight. He had lost ten pounds the first two days, two pounds a day afterwards. Sometimes it felt like he was digesting his muscles. But the muscles were well defined, now. He could see each one move as he lifted or ran. The muscles of his face were firmer, too. There were no bags or frowns. After the third day, it didn't hurt. He slept longer, woke faster. His breath smelled sweet like pineapple.

Then the next weekend was upon him. Marie was waiting for him, in front of his lean-to. She went in and started a fire. The sun had set.

"Let me tell you some of our myths, so you will understand more. Some of them explain the way things came to be in a certain way; others are lessons that show the sad results of theft or dishonesty."

"About Coyote?" he interjected.

"Yes, Coyote was a changer. He was always getting mixed up,

dismembered—"

As she described Coyote, Walker remembered Jung's commentary on the trickster: He was god, man and animal at once; subhuman and superhuman, divine and bestial.

"—he acted out the disasters of violating society, but taught also the superiority and morality that is possible for human beings."

"Tell me a story," he demanded, tiring of abstractions.

"Once, Coyote killed the sun. It is a long story, involving deer and rabbits, so I am telling the short version. Here is how it happened. Coyote's children stole the disk of the sun people, who chased them and killed them one at a time, as one passed the disk on to the faster, until it was passed to Coyote by the last one. In his grief for his children, Coyote threw it away. Only later did he decide on revenge. He traveled day after day to reach the sun, but got no closer. Then he encountered a meadowlark on the road, who suggested that he travel at night, when the sun could not see him, and trap the sun at a pool where he stopped to drink at noon. Coyote took the advice. On the second night, he found the spring, and dug a hole for himself opposite the bank where the sun bent to drink. At first the sun circled warily, suspecting something, but finally reached down to drink. Coyote reached up suddenly and cut off the sun's heart, which was hung around his neck by a thong. The sun fell down and died. It became dark, only a few stars showing. All the Indians murmured, "Coyote has done something." Coyote kept stumbling over the sun's body wherever he walked. Worried, he asked his powers what to do. They said, 'Put down the heart you are holding in your hand.' He did, and it became light again."

Walker knew that the Greek Heraklitus thought the sun to be masses of pure fire. Anaxagoras, too, claimed that it was nothing but a fireball, before he fled the city in fear of his life for doubting the divinity of the sun. In a way, the sun is divine, he thought. Everything on earth depended on it. Among the Zuni Indians of the Southwest, the very word for life, 'tekohanane,' meant daylight. Other peoples revered the sun, and with good reason. Whenever the sun was blocked for long periods of time, by volcanic ash for instance, crops failed. Parts of the Northwest America and Europe had suffered that. He knew of research on the sunspot cycle and its relation to climate. The annual growth of trees was linked to the sunspot cycle of eleven years. The earth's climate was linked to that cycle. From 1645 to 1715, when the cycle mysteriously stopped and there were almost no sunspots, a 'Little Ice Age' occurred in Europe.

He sat quietly, thinking; she sat quietly, not thinking. They were both comfortable with silences.

Another time, they discussed the soul, again.

Marie warned: "Men who do not see are dangerous. They are not fully human. They walk in the form of men, but are not men; they are soulless, their souls have died."

Walker didn't recognize one of the phrases, and asked her about it.

"Ikhwl tts'silshn khwe gul tt'mikhw," she repeated, "some animals have two legs, a phrase for men. For white men, it is—was Ch'salqikhw khwe, 'they have a bad odor,' " she explained, laughing. "Your odor is good, now. For the soul is more delicate than life; the pattern is more delicate and precious and more easily destroyed. And human civilization is intent on providing pitfalls for the souls of the living.

"Animals have humaneness. Bowerbirds construct a nest of color, texture, and fragrance for their females. Dolphins have compassion for the fallen and those left behind by the fallen. Elephants have law and justice. Raccoons and coyotes, wolves and snakes, tenderness. Their souls are stronger in simplicity.

"Listen to every being. What does the thunder say? It warns. Feel the sky, feel the earth and all living beings. Listen, be watchful; there are inner meanings in rain and trees, and in those who hide from the rain, in beings with legs and those without legs."

She was worried. He had not told her of being contacted by a power, yet. Sometimes she had the feeling that he was the father of all powers, yet sometimes that he was not awake. She could no longer keep track of him when he left on a quest or when he came back. She did not know if he was ready or not. She would see Helen and talk to her.

"Listen to me!" she hissed, angry at herself for becoming angry. "Powers are not toys, not to be played with. I do not know if you have been contacted, but listen to what I have to say."

She lifted his chin up sharply, so that their eyes met, blue and black, deep sky and deep soil. "Powers can not change the world. A bird may have more value than a thousand men with guns and bows aimed at it. But a power cannot stop one of them from killing that bird. Powers can give you strength. And with spiritual strength, you can live in the world with love and understanding; not change it by force, but by example. Be simple, breathe deeply. This air cannot be, unless the animals, grass and trees breathe it out."

She pushed him away, gently and firmly. He noticed her for the first time, really.

"But I have no power. No thing, no being has made himself known, yet," he protested.

She spoke again, "You will, in time. Their time is not your time. You have a long journey to reality. Like the hunter, you must know other beings, or you will starve. Like the warrior, you must know yourself, or you will be lost. If you take both steps, you can become a shaman, a person of knowledge. But you must start by yourself. I cannot go for you."

He nodded and turned away. He reached out and touched a pine as he went. The contact gave him as sense of belonging, and he was calm. Dreams seem to have left him again.

The next week, he stayed away from the shaman. He convinced Helen to try St Mary's Catholic church. They offered a mass at 11:30. The reverend Tim Westlake proved easier to talk to. In fact, he was a disciple of Teilhard de Chardin. So he believed that evolution was real. With Teilhard, it was possible to be Catholic and a scientist, in spite of the reaction of the church. He had hypothesized that all matter, to varying degrees, was transfused with consciousness. After billions of years of evolution, this consciousness blossomed in Man. The final stage of development he called the Omega point, where all humans and matter would be elevated to a unity in Jesus. With Teilhard, God was no longer divine, but mysteriously internal to the world. Jesus was only a pinnacle of evolution, the result of a cosmic accident. But he did not believe that it compromised the teachings of the church.

"If evolution is good, then why are some animals considered evil by your church?" Walker asked.

The reverend Westlake was sucking his lip. He leaned back in his chair, considering his answer. He loved a good talk. "Every animal that was venerated by the gods of other peoples was consigned to the devil by Christianity. Every animal that was feared by man, that was inimical to him, was diabolized. Animals that were treated as demons by animistic religions were added to the list. The elephant of the Buddhists, the bull of the Egyptians, and the pig, bear, and fox; the goat of Assyria, were considered incarnations. The bat and rat were merely abhorred. The fly of the Persian Ahriman; the raven of the Scandinavian Odin. The cat of Freya. Wolves are dangerous, were dangerous, believed to be dangerous. The devil was even called a lion."

"Before Christ was?" Walker interjected.

"Why yes, in Peter 2.8, I think. Jesus was called the lion of Juda, in Revelations 5. Then, too, medieval writers converted metaphors into facts. If the Devil was called a roaring lion, a dragon, or a serpent, then it was supposed that he assumed the forms of these animals. The ape of God was another literal interpretation. In Hindu mythology, the serpent is a guardian of treasures."

"Why were Christ and Lucifer—"

"Satan?" Westlake wondered.

"Lucifer. Why were they called the same? They were also referred to as 'Son of Morning' in different places in the bible. Could they be twins of a kind?" Walker asked awkwardly.

"No, the devil copies. The devil has worn many forms. He is polymorphous. He is a master of the art of physical tergiversation. He can contract and expand at pleasure. A spirit, yet, he has the power of manifesting himself in material form. St. Paul warns that he can transform himself into an angel of light."

"But, that much is logical isn't it, since Lucifer started as an angel of light?"

"Angel, ah, yes I suppose. God created angels before the universe, giving them free will to choose to serve him. But one, one, said he would not serve. Admiring his own brightness, he contemplated himself and then set up a stronghold in heaven for himself, in the northwest, he built himself a throne, summoning other angels to rally around him. God threw them down. For three days and nights they fell, into the pit. Undaunted, Lucifer raised a castle in darkness. He spoke to his retainers saying that God will fill their spaces with humans, a new creation of dirt and soil. And vowed to turn them against their creator. And so he did, against God, but against Man as well, hmmm." Westlake sipped his coffee, in a Chinese mug wrapped by a white dragon, whose tail formed the handle.

"Angels are divine messengers," he continued. "They are invisible because their speed is that of thought. Lucifer became his own messenger, the Messenger of nothingness and its mysteries."

"Yes, but nothingness is really the glue of existence. Even the brightest star is nothing without emptiness around it." Walker offered.

"Nothingess does not exist," the reverend said with certainty.

"Nothing exists alone, all else is a dream. Only empty space and you. And you are nothing but a thought squeezed from nothingness."

"Do you believe that?" Westlake asked.

"No, I thought you did. Why else would you worship the author of the dream?"

"I worship God, not Satan. When Satan was asked why he left Paradise, he answered that he wanted to be an author. The author of everything is the authority of all things. The need to write, to create, is to want to become like God."

"How is that bad, if we are in his image and want to create?" Walker asked.

"We lose ourselves when we create, and when we lose ourselves the devil finds us."

"So, we should not lose ourselves in creation? Nonsense. Where better to be lost?"

"Creativity leads to vertigo, like looking down the tower of babel. It results from the incapacity of humans for inhuman attitudes or dimensions."

"Yet, those dimensions help us to be human, by allowing us to expand into those dimensions," Walker reasoned.

"Satan is the one who denies everything. Goethe had Mephistopheles say: I am the spirit that always denies! A good thing, too, for all that exists deserves to be destroyed. It would be so much better if nothing were ever created. So, he denies."

"How can he deny? I thought you said he wanted to be the author of everything?"

"What? Never mind, Satan is fallen," Westlake stated. He looked unbelievingly into the empty cup, wondering if he could have more coffee, now.

"He may be fallen but he has kept his spirit pure."

"The void in his heart is the consciousness of his loss of his rightful place."

"No, he is conscious of finding his rightful place."

"Well, yes, he is the Prince of the world. Christians condemn that he will never have anything but this world."

"Maybe. Do you know how large this world is? How connected to all the universe?" Walker asked, thinking that the emphasis on the infinity of the universe devalued the infinity of planet and inhabitants.

"Satan can do nothing but to incite us to, to abuse our liberty and the goods of the earth."

"Ridiculous, he is the earth; he wants your liberty from divine mechanism. By the way, I am talking about Lucifer, not that little local Satan fellow."

"Responsibility is the opposite of liberty. Every responsible life is a defeat for the devil."

"Nonsense, that would mean that every freedom is a defeat for God."

"It is through freedom that we have the power to sin."

"It is through freedom that we have the choice to sin or to do good. That freedom is necessary for either."

"People are not as free as you make them," Westlake chastised his visitor.

"I agree that they may not want to be free. Look at all the books about the devil, devil worship, demonic possession—I think most are just people's way of saying 'it's not my fault,' 'don't blame me,' 'I'm not responsible,' and so on."

"There has to be a choice, though," Westlake paused thoughtfully. "What is beyond good and evil? Boredom."

"No, that is the newest evil, boredom leading to indifference. Anything is tempting to the bored. And they try anything to relieve the symptoms."

"Can they be blamed for not knowing or choosing?"

"Ecclesiastes was right: humans know nothing. All, happens equally to all, righteous or wicked, God-mocking or God-fearing." Walker paused and looked at the ornate ceiling.

"Do you hate God so much?" Westlake asked.

"What a foolish question. I love God as I love everything. I am not the same, though. I have different ambitions. And God loves me. If you cannot believe this, think of us as metaphors for your longing to be one with nature again."

"Metaphors? No! God is real."

"A metaphor is just a way of understanding, by connecting something not understood with something understood. For instance, we make a woman into an angel or devil, partly because of that apple incident that had Eve's desire set off the old Man, er, that is, man as metaphor."

"All right, I'll accept that in a literary sense. In Faust, I remember, he, 'with greedy hands he digs for treasure, and he is happy when he finds earthworms!' Thus, the devil is identified with the smallest and slimiest things," Westlake smiled.

"Not exactly. Earthworms are an important part of the earth. We are blamed for finding charm in the most disgusting things, as Baudelaire contends, but there is charm in everything; not knowing that limits you to those very few things that appeal to humans, out of the infinity of God."

"Baudelaire, yes. He also said: The devil's cleverest wile is to convince us that he does not exist."

"You have good quotes but you seem to understand them backwards; the real evil in this world is the loss of awareness of evil, the evil of individuals, of indifference, of the system which directs our lives—much more than the simple metaphor of one individual who is supposed to cause them.. We need to become conscious of our actions and their context in the corporate life of society."

"Satan exists, but he fears to show himself in his ugliness, which is why he relies on masks."

"No, Lucifer wants to show himself. The masks are just for play," thinking that play was a way of teaching and learning, Walker smiled.

"No. He tries to hide his wickedness behind masks."

"He doesn't care who sees his wickedness or good. Why should he?"

"Do you think you are God?" Westlake asked, beginning to get tired of this debate.

"God, nature, me. Does it matter? I am Lucifer, Lightbearer, and my light is not the cold light that you imagine, but the creation of the greatest pressures and releases."

"God is the owner of the universe and you."

"There is no relation now between God and the Universe. He poured himself into the big bang and is now enjoying universal consciousness. The difference is that I, Lucifer, limited myself to one place, one planet, one star. I went the opposite direction and concentrated. We were both faced with the old problem: How does one renew one's self? God went to renew everywhen, everywhere and in everything. I went to one place, then to dive in and out of time."

"God is King of eternity. The devil is prince of time. God is a Lamb. The devil is a wolf."

Walker could hear the upper and lower case letters being spoken. He answered, "You might have that backwards, too. God chose the wolf to be his dog, according to Grimm's fairy tales, so the devil chose the goat to be his. This is a cute story, listen. The wolf got along famously with God, following him everywhere. The goats wandered all around independently, getting their tails caught in the bushes, so the devil had to go and untangle them all the time. God asked him why he chose such an evil-smelling, trouble-making animal; the devil said it was his nature, but later he got so angry that he bit off all their tails. The goats then ate all the acorns. God bet the devil that they could not eat all acorns. When the devil came to collect, God mentioned that there was a tree in Lebanon that was still green. The devil raced off to look. By the time he got back the other trees had become green again with acorns, so he lost. He became so angry that he put his own eyes in all the goats so he could see the trees all the time. That is why goats have short tails and evil eyes. That is why Pan, with his goat parts, was feared for his association with wilderness. And, for sexual passion, which suspends reason. Then, almost anything can suspend reason, which is held by the very weakest clip to—"

"You are a Satan."

"No, The name Satan comes from a word meaning to oppose or obstruct. Satan is not a being, just a noun that an angel is when the angel blocks the road. As when David asks what right someone has to play the Satan against him. No, I'm Lucifer."

"You are terrible, to say that, to think that," Westlake shook his head.

"All angels are terrible, as the poet Rilke said."

Westlake knew in his heart that Lucifer was an angel of darkness, but he chose to be silent for a moment.

The reverend looked at his watch, Walker thought, with a rather time-worn gesture. As he looked up and saw Walker regarding him, he thought Walker looked like a wolf.

Then he broke the stare. "I, uhhmm, have to prepare for 1:00. Those condemned for the 'sins of the wolf'—the seducers, magicians, thieves, and liars—occupy the eighth circle of Dante's hell." Now, why did I say that, he kicked himself.

Walker smiled and left the office.

That night he talked to Helen.

"What do—Am I strange to you?"

"No," she answered, writing notes for tomorrow's staff meeting.

"Can Lucifer change himself into a wolf?"

"Just a minute," she said, looking up and putting her pencil down.

Walker kept looking at his hands.

"There have always been connections," Helen started, drawing on her wide readings. "In mythology. Apollo's mother, Leto, disguised herself as a wolf to escape the attentions of a jealous Hera; she ran with a pack of wolves. Later, Apollo took on the shape of a wolf, once, to fight and destroy the, ahh," she bit her lip, her eyes unfocused, "sorcerers of Rhodes. Yet Apollo was also patron of shepherds and was supposed to kill wolves to guard sheep. Mythology always starts or ends in contradiction, it seems," she finished.

"Apollo was also the sun god," Walker subvocalized.

"What?" Helen asked, leaning forward.

"Inter lupum et canem," Walker said.

"What, oh, between wolf and dog," Helen translated, wondering how Walker knew Latin, and why this Latin. "It means dawn, between wolf and dog, between night and day."

"Is the wolf a creature of dawn, the son of morning?"

Helen waited, not knowing how to answer. She reached over for the dictionary, suspecting another kind of connection.

Lucifer/Wolf, thought Walker.

"Here," Helen motioned. "The Greek word for light is 'leukos' and the word for wolf is 'lukos.' In Latin the word for wolf is—"

"—lupus," continued Walker, "and light is 'lucis.' Lucifer, 'lucem ferre,' bearer of light."

He kissed her on the forehead, and left. She shrugged and went back to her notes.

He was sitting by the lake when he heard the music. The notes came over the lake and wound around him, gathering together the vibrations he had diffused. It told him of others. It pushed him and pulled him to get up and move. He ignored a flash of silliness and got up. His legs and arms moved rhythmically. He felt he was entering a trance. His awareness expanded beyond the body, encompassing the worms and fish, birds and chipmunks. He touched a deer.

The body began shaking with power. He felt it being dismembered by possession. Red spots appeared on the fabric over his shoulders and hips. Blood stains. His joints popped. The body was lifted and dropped, lifted and dropped, by some force. He saw the eyes. Through the eyes. Into darkness.

Walker missed class the next day. When he showed up on Tuesday, he seemed gaunt and hungry. The first lecture was on consciousness. His introduction was a presentation of facts. When he got to the section on 'Consciousness in Dreams' he decided to read from the book. The students would think it was a new tactic.

"Fischer describes a series of dreams where the dreamer believed he could fly. Since the dreamer knew that human beings could not fly, he tested himself during every dream to make sure that he was awake and really flying. For several months this series of dreams continued; the dreamer was sure that he could fly, but when he waked he never remembered dreaming. The two consciousnesses did not have access to each other. So no experiences of flight were exchanged between them, on either the possibility or the impossibility. One day something happened that gave the waking person knowledge of his dream; he remembered dreaming that he could fly, and even recalled the whole series of dreams. The dreams of flying did not occur again. Apparently, the dreamer no longer believed that he could fly. Freud, who carried—" Walker stopped.

He never remembered his dreams. His memory itched. He looked back at the page, and started, loosing his place.

"—two levels of consciousness: one observing the dream, the other participating in it—"

Schizophrenia, double consciousness. Was he going mad? He heard the class stir.

"Oh, sorry, you can read that on your own. Why not tell each other about our dreams? Let's start down the front row," he gestured. Most of the dreams related were hodge-podges of adolescent desire. If the dreams are the same and shallow, perhaps it was because all of their experiences were the same. He noticed the same trend in song-writers, whose most memorable experiences were writing and singing songs. The songs became about singing, or grouping after singing, more convoluted, like seeing an image of oneself on the toilet, reflected in mirror after mirror. He did write some of their dreams down: —in a strange city, in an

257

apartment over water looking at pictures, packing a suitcase captured by
the Salvation Army band for drunk and disorderly   kept in detention by
a tuba (good) chased through a parking lot by a truck towing a gangster
on water skis in a swimming pool with two Eskimos having a picnic with
Sheila in the park, undressing her.

"What about one of yours?" came the question. He looked up and
realized that everyone had finished.

"Well," he invented, "I was once the dark world dream director for
the Dream Travel Agency in downtown Burbank. My best customers
were people just like you, too broke to travel on their own." The class
ended with good-humored kidding.

Chapter 14. Transformation

There was a way of knowing, that was the way of the deer. Walker
realized that he knew it, he knew the feeling. Fridays through Sundays
he reserved for his 'explorations' as he told Helen and his colleague,
Busby. At first he remembered walking on the edges of wheatlands and
clearings, then running for the joy of it. He was always hungry, always
wary.

One Sunday night he was reading a book of poetry, and came across
one entitled, 'The Way of the Deer.' He transcribed part of it into his
journal. "The vitality and wisdom of its body ruin

      Complete rationality and loosen up mind's categories—
      No monster Pan, but a small being pleased
      At fitting between the woods and fields so well. .

How can you browse grass or rub a tree without becoming it?
Dizzy with eating, exposed, she scratches the surface
Of wholeness with her hooves ...

Walker wondered if the writer were male or female; female probably. A.M. Caratheodory. Sounded French or Greek. A relative of the physicist? He remembered that all animals were called 'deer' once, just like they are called 'animals' now. He fell asleep in the chair.

Sam Morris woke up before the alarm. He looked at the clock: 7:00 a.m. and turned off the alarm before it woke Margaret. He no longer got up at 3:00 a.m., although he still dreamed of the huge buck peeping from between two trees. But then this was his eighteenth season. He went down to the kitchen, but wasn't surprised to see his son sitting at the table affecting a nonchalance over his cereal. He grunted a greeting; his vocal chords were just slower than the rest of his body, although his stomach was awakening, now. He cooked himself sausage and hash browns; he knew he should move faster, before the boy screamed his impatience out loud. He noted gratefully that the black coffee was steaming in the mug. As he ate, he thought about his totals: forty deer, about evenly divided between mule and whitetail, on all kinds of terrain. He remembered with slight embarrassment even now the one season he didn't get any. He had spent one weekend watching an obvious deer trail for two days. Then old Harv had told him that the deer only used it at night probably. He could still summon up Harv's harsh laughter.

"Dad?" his son asked.

"Hhmmm?" He answered through his mug.

"Can I get the three wheelers ready?"

"Good idea, Buddy," he praised earnestly. "But don't try to load them until I get there."

Then he noticed the boy had own his jacket already. He salted the potatoes again and gulped the last of them. Ever since Margaret had started to buy A-1 sauce for hamburger, to make it taste like steak, he had started to use it on potatoes, to make them taste like hamburger, he supposed. He would have preferred a steak this morning. As he clumped down the stairs, he wondered again how wise it had been to buy those three-wheelers for hunting. Gear was important, everyone knew. Hell, they were up until one cleaning the rifles and loading their vests. But those Hondas were not really necessary—electric start, shaft drive, reverse—he catalogued. Maybe hunting was better without them. He made up his mind.

"Buddy, let's leave those behind, today. We ought to scout out our territory anyway."

"Aw, damn it, dad, I want to take them," Buddy protested, testing his profanity in front of his father.

"Stow it, boy," he closed down the argument more finally then he meant, so he softened it some, "Them are orders, soldier."

"Yes, sir," Buddy answered, still feeling trapped by childhood patterns.

Sam loved his son, he realized. He remembered his own first hunt.

"Guns stowed?"

"Hours ago," was the answer.

He laughed, "Let's go, you drive."

They got into the pickup. Still almost new.

"A good hunter knows the territory and the woods," he said to said to Buddy as they were driving, knowing he was lecturing, but knowing that it was important. "Hunting is as old as humanity and deer. The skills of the hunter were passed down directly, by verbal and nonverbal communications. Words often don't belong in the wilderness.

"I remember my first kill; jumping a mule deer in a stand of ponderosa. The pine needles were all frosted; there was no wind." He gazed at the road. Miles passed.

"I want to make sure that you know what is a good hunter. Someone who enjoys the wilderness more than the shot; someone who only tries to even out the imbalance caused by others, who have killed most of the cougars, wolves and coyotes, by killing only the weak and old, like wolves and cougars. Someone who eats all of the kill, who does not freeze it until the freezer falls apart.

"There is equipment, skill, and most of all, luck. Deer and elk follow patterns of movement, but bear are more random. They feed continuously, on ants, acorns, termites, until fall when the berries ripen. Hawthorns and chokeberries, raspberries, rose hips, ants—"

"Dad, the deer, just the deer."

"Oh, sorry. When you can find the pattern of movement of the deer, then it's just a matter of watching and waiting."

"Life is too short to spend it watching, can't we just go after them?"

"Life is too short," Sam sighed agreement, but watching is the soul of hunting he thought.

Then they were at the wilderness. The wilderness was eight acres of clearcut. Near the open parts were red fir and bull pines. Logging trails cut out in several directions. Sam remembered that there were dormant fields to the north and south of the clearcut. Deer could be in either.

Then they were walking out into the cold morning. After about twenty minutes around the edge, Sam suggested that they wait under a white fir. He was sure that there would be traffic in the clearing before long. They waited for fifteen minutes. Buddy kept fidgeting. Sam didn't want to talk.

Then Buddy spoke in his ear, "I'm going to go walking over that way."

Sam didn't want him to go, but didn't want to ruin his own chances, so he warned, "Remember where I am, and what I look like, and don't go far—don't shoot any cows."

Buddy nodded his head as he walked with a springy step into the trees.

Sam guessed that an hour had gone by. He knew that some of his friends still got up at 4:00, but he didn't think the deer ate any earlier during the season. Then, just like in his dream, he saw a buck between two trees, exhaling steam. He slowly raised his gun, and sighted his chest. The finger, no longer his finger, tightened on the trigger as daintily as it would on a teacup, and no less intimately. Before the trigger was pulled, the buck was standing, afterwards it was lying down, bleeding slightly. The bullet had made the kill and threaded them together before he could even make out the details of the buck. He hoped Buddy would be drawn back by the report.

He watched the hunter, the shuffling feet, the hands digging in the pocket for another cigarette. The head swiveled. Then, they both heard the report of a gun.

Buddy started to run back to where his father was. Then he heard the sound of running hooves. Suddenly he stopped, thinking that if the report had scared something his way, he might as well take a chance at it. There was silence. He kept his gun up.

A snort behind him; he turned with the barrel. Then hooves behind him. He started running. He wanted to scream his fear; it tightened his throat; it banded the muscles of his neck until they felt like iron. His jaw was frozen and the cold went down into his stomach. Then he remembered his gun. He stopped running and turned around, lowering the gun to his hip. He saw nothing. He searched where he had run. The hoofprints had veered of twenty yards back. He scanned the trees.

He saw it! It was a naked man, looking at him. The man ran off to the side. Buddy watched. The man was lost momentarily through the trees. It looked as though he was part deer. Buddy was paralyzed. Then, he turned away. He would not face it. He would die with his face in the ground if necessary. He heard the hooves thud into the ground. Die? He had never thought about it before. Goddammit, he didn't need to be hunted like an animal. Could he reach safety? He recognized an old logging road.

He launched himself with a speed that surprised himself. His own heart and lungs started making so much noise that he couldn't hear it. But he felt its presence, its breath. He knew that wherever he ran, it would be there. He threw his rifle away and ran faster. He tripped over a root but got up immediately. He could hear brush be pushed and torn beside him. He started looking for a tree to climb, but they all looked too small or had limbs too high. Why didn't it attack?

Sam saw Buddy running toward him like a bat out of hell.

He picked up his gun again, and shouted, "What is it?"

"Run! run!" Buddy screamed, "Truck."

Sam didn't argue. He glanced once at his ideal trophy and bolted toward the road. Buddy caught up to him two thirds of the way there. Sam couldn't see anything chasing them, so he slowed down. When he got to the truck, Buddy was leaning over, breathing with a rasp. After he got in, Buddy suddenly reached over and locked the door.

"Later," he panted, "tell later. Go!" Sam peeled out, spinning on dirt and leaves.

Walker got up. It was 1:45—too early to stay up. He was tired from the previous day, but remembered nothing. He must have run a marathon. But he went for a walk, out around the lake. At his favorite spot, he took off his clothes and threw them over a branch. A fast swim should make him tired. After he got out, he lay on the needles for a rest, and fell asleep.

He heard barking a couple of hundred yards away. He answered.

The next night, he went out again. When he heard the series of barks, he made his way towards them. Soon he was running. And changing as he ran. He was different. He was smoother. He was ecstatic. And ecstasy was needed for change. He had stood out from himself and looked upon a different world. He had a spirit, now.

Then he saw her; small, delicate, her coat was gray, with rust, black, and white accents. He paused and snapped down at a flea. His own underfur was riddled with black guard hairs. He walked forward, wagging his tail. She was shorter and slighter, probably younger; he was larger and darker brown. They participated in a polite ceremony of nose touching. He was curious and sniffed her flanks, but she nipped him coyly. They hunted together for several hours in the night grass, wolves of the prairie, coyotes. They each stalked a mouse, approaching cleverly. Each ate his or her own catch. Then they parted before dawn. Her hiding place during the day was at the edge of a meadow, near a stream. His was in town.

The next night, they met again, guided by barks and howls. Their hunting world was chiaroscuro, colored only by the smells of blood, feathers, urine, leaves, dirt, sometimes steel and oil. On the third night, they caught and shared a rabbit. A rabbit was easier to catch as a team. And it was easy to communicate the idea; she flushed the rabbit and tired it, driving it toward where he lay waiting in ambush. Then it was theirs. At the end of the sixth night, he did not leave her, but followed her to her hiding place. She turned and looked back at him several times, in warning or invitation; he thought invitation. So when he caught up, she accepted his presence with feminine nonchalance. They slept together and played. They ran and hunted together. Life was more interesting. They were friends. Sometimes they would point their muzzles to the sky and howl an ode to joy, long controlled tremolos in a chorus of two.

He tried to tell her the Indian stories of Coyote; Coyote starved, defeated, drowned, crushed, or broken, but always reborn for mischief. He vocalized that Coyote was even more beautiful, once, than they were, now. Coyote had come across a very ugly brown little bird, bathing in a lake. Since the behavior was not normal, he watched. Four times a morning for four mornings the bird immersed himself in a blue, blue lake. After the fourth morning, all its ugly feathers fell off. They grew back blue that afternoon. Coyote, who was a bright green, wanted to be blue, also. He approached the bird and asked him for the song. As his feathers were drying, the bird taught Coyote the song. Then Coyote too bathed for four days. As soon as his fur grew back blue, he went running along the road; he was so proud and happy. But when he looked back to see if his shadow was blue, he tripped and rolled in the dust. He has been the color of dust ever since.

Often, during the day, he would leave her for hours. If she tried to follow to his hiding place, he would bite her firmly. He knew he could not stay much longer. He had two powers, now, elk and coyote. But he did not want to just be a coyote. One evening, he did not return.

Walker pushed up to the bar.

"Where a you been?" Regina asked, from behind the high counter.

"Out listening to coyotes." Walker spoke truthfully.

"For weeks?"

"I have to work, too."

"Anything new tonight?"

"Why not? Let's start with a cuba libre, but put in a chocolate liqueur instead of lime juice."

"Hmm, what kind of chocolate?"

"Dutch Chocolate, if you have it."

"I'll have to add a dollar," she warned him.

"How much?"

"2.50. I don't make these custom drinks for just anybody. You wanna name it this time?" she asked.

"No, your turn," he gestured.

"Richmond," she said with new enthusiasm. "I want to name it after my cat, who is that color. Besides, it sounds like a southern drink."

Walker paid and sipped the drink; Meyer's rum, she remembered. He noticed she made a smaller version for herself, to test it. So far, she had added only one of his neobarbarisms to her list, that was the 'Tired Horse,' composed of vodka, rum, galliano, coke, and cream, in about that order. He didn't think any one had ever tried one, except Helen.

One of the north Idaho regulars, looking a bit like Elmer Fudd after a radiation accident, came over and stood next to Walker.

"That a commie drink?"

Walker appraised him, in case there was a fight.

"You like commies and coyotes?" he persisted.

Walker stared at the veins in his nose before answering, "Just coyotes—the drink is pre-commie." He looked at the bottles arranged neatly in front of the mirror.

"All um ought to be shot—kill every sheep they can." Elmer raised his voice a little, hoping for an audience to the debate.

"Coyotes or commies?" Walker asked, knowing which Elmer meant.

So, it was to be an argument. Another pro-something or anti-something, or someone. A few men turned toward them. The men with women didn't pay much attention. The women were ignoring the large-screen ski film showing off to one side.

"Coyotes, whad ya think." Elmer confirmed, establishing his superiority early.

Walker spoke thoughtfully, "I heard that in the early days, when ranchers took care of their sheep, shepherded them carefully, they never had problems with coyotes. You think a ewe or sheepdog would let a coyote kill a kid?"

"Damn right!"

"Unless there were too many sheep, left out too long without a shepherd?"

"What'r you saying?" Elmer menaced.

Regina smiled. Entertainment tonight.

Walker shepherded his drink. "Coyotes are scavengers," he explained, "They keep down mice and rabbits. They clean up carcasses of animals that starve or injure themselves and die." He held off Elmer's protest with a hand. "Cattle and sheep already provide for coyotes; afterbirths at calving time; calf droppings rich in undigested milk—"

Elmer made his protest, "Just no room for coyotes. They steal our food outa our mouths."

"You mean, there shall be no other predators before us? to compete?"

Walker asked uselessly, realizing that ecology was not spoken here.

"We aint predators. We raise those animals."

"You don't eat them?"

"Coyotes are no damned good," declared a short bearded man Walker recognized as Ben Hoffman. "If you left it to them there'd be no deer left. Most of us feel this way," he added.

Walker could tell by the sound of hard peas in an iron pot that heads were nodding. He started again, "If the coyote's such a villain, why were there so many deer around before we started bringing in sheep and cattle?"

"We're the ones that kill the deer," Regina added, "hunting."

"Starving to death or being eaten by a lion is much worse'n being shot," Ben judged.

"Did you ever ask a deer that?"

"No, but it aint human, neither!" Elmer butted back in.

Ben elaborated, "Sometin always has to die so we can live. We out west accept death better than a lot of eastern liberals." He implied that Walker was one of those despicable perverts because of his opinions.

"What would your choice be if a grizzly offered you: die mercifully now, or linger on with cancer?"

Ben brandished his cigarette in one hand and his whiskey in another, but before he could speak, another voice offered, "They sure raised hell with the calves last year."

"How many did you loose?" Walker questioned the tall mustache.

"Well, four, we think—"

"You think?" Walker stabbed.

"Yea," Mustache reflected honestly, "four had bites on the carcass. Others had prints around them."

Walker sighed, sure, I just said they're scavengers didn't I? "This year?" he managed.

"Well, we haven't lost any this year. But we haven't started calving, yet. That's why we ought to thin 'em out—before the calves come." Mustache explained.

"Killing them before they can disgrace themselves?" Walker dripped with sarcasm.

"Isn't it better?" Mustache asked seriously.

"Would you tolerate euthanasia fir yourself if there was the possibility you would be executed for killing a clerk during a robbery? Humans do that, you know."

"—nasia?"

"Mercy killing. Like Andy did with his mother." Regina explained over drying a glass.

"No, but it's not the same. We're talking about animals." Mustache reasoned.

"The Indians have many stories of coyotes leading men to an injured hunter or a lost child, even standing guard or licking a wound. Does such an animal deserve our kind of death?" Walker asked.

"Yes!" Elmer proclaimed, irritated at being left out of his argument. "Those shits make up 'em stories." But it was an unpopular thing to say, where many people respected the native Americans, so Elmer went off to a table by himself with a new drink.

"So you went out blasting first?" Walker pried at Mustache.

"No, one of the hands thought he saw some tracks. And there was a bobcat last year. So we thought we'd better get some traps."

"And did you catch anything?" Walker dreaded the answer.

"Some pests." Mustache evaded.

"What?" Walker pressed.

"Three raccoons, a skunk, two foxes, a w—" he mumbled. Walker had heard the last word, however. They had trapped a ewe.

Ben came forward in defense, "Our hunting helps the ranchers out. We control the numbers of coyotes. We don't want to exterminate them. Hell, if they get scarce, like bobcats, we ease off on 'em."

"And how do you hunt them?"

"Helicopter," Ben confided, "better success rate."

Walker had an image of thousands of dead coyotes impaled in barbed wire fences, symbols of the new, human order. He ordered a straight rum.

Regina accused Ben, "You men! You take life so casually. And shoot anything in your way. Kill some wonderful sentient animal with hopes and a family of its own. For what? Food, trophy? No, for a count! You're sick."

"You wanna save the cuddly aminals, sweety?" teased Ben.

"I'll piss in your beer, cowboy," she promised, emphasizing 'boy.'

"Hey!" Walker warned Ben, who stepped back.

"Some people are hard-hearted and some ain't." Ben said.

Walker rebuked, "Some are soft-headed and some ain't," smiling at Regina with her hackles up.

"Despite that," Mustache was saying, "human needs rightly take first dibs over coyotes."

"Their needs are our needs, in the long run. We need them, to keep down pests," Walker wound down.

Everyone was tired of the conversation, but unwilling to let it end without conclusion.

"You think all this beauty was made for humans? The grass feeds the deer for your table; the berries feed the bear for your warmth? Nature isn't made for us. It isn't a part of us—we are part of it, a small part."

"Yea, well, we have to cut our losses," Mustache affirmed.

"It might be easier to cut our desires," Walker replied.

But Regina ended it, "The wind is invincible; the voice of the coyote will never be silenced. Now shut the fuck up."

Chief Packard was bored. He had been retired for four years now, and the golf course of life stretched further ahead than ever. His wife of forty-two years, Margy, had come to enjoy their weekly game. He would rather have been fishing, but he was so pleased that she had found something that interested her and got her outside to exercise. Now that it was getting cold, too cold to play in Moscow, he was sure that she would start getting ready to go to Arizona, to play golf for a month. It wasn't that he missed the humdrum of police work—there had been plenty of that. But he had always missed the big excitement: the terrorist attacks, hostages, mass murders, brutal rapes. Not that he ever wanted anything like that to happen. It was just that routine police work was so boring. The department should have hired more family counselors as officers and equipped them with black robes and gavels for household arguments.

He was proud that Moscow Idaho had been called one of the ten safest cities in the United States. He had read that book, whatever its title was, as soon as it came out. Safe Cities? or whatever. Then, Moscow was a small college town with an attractive downtown, a hotel, a Penney's store, two big, complete department stores, David's and Fonk's—well, he liked Fonk's, even if it wasn't really a big store. Then, as he got ready to retire, things started to go wrong. Greed reared its ugly head, and California was upon them. Moscow had been californicated—good word—only it was a repeat of the fifties in California; the same bad things, as if no one ever learned. He had to watch as the new, neon 7/11 store was robbed twice in its first two months, by ski-masked thugs, probably from California, too. Then he had to listen as the city council voted to invite development of a fifty-store shopping mall on land owned by the University of Idaho and rented for a dollar. A dollar! So much for the fiscal acuity of those hot-shot, corduroy-covered turds. They could have rented it for $300,000.00 a year and endowed three professorships and 30 scholarships. Maybe his son would have gone to Idaho, then, instead of Weber State.

He was sure the ruination of his town stemmed from that tub of lard, Tony Laird, who held an exclusive patent on the secret of stretching polyester 10% beyond its limits. Immediately after the mall was approved, he invested heavily in it, quitting his Italian sandwich business to be the first manager of the mall. The mayor benefited quite a bit from that mall, he recalled. Then, if that wasn't enough, some other developer raced to build another mall on the east side of town. Some schmuck in cowboy boots did that one, finishing before the first one, then prowled around it looking for a horse to ride, or something to put between his legs. Packard was still bitter about what was done to his town in the name of profit.

He went into the study and looked over his mineral collection. He used to collect rocks whenever he had to drive out of the city. Then he started trading and buying whenever he could. 'The earth abides,' he thought; and no wonder, it was made of rock and metal. He had just gotten another amethyst crystal and mounted it in a plastic case. Such beauty. He rotated it in the light, watching its facets bend the light. Idaho was the gem state. But he continued musing on the lack of excitement; drunken students, not to mention staff and faculty, crawled or raced between Moscow and Pullman, where Washington State University huddled eight miles away. Plenty of wrecks and near misses; no complaint there. That was east and west; north and south, chip trucks rumbled all day and night, sliding off the highway sometimes. Making driving more difficult. He wished that they still had the railroad between Potlatch and Lewiston; it was more efficient and romantic. His old friend, Mel—high school together—had given him a ride on the diesel before he retired—wonder what Mel's doing? And there were plenty of runaway or deserted animals. He remembered picking up a frothing Doberman early one morning. The first officer on the scene—young Murphy—was waiting to shoot it, positive it was rabid. He was sure it was old Brown's dog that had climbed a 12-foot chain fence to get out again. No wonder he was frothing—he must have been exhausted. The dog fell asleep in the back of his car.

Life was good, though. He wished Margy would get back from the store. He wanted to eat lunch at that new motel, next to the big mall. They were rumored to have a good salad bar. He still refused to shop at the mall, but eating near it was something else. Merchants were deserting downtown like rats from a ship. A lot of the older merchants, his friends, kept their stores downtown. Other old businesses went to the malls. Fortunately, the buildings were being leased again to people who wanted to start their own small businesses; wine shops, gem stores, furniture, and hardware stores. He sat down and opened the paper. Then the phone rang.

Packard was horrified. He listened as Joe asked him to drive up past Plummer. Slim Hoffecker's body had been found draped over a barbed wire fence. That wasn't all; his head wasn't with it. Putting a lid on his imagination, he agreed to drive up and look over the scene. Putting down the phone, he thought 'Well, I asked them to let me help with anything interesting.' He wrote a short note to Margy and left the house. He wondered if his coat would be warm enough as he started the car. Who would kill Slim? Driving past Viola, he wondered if the murder—he was assuming that it was murder—was related to any other recent ones elsewhere. He remembered the contents of his journal: In Seattle, a professor bled to death in a monkey chair—what in the hell was that about? In Pullman, a year later, another professor—this one choked with cookies. He wondered if the murderer was the same man—it had to be a man—few women were that demonstrative—'de-monster-ative'—he grunted at the monstrous pun. Then the Nazi slaughter that Edelman had told him about. Serial killings were big this season. Perhaps the killer was working his way east.

The first report was wrong. The head had been found shortly afterwards. Noticed sticking out from the trunk of a tree. After the photographer finished taking several sets of photographs from various angles, Doc Jefferson looked over the head and pulled it straight towards himself. It barely moved. Jim Maynard, the deputy, reached up to help, averting his gaze and trying to control his stomach.

"I don't know how it's up there," gritted the Doc. "Mac, could you help us? Grab the ears or something."

Mac hurried behind the tree and wretched loudly and uncomfortably.

Doc gestured to Chief Packard, "Com 'ere, Leslie, pull on this."

Packard flinched automatically at his first name; it was brought home to him again why he encouraged people to call him chief, to avoid his mother's revenge on his father, and on him.

He regarded Slim's head as meat. That helped. He had once helped his cousin, Wilbur, who farmed up past Viola, slaughter an old dairy cow, too old for milk. Wilbur was a lean sonofabitch. He thought of Wilbur while pulling on Slim's head; they ought to recruit farmers for officers, too. Wilbur was a survivor; there was no luxury in his life, there never would be. Suddenly the head, with three of them straining, sucked and popped loose. The release caused it to fall and tumble towards Slim's body, still hung upside down on the barbed wire, legs and arms spread. The head rolled so that it appeared to be gazing wistfully at its body. Mac came around the tree and then retreated again. Packard looked up at the piece of metal jammed into the ponderosa. Doc was looking at it, too.

"Damn," Packard recognized it, "that's the gun barrel." He and Jim tried to dislodge it, while Doc bagged the head.

"Jesus, we can't budge this thing," Jim realized, "gotta find a crowbar." Packard just looked at the broken barrel, wondering who or what had broken the gun, rammed it into the tree; then ripped off Slim's head and rammed it on to the barrel. He never wanted to meet that person without two sets of bars between them.

The body felt the same as that cow had: heavy, cold and wet. He had been irrational about the cow, and had never eaten any of it. They had to unwrap the arms and legs first. Doc held the bag open as they lowered the body.

"Slim always was a headless wonder," Jim tried to joke.

"Shut up, Jim." Doc ordered. No other words were exchanged. Jim and Mac accompanied Doc back into town to store the body. Packard agreed to come in later, for the bull session, as the official investigation was called.

Driving the long way back, through Potlatch and over the mountain, Packard reviewed what the others had found—basically nothing. He stopped at the top of Moscow Mountain, at a scarified area where people had cut trees for wood fireplaces. From a distance, the mountain had looked like a head trimmed by a mad barber, with some mad private design. He picked up a twig and twirled it in his fingers, breaking it into smaller pieces. He wanted to be at home, watching the cat pouncing on a piece of ribbon, and listening to Al Hurt's trumpet. He wanted to be in Arizona. Most of all he wanted to be fishing. But he realized that he had gotten his excitement. His career wasn't riding on it, but he wanted to ride it anyway, filling it in like a puzzle. Driving down the dirt road, he knew what other bodies he had seen displayed like that—coyotes. People used to leave coyotes like that to warn other coyotes to stay away from their pigs and chickens. He wondered if Slim had been hunting coyotes. He would have to find out.

Doc Jefferson worked alone at the table, a large piece of butcher block supported by pipe fittings. He stood on a low wooden platform with a rubber mat on it. In back of him, on a wall of shelves, were bottles of specimens. A large fluorescent light ran the length of the table, slightly longer than the body and the head on it. He looked over at the table with the microscope on it; his notes were scattered around it.

"Rats," he said out loud, "extra movement is the bane of the elderly. I should be more efficient by now."

'We may have to train a younger man' he thought. Jefferson was only associate medical examiner. He did autopsies because Grinnell was even older than he was.

"The body appears to—is—that of a caucasian male, five feet nine inches, weighing 140 pounds five ounces. Brown hair; dressed in camouflage clothing."

'Didn't do much good against whatever caught him though' Doc realized.

"There is virtually no decomposition of the body. On the sides of the neck and jaw are abrasions. In the eyelids, small petechial hemorrhages, suggestive of asphyxia. The lungs are congested, but have no evidence of natural disease. Regarding the gastrointestinal tract, the stomach is filled with moderate amounts of ingested food."

'Tacos and beer' he identified, but not for the report.

"It is partially empty, indicative of a post-digestion period of at least five hours before death."

He turned off the recorder. As in most homicides, the cause of death was obvious; he was only looking for other findings that may influence the course of the investigation. Maybe the scrapings under the fingernails might help. No buttons, no footprints, no hairs—at least other than Slim's and from a coyote. It was clear that Slim had been strangled and suffered a rapidly acute asphyxial death. He had not been dead long, if at all, when his head was ripped off. The evidence was clear, but it wasn't going to help the police in their search for a perpetrator. 'Sure as shit, they'll need their crystal ball on this one,' he relapsed into detectivisms. He thought again about the body. Judging from the brain damage, which resembled a contre-coup, he knew that the moving head had impacted against a hard, stationary surface—the tree. The question that nagged him was, 'was the head attached or detached on impact?' The shoulder, deltoid, had been heavily bruised on one side, with puncture and cuts. The sternocleidomastoid was torn. Possibly, the body had been used to lever the head onto the barrel, then ripped from the head.

Helen almost didn't recognize him, he looked so healthy and rested. So, he was coming into the library before classes, again. That was a good sign. Maybe he was rekindling his interest in psychology. She had overheard several students talking about how pedestrian his lectures were getting. Maybe if they had gotten much worse, he would have been made department chairman or vice-president of the college. Helen knew the college and the inexorable laws of academia. She was a victim of one of them: Librarians were expected to have two Master's degrees so they could be paid even less. She wasn't bitter; she was doing what she wanted, but then so were actors and ballplayers, for a hundred times more reward. When she looked up again, he was standing in front of her grinning, no, smiling.

"First day with the new brain?" he asked. "Try to follow this: 'George, kiss me'" he mugged the words with his lips. He started to breathe funny. And ducked behind a stack. She leaned after him, concerned. His arm shot out from the stack, grabbed hers and pulled her in and hugged her.

"George, this is a library," she chastised him, wishing he weren't so demonstrative at unpredictable times; or maybe that she was more so. "I have to live here."

"That's strange," he considered. "There's an apartment in your name four blocks from here. Ever been there?"

"In town, I mean; this town."

"What are you doing for lunch?"

"Going down for a burger at Hudson's?" she asked hopefully.

"No, we are playing football."

"What!" she exclaimed. "Not me! Too old, too dumb, old sport."

"It's for charity. And if Professor Wilkins can play, so can you." Professor June Wilkins taught anthropology. Everyone at the college knew that anthropologists had beards or were overweight or both. June didn't quite have a beard, but she had the mass and a primitive energy.

"Even Tran has agreed to play, if she can be quarterback, said she always wanted to be quarterback. I agreed to back her claim if she would agree to throw to me instead of that bozo Roberts."

Helen smiled at the mention of both of them. Tranquillity Evans was a secretary in the English department; her husband was a coach; she and

Walker had had dinner with them once. When her husband Bubba had said that everything he worked with had balls, Tran had said that was true of her too—before Bubba got angry, she listed the typewriter balls, and the bald heads in the department. Roberts taught biochemistry, and was a self-taught stud with very large and wandering feet.

She sighed, "Okay, who do we play, hunk?"

"Students, it's their scholarship fund," he answered remotely, looking at the call numbers of the books.

"KF," he announced, "we've never kissed in law before. This is a first."

He already had her arms pinned to her sides; she was kissed. Then she pinned his arms and he was kissed.

The faculty lost. Tran had a tendency to throw to the biggest group of players, hoping to improve the odds. Walker played quarterback for the last quarter, saying that it was one of his dreams. He made a couple of good runs, dodging students and his own defenders, but he had too much fun to run straight to the goal. On the last series of plays, he pitched out as he was tackled and Tony Roberts made the touchdown, holding his left arm straight out as he ran, spiking the ball efficiently as he carried it in.

"Weights," he smiled superciliously to Walker as they went to kick off.

After the game, Walker asked Helen, "How come you wanted to be a guard?"

"So I could keep close to our lummox of a center and he could block for both of us."

Walker recognized the lummox as Joe Sullivan, from Business. "Listen, tell me if any of those little savages groped you and I'll plant their teeth in the field," he offered.

She laughed, "No, but some goon kept feeling my bottom on some of the short runs."

"Couldn't have been me," Walker protested, "I had a football in both hands."

"Well, off to the showers," she suggested cheerfully.

"Did you play football in school?" she asked.

They were perched on stools at Hudson's, eating good all-American dinners—hamburgers.

"No, no time."

"Didn't you ever play anything?"

"Well, the armed forces, but they have a different version of sports. Did you?" he changed the topic.

"Yes, volleyball and swimming."

"That was fun today. Did you enjoy it?"

"Oh, I guess so," she reflected. "Did you?"

"Immensely, except for bozo."

"Why? I mean it seems so juvenile."

"It's a necessity."

"No!"

"Yes!"

"Prove it," she challenged, "prove it and I'll pay."

"It's how you'll pay that interests me," he hinted lasciviously. He chewed on a fry before offering his proof. "But, consider the human species. When humans began working as cooperative hunters, they left behind their shuffling, gathering, and began chasing, aiming, and throwing. With the pressure of a growing population, farming and domestication replaced hunting, which became a sport for the rich. The skills and urges of most people were applied to other sports."

"Such as."

"Target games, mostly," he considered. "For the rich, the chase became an end itself; the trophy was the head, not the ribs or thigh. As the population still increased, bloodless sports replaced blooded ones.

Cooperative target events required all the skills of the hunt, running, jumping, aiming, but without the blood."

"Oh, boxing is bloodless? Fencing, skiing, hockey," she added.

"Blood isn't the goal. It's incidental."

"But people get excited about blood," she insisted.

"That's right, but the goal is excitement. The blood just means that it's real. Think, mass production is boring, mass civilization is boring. Repetitious, boring work creates high levels of frustration for workers. Sport relieves that. It returns the excitement of the hunt, with all the same skills. The sport is not merely exercise, but chasing and aiming, catching, and scoring—the symbolic kill."

"Sometimes it's a real kill. People die. Is that good?"

"Yes, it is," he gritted his teeth, "no risk, no reward. Wait, wait," he held up his hand.

She transferred her aggression to tearing some cheese of her roll.

"Why are we out there playing football, jumping and wrestling in the dirt? Because it feels good. Because it is a good experience. So there's some risk. That amplifies the feeling and the meaning. There isn't much risk, because we pay with rules. We should be free to risk our lives, our health. That is what modern weapons against animals, modern safety regulations, and other improvements, have taken away. The guardians against change—the lawyers, doctors, ministers, politicians—won't allow any risk. Their universe is bound by paychecks and bills, bread and circuses. There are already ethics in sport. There are ethics, which are just rules for living together."

"But it's so—" she paused, "so unimportant. It's pleasure."

"Unimportant compared to what?" he wanted to know.

"Well, government," she considered, "meeting the needs of the poor, reforming government."

He turned toward the counter and sipped some coke. The cook looked at him, as he was drying a glass, ready to answer any request for more food. Walker shook his head microscopically; the cook bent over for another glass.

"Food, shelter, clothing medicine, education, are needs; they are problems if they are not met. Many people work to meet those needs. They derive pleasure from their work, even if they are not always successful."

Helen had a sudden feeling that she was going to pay for dinner. That Sophist!

"Groups that hunted and gathered food took pleasure in their hunting and gathering. Sports are fun. Participating in them, or watching, makes people feel good. When people feel good, they are more positive about their work and fellows. Maybe a few more problems are solved," he concluded.

"So, sports is a panacea for modern life?" she asked sarcastically.

"No, sports won't replace government. Government may be separate, but awareness and conscientiousness can be fostered in many ways."

"But that implies that pleasure is the chief purpose of the universe?" she tried desperately.

"Pleasure?" he asked; his hand dropped and brushed her thigh through the jeans. "Pleasure is an experience. Experience is a better candidate for the purpose of the universe. Think of how diverse life is? How many ways of seeing or feeling?" He thought for a moment, glancing at the curve of skin under her jaw. She had eaten all of the bun and cheese from her hamburger. He moved the half crescent of meat to his plate. Her eyes followed it.

"Why else would God have created the multitudes, if not for the experiences that he could not have as God? Being the whole universe is not the same as being the parts. In radical theology, the sum of the parts is greater than the whole," he smiled. Then asked, "Who pays?"

"What about trash sports, like motocross motorbiking, or hunting?" she asked.

"Those aren't really sports, those are perversions that result in the wasteful death of animals and plants. A sport must be joyful on both sides, said Plutarch. Even if one side consists of animals or land."

"I'll pay," she conceded. She was writing a check when she noticed him put the meat in his pocket.

"You have another date, with someone else?" she added, with mock-injury in her voice, trying to look hurt and smile at the same time.

"Four-footed. Canid," he added when she opened her mouth in sport.

The hand finished scissoring a short newspaper article, then taped it below three similar ones. The four articles, in chronological order, read:

1. Washington Mercy Kill Nets 731. Due to unusually cold weather east of the Cascades, thousands of deer are threatened with starvation. The Washington Game Commission announced plans to hold an emergency deer hunt in an 800 square mile area of central Washington. Earlier attempts by conservationists to provide adequate hay and forage were considered a failure. 1,600 people, with 800 vehicles and packs of dogs took part Saturday. One official stated that the hunt was necessary to save the deer from certain starvation. It was reported that the weights of slaughtered deer were "below average" and infested with parasites. The remaining numbers should have no trouble foraging, now, reported one hunt coordinator.

2. Low Forage Due to Poor Range Management. It was revealed today that the critical lack of forage on open ranges in Washington was the result of poor range management by state officials, who had issued more permits to (continued, page 9)

3. Humane Society Groups Protest Hunt. Humane Society officials decried the need for last week's slaughter of over 700 deer. There were other nonlethal alternatives, according to Martha Sloan, state director. Providing access through fenced

lands would have saved hundreds; but area ranchers have increased fenced areas. The deer killed were in good shape, according to one veterinarian, who examined six of them. Furthermore, the parasites mentioned were a typical assortment of fleas and flies that deer always live with. Dr. Jane Lantier commented, "Killing animals for their own good is absurd. I certainly wouldn't use that argument with cancer patients." Ironically, many orphaned fawns were found days later, starved to death.

4. Two Hunters Found in Double Tragedy. Craig Old, 46, and Roger Davis, 32, both of Spokane, were found dead in an area east of the recent deer kill. Both men were reported missing Sunday morning, by their wives. The bodies were a hundred yards apart. Both men apparently became lost and died of exhaustion and exposure. No foul play is suspected.

Packard noticed that the headline type point size decreased as the articles got older and the page numbers larger. He closed the journal.

When Sam Morse read that last article, he shuddered. He wondered what Buddy had seen. The boy had been tense and jumpy for weeks. He was still spooky. Must have been something to put the fear of God in him like that. He wanted to take him hunting in a couple of weeks, if he could.

Water burst out of him, like blood from a wound.

"Shit!" he barked, glancing at his pants and immediately back to the apparition in front of him.

The beast stopped three feet from him. Werewolf, Stuart thought, it's a werewolf and it's going to kill me. He felt the urine running into his socks, and the wetness of his pants against his leg. In his terror, he was drawn to the face, noticing every detail. The glint of saliva on a whisker, the muscle pulling the upper lip back from the teeth.

Neither moved. Man and not-man searched each other's eyes. Stuart was acutely aware of the other's rough breathing, from some recent exertion. He looked beyond the pelted shoulder to the hall door. He remembered that the other exit was around a corner. The only light was from an exit sign. He felt his mouth open and close, fishlike, only no water, no air, no words. His eyes noted the clawed gnarled hands. It had an erection. Oh, God, what if it thinks I'm a female. No.

Then the knees straightened; the hair smoothed out; the spine straightened as well; the face retracted; the eyes did not change. He found himself looking into the face of George Walker, his teacher this summer.

He found that he could speak, "You're ... naked."

Walker looked at him and shrugged, "Laboratory accident. I had to tear my clothes off. Acid burns." Stuart noticed that Walker was not excited.

"Are you all right? Cold?" he asked Walker suspiciously.

"It looks like you need to restore your fluid levels," Walker noted politely.

"You scared me." Stuart started, remembering the apparition. "I thought that you were a- a—"

"Monster?" Walker finished. "Must have been the light, or something, caused a hallucination; it happens. Let's see if my clothes are damaged."

"I, aahhh, I'm thirsty. There's a coke machine down the hall."

"Good idea, I'll go with you. Then we can go back to the lab and get us both a coat or something dry," Walker suggested.

"Ahh," Stuart started.

"Don't worry, if any one sees us they'll just think I'm naked. It's dark," he added.

The hall was cluttered with old furniture. Walker let Stuart go first. Stuart bought two cans, exhausting his reserves of cash. They proceeded in reverse toward Walker's office. Stuart looked over Walker's shoulder as he opened the door. It had not been locked. There, on the center of the floor, were torn and jumbled clothes. Walker went directly over to another room—Stuart knew that it had a sink in it—this building was once a dormitory—and looked in.

He clicked his tongue and closed the door. "It must have been water, not acid. What a waste." As Stuart looked into his eyes, he realized that Walker had been moving towards his office when they encountered one another.

He gathered his strength, "You were going to kill me?" How could he have said that? But Walker was tucking his buttonless shirt in.

"Naked? That's amusing," Walker smiled as he put on his tweed coat.

Stuart wished for something to say.

"An intelligent conversation is worth the risk." Walker added, handing a white long lab coat to Stuart.

"I am no threat to you," Stuart waved the coat away. "I have my own coat."

"Thank heavens, I thought you were going to steal mine." Walker threw out the absurdity.

"But I saw—"

"You saw a naked man in a dark hall paralyzed by fear."

Stuart said nothing, thinking 'I am no threat to you.'

"Let us react in a civilized way, like two British gentlemen, and say nothing of our two messy accidents," Walker offered graciously, thinking 'If you get too close, I will kill you, regretfully, but kill you.'

He was furious with himself. He thought that it would be fun for a run in the starlight after an evening of academic solipsism. He must never, never try that again. He really needed a drink, now.

The bar was almost deserted.

"Vodka on the rocks," he ordered.

"Nothing new?" asked Regina unbelieving.

"When do you study? When do you graduate?" he changed the

subject.

"I was studying before you came. I study in class."

He watched her pour.

She pried at him, "What are you studying?"

"Wolves," he replied without thinking.

"Wolves? Why would a psychologist study wild animals?"

He sipped slowly, then responded, "What makes you think wolves are wild?"

"Well," she was surprised, "wild animals aren't domesticated."

"What's that mean?"

"It means that they can't talk—can't be trusted."

"You mean has no social skills, like dogs?" he led her.

"Yes, I think so, wolves don't interact with humans," she struggled with the concept of wildness.

"But you can't interact with wolves."

"Why would I want to?"

"And having no wolf social skills, should they not regard you as a wild animal, dangerous and untrustworthy?" he asked.

"That's different. We're superior," she asserted.

"Oh," appraised Walker, "can you smell a storm, catch a mouse, or dig a den with your hands?"

"No, but I have weather satellites, mousetraps, and shovels," she snapped quickly.

"When do you make these instruments?"

"Well, others make them. I do other things."

"So, you're more like a termite than a wolf," he guessed.

"No!" she protested. "That isn't fair. Humans have a culture, and noninstinctive divisions of labor."

"So do wolves, so do wolves," he walked away.

He thought about wolves as he walked home. The wolf's clothing that men saw was a hide of their own invention. Legend, nonsense, fears, symbolism, ignorance. The wolf is a carnivore; it eats mice, moose and anything in between. It hunts in packs, families, or alone. It is intelligent. It has a language and a culture. Wolves take easier kills if they can. That is why the weak and sick, old and young, are taken first. Since domestic stock is often dumber and weaker than wild, sometimes it gets eaten. As a predator, wolves are dependent on prey animals. Except in rare circumstances, they kill to survive.

Chapter 15. Life And Death

Running naked pulled memories from the trees, from the soil, memories of wolves, of prey. The vibrations of thousands of pads and bodies, welcoming howls and warning snarls. He leaned forward, his face subtly altering shape, until his forefeet touched the ground. He slowed when he came to the tracks.

He liked to walk railroad tracks. He could go for miles on a rail without stumbling. Tonight he whimpered a bit with happiness. With the joy of motion. He stopped to watch a hare tear off the buds of a green alder; it did not eat them. He kept going, until he smelled deer. Then he turned off the tracks and followed.

The deer was numbed by winter ticks. Over six hundred had fastened to her and were draining her blood. Whenever she shook, a faint shower of blood stained the snow. Now, she was way behind the others, too tired to catch up. He spotted her. Her peculiar gait gave her away. She was hundreds of yards behind the others. He recognized the tiredness in her stance. She was aware of him. As he approached, their eyes met.

He measured her pupils. He decided to test her and charged. She turned and bounded away, but began slowing. He could smell her rank breath, the smell of sickness. He loped gracefully towards her. As an invisible line was crossed, she bounded away, pounding with exertion.

He caught her from behind and to the side, with a neck hold, and suffocated her. He worried the neck to make sure she was dead. Then started eating from the muscle of the thigh. He ate some of the fatty tissue, some of the lung and heart, liver and kidney. He ignored the stomach and its contents.

A raven flew from one fir to another, arcing closer to the kill. She had the luck to spot the wolf before others came. It was just a matter of waiting. She looked for other wolves, before hopping within thirty feet of the kill. She looked at the wolf's expression, accentuated by a set of dark lines marking the ears, eyes, and muzzle. He was almost as dark as she. A movement of the eyes and lips conveyed the intention to eat a raven if she came closer. She waited, listening to the snaps and licks of dining. When he finished eating, she abandoned her pecking at bloody snow and approached the carcass. He stopped fifty feet away to clean his fur. He watched her eat.

Bill spotted the deer struggling through a drift. Apparently, it had been frightened by the roaring of his engine and had bolted for safety. He headed his machine directly for it.

'This is sport,' he understood, overtaking it in his snowmobile. He butted the side of his machine against it, the first time, causing it to stumble. Then he backed off and kept directly behind it. When it turned its head in terror he could see specks of foam. He charged it. A ski hit its hind leg and made it fall in a cloud of snow. After he lost sight of it, he traced a large circle. Then he saw it up and running in the opposite direction.

"Stupid bitch," he mumbled.

His sport began in earnest. After a few minutes, he hit it again, letting out a whoop of victory.

For over an hour he chased it, hitting it fourteen more times. He was worried for a moment, when the animal crossed a small stream, but he forded it thirty yards away and took up the chase again immediately. Finally, it fell in exhaustion in a snowbank. Getting a good run, he jumped his machine on it, relishing the thump. He jumped on it again and again, until it was crushed.

"Stupid fucker was no good anyway," he said under his breath.

"Wow! If only someone could see me!" he proclaimed happily, turning north to look for another deer.

Someone did. Stunned at first by the broken images that traveled over the snow, he screamed with pain and beat the snow. He raged.

He ran a mile to the crushed body, examining her first, and then the snowmobile tracks everywhere. The chase had begun far away. In the north, he heard a slight buzzing. He tracked it. He kept going until he reached a granite outcropping, bare of snow. He could see a noisy black dot several miles below. As he watched, it turned back towards him. He waited.

Bill was irritated. He had seem tracks, but had not found any more deer to test his skill against.

'Might's well call it a day,' he resigned. He headed back to his truck, eight miles south, off Highway 8. He steered just west of the windblown hill. He was reliving the chase, when something heavy struck him in the chest, knocking him backwards from the seat. He sat up, breathing painfully. He saw the snowmobile turning back towards him, with someone inside.

"Hey! Whatsya doin!" he shouted angrily.

"That's my Scorpion!" He was really pissed as it came back, slowing slightly. He had over $3,000.00 in that sleek, black machine. It had a special engine and leopard upholstery. If that damned fool damaged it, he'd have his ass in a sling. Then he was apprehensive. It was aiming at him. The engine revved. He leapt out of the way.

"Ahh!" he screamed, the pain in his ankle testifying to the closeness of the miss. He brushed the snow off his face and looked around. No doubt of it. That maniac was coming around again.

"Hey! This isn't funny. You hurt me!" he shouted, with a trace of panic in his voice. He saw the outcropping twenty yards away and started hopping towards it. The engine was louder he started to run, damning the pain. He wasn't going to make it. He dove to the left, knowing that his Scorpion couldn't turn fast.

"Aahh!" his ankle was hit again; it was going to be purple tomorrow. He moaned.

Another turn. He tore off his heavy gloves as he stood and threw them at the approaching roar. They bounced off the front. He tried to jump over, but was bounced by the windshield.

'Jesus!' he choked painfully, 'he's trying to kill me.' He rolled over and churned his way toward the outcopping and safety. The pain in his legs was making his whole body throb. Wait! He couldn't hear it. Fucker must have stalled it. He turned back north to look for it. Then he heard the roar in back of him. He hobbled around to see the black shape come flying off the outcropping. He noticed the dents in the front, just before he was snapped backwards.

Packard clipped another newspaper article for his journal.

Sportsman Found Dead

A sportsman was found dead today of a freak snowmobile
  accident. William Stark, 35, was found with lacerations and
  a broken back in the snow twelve miles east of Princeton.

A spokesman for the sheriff's department revealed that the
  snowmobile had been found a half mile away, out of gas. There
  is speculation that Stark had fallen from his machine or gotten
  out, and was run over accidentally. Foul play is not suspected.

An autopsy will be performed.

Ran over him four or five times? Packard wondered. Ought to see someone at the dealership and see if that's even possible. Was it related to Slim's death, and the others? Worse, Doc Jefferson had identified the blood under Slim's fingernails. He said it was the blood of a chimera. He remembered the conversation.

"What is a chimera?"

"Just like what it sounds," Doc said dryly. When Packard waited, he continued. "A chimera is a fabulous creature in Greek mythology—"

"Myth!" Packard exploded.

Doc frowned, "a creature with the head of a lion, the body of a goat, and the tail of a serpent. It spat fire.—"

"I still don't see—"

"Don't interrupt," Doc chastised him, "and you might learn something." He continued, "Biologically, a chimera is any living structure in which the chromosomes of different species are combined—believe me, I looked it up. Now you're going to ask, so what? All I know is that man cells and mouse cells have been combined in the laboratory. Human combined with the chromosomes of other animals."

"What animals?" he demanded, unable to understand what this all meant.

Doc waved his question away. "I don't know what it means, either."

"Well, what kind of things were in the blood, then?"

"Oh, man and coyote."

"Just like that?"

Doc shrugged. What could he say?

Packard pursued the possibilities. "Slim was killed by a man with coyotes? and coyotes? with coyote blood?"

Doc shook his head.

"Slim was killed by a werecoyote?"

Doc nodded.

"Well," Packard breathed, "it should be easy to find."

"One more thing, Leslie, it wasn't a full moon."

Someone made the killer? Packard was really confused. In a laboratory?

Knocking woke him up. It was Helen.

"I know it's early, but I can't seem to reach you at other times," she apologized.

"How early?" he grumbled.

"Five," she coughed.

He closed the door and took her hand. He pulled her into the bedroom and under the covers. She threw her coat out onto the floor.

"That's all you have on?" he spoke through the pillow.

"Yes," she confessed, "I was hoping for an invitation."

He rolled over and started breathing regularly.

"Aren't we going to make love?" she asked.

"No, you're too cold. Let's sleep," he suggested, pulling her close. She slept.

He woke up. Helen was shaking him.

"You were shouting in Spanish," she observed with concern.

"Italian, I think," he answered.

"Italian? Where were you?" she asked, her manner asking more.

"Never—" he started to say, almost remembering the time and place from his dream. He lay back down and she hugged him.

"Have you ever felt you lived before, in other times?" she asked.

"I have memories—of sorts. Languages ..."

"What do you remember?"

"Nothing much," he stated.

"Then it can't be reincarnation, can it?" she reasoned.

"No, but it could be. Think about," he suggested, waking up. "What did you do last October fifth? Where were you? Or July twentieth? Can you tell me who you met and what you talked about?"

Helen was trying to remember.

"Does that mean you were not living last year? No. Now you ask me about another lifetime. Can I describe people long dead and roads I've forgotten? No. Only a few traumatic experiences, or great emotion. I'm sorry," he sighed.

"In Italy?" she asked.

"All over—different places," he shrugged.

She kissed him and started to go back to sleep.

"Perhaps there are floating memories, vibrations that are trapped in organic patterns and released to a sympathetic mind. Who knows?" he asked before sleeping himself.

"I thought you might be interested in a good sermon, that is, if you are still going to church."

"The world is my church," he expanded later, pulling two pieces of toast from the oven.

"That's what this is about," she said.

"Oh, who's giving it, what's it called?"

"The War for the World, by Reverend Smith."

"The war's over. I won," he joked. "Have we listened to him before?"

"Yes," she answered between bites. "During your religious marathon months ago—what do you mean you won?"

He ignored her question. "That long? Really?"

She nodded.

The church was a long white barn. Smith's large voice filled the church.

"The ruler of Heaven and the ruler of Hell are pitted against each other in a war for the mastery of the world. And man is the bone of contention in this combat.

"Jesus lifts man upwards, Lucifer drags him down. From the moment God made Adam, Lucifer tempted him. Through cunning Lucifer turned man from the high-road to heaven to the path to hell. He even tried to sink Noah's ark. Having failed to win Jesus from the Lord, he had him persecuted and betrayed.

"Even Christ's vicarious death on the cross has not delivered man from Lucifer. Although sealed in the pit, his tail wags the world, now. He lurks in the strongest of hearts and influences the best of minds. It would seem, then, that in this war for the world, victory lies with Satan, not the Savior. Satan is the Prince of the Air, the prince of this world. (John 7:31). Nay, even the God of this world (deus hujus seculi, 2 Cor. 4:4). The earth is his property."

God of the world, Walker thought. And when will the God recover his strength and memories? Walker wanted this man to tell the truth about Lucifer. And Christ; Christ, how many others have there been, who loved woman and man, and left them for a promise? Was it happiness to go? He concentrated on shaping the words. He listened.

"And on his earth, he is not always evil. Many times he has rendered good to advance his cause. In fact, he seems to have a love for the clergy. I heard once of a Scotch minister riding home day being warned by Satan not to eat the chicken his wife was cooking; it had been accidentally poisoned. Again: A French monk who had befriended Diabolus was sick one Sunday and asked his friend to occupy his pulpit to edify the congregation. Satan preached a masterly sermon, covering himself with shame. When the monk asked if he had ruined himself with that stroke, Satan replied; 'No, no harm done; there was no unction in it.'

"In as much as the Devil is the master of matter, the church considers him the sponsor of human endeavor based on mundane interests. The church is concerned with things spiritual, consigning to the devil the possessions of the world. The church depreciates reason, as Satan is the incarnation of human reason. And reason vindicates the rights of matter. The Savior represents faith. But the devil does not believe; he does not accept authority blindly. He reasons; he relies on thought. The devil is a scholar, a logician, a philosopher, a scientist. "All the inventions of science are inspired by reason. And reason is the domain of evil. The art of printing was ascribed to the devil. Paper money was ascribed to him. Pope Gregory XVI called steam the invention of Satan. The steamboat, the locomotive were his devices. The radio and telephone. His. Satan was regarded as the pioneer of progress. The church even contended that he filled man with the love of liberty, and equality and fraternity. Satan was discontent with the existing social and political and even ecclesiastical conditions.

"Lucifer was the first rebel. His words—non serviam—I will not serve—burn on the lips of revolutionaries everywhere. He was the symbol for the liberation of the human spirit from absolutism. Beginning with the French revolution. Theologians, who benefited from the wealthy, represented Lucifer as the arch-fiend, the bitter enemy of the good and holy, But the common folk, the poor and helpless, saw him as a protector, a democrat. He appears in folklore as the defender of the innocent. Medieval legends report his gratitude when he is treated with justice. Have the sons of Adam done better?

"Despite the urging of monks to emphasize the power of the devil, the tendency of folklore is to make the devil seem ridiculous and impotent. Comedy relieves the threat. Common people could defeat him with wit and common sense. For example, the devil built a house for a cobbler after the cobbler promised he could have his soul as soon as the candle on the table guttered out. But, at night, the cobbler blew out the candle before it burned down. The devil is a fool who understands nothing.

"I love those stories, they are fun, aren't they. I think that's why God never gets involved, so he can never be fooled by those wise peasants."

"To continue then, the church portrayed Satan as the prince of pleasure. The joys of life, laughter and gaiety, came from the devil, according to St. John. He was looked upon as the lord of love; the affection between the sexes was supposed to be under his control. Women were called his instruments, the gloves in which he concealed his claw. Love was a demonic factor that makes humans into puppets moving to another's purpose.

"Thus, Lucifer represents all terrestrial interests. He excels in the dialectic. He stands for every glorification of the flesh, in dance, in painting, in fiction and in life. Man, we know from Genesis, belongs to the earth. He is made of the same stuff. His health depends on his connections to the earth. Lucifer has won that war. For the world. For all matter." Smith paused in distress. Somehow, he had lost track. What had he said? He searched desperately for a suitable conclusion.

"But God has the worlds of the spirit. We can give our spirits to God. But only when matter is reconciled with spirit. Only then, when the two kingdoms are one, will we be, will we ever be, at peace."

A long silence followed his sermon. Walker was pleased. It was the most truthful sermon he had ever heard.

Helen whispered, "I arranged for us to talk afterwards." They sat while the throng filed out. They walked back to the chambers.

"Oh, yes, pleased to meet you. Helen has mentioned you." The reverend extended his hand politely.

"The two kingdoms will never, can never, be one." Walker stated.

"Why not?" reverend asked curiously.

"Because. Their contrasts are needed for creativity, for life itself."

"I'm not talking of life," reverend stabbed his finger. "I'm talking of the end of the universe. The reverse of the big bang, the big crunch."

"But even the bang or crunch cannot be all of one thing. It contains the seed of its own opposite, as yin and yang. It has to," Walker argued. "And it seems strange that man can deal with matter better than spirit."

Reverend Smith considered: "Man has trouble dealing with God and his neighbors. This is because of what happened in the Garden of Eden. Man rejected revealed knowledge from God (Genesis 3:23)! God sent them forth and cut off the tree of life with a flaming sword."

"Perhaps it is because that man has faith in matter," Walker proposed. "His faith in life and in the spirit has been taken by the church. Men were liberated from the garden, which was surrounded by wilderness. It is in gardens that everything is controlled."

"You argue like Satan," Smith commented.

Walker smiled, "Thank you. And you admire the body of Man as God's handiwork, but consign it to Satan. It is not bodies or souls that Satan wants. It is freedom. He has the bodies and souls already. The soul is made from the ground—read your bible—it is mortal. And, as you so aptly spoke, he is God of the earth."

The argument petered out. The reverend was tired and needed to take a nap. Helen and Walker walked to her house.

"Why are you so interested in Satan or Lucifer?" Helen asked.

Walker shook his head. "I'll tell you later," he said.

"I have a surprise for you," she announced, changing the topic. "For Christmas."

He sat down and looked up at her.

"I have a gift membership for you in the Sierra Club."

He didn't say anything.

"I thought you would be pleased," she complained.

He tried to be polite, "Thank you, for thinking of me."

"You don't like it?" she questioned.

"Well, I had the impression that it was a hiking interest club, dedicated to human pleasure."

"No," she protested, "we believe nature is valuable."

Walker sighed, "What is valuable in nature is its nonhumanness, its lack of purpose, its lack of importance, significance, and abstraction. Tell, me does your club protect the beautiful animals, only?"

"No," she frosted his eyebrows, "ecosystems. Lovely animals raise more money, but aren't the only goal. What's wrong with you today?"

"I'm tired. I think I'll take a nap."

Walker lay looking at the ceiling.

"I guess the killing disturbs me," he rambled. "Animal life is not sacred, anymore; but, everything human is."

"It's always been like that," Helen commented into her pillow.

"No," he corrected, "it hasn't. Human life never used to be sacred; murder was not sacrilege. Desecrating animals was sacrilege; disregarding taboos was sacrilege. It's been reversed by modern religion. Human is sacred. Killing animals is regarded as victory over nature; courage over ferocity."

They drifted in and out of sleep for a half hour. He was conscious of his hand touching her hip.

"I know how to save animals. Let's form brotherhoods, like the Elks or Moose, for the protection of species," Helen proposed.

"That's just totemism."

"So what?"

"So, who will choose the rats and grasshoppers—or any ugly animal?"

"I—I don't know—someone," she hesitated. "Why not have them assigned by phone numbers. Then, everyone in world would have brothers and sisters in the same family—or totem? They would represent each their animal, protect them."

Walker sighed, "Wouldn't work. It's based on a wrong belief: that individual species can be saved; that pupfish, louseworts, tigers, elephants each exist in isolation, unchanging, unaffected by climate, environment, human activities, other species. They are not separate; they are members of chains, nets, families, communities."

"No," she disagreed, "totemism is more general. It regards animals as relatives; there is direct descent from an animal or an ancestor associated with the animal. The word 'totem' is derived from the Algonkian language of the Ojibway, 'ototeman,' which translates as 'he is my relative.' The totemic animal is protected by rituals of permission and apology. They are protected."

"They were protected, under native traditions," Walker agreed. "We no longer have such traditions. The money for the hide is valued more than the bear. We couldn't start modern totems."

"Well, how about land totems?" she tried.

"Better—if the local system is saved, then the animals could be saved as part of it. That is the major threat—competition for land, the destruction of marshes, forests—habitats. But it'll never work. People want too much—shops instead of marshes, toilet paper instead of trees, cheap beef instead of rainforests—and industry provides it." He was quiet again, thinking.

She said, "It's hard."

"How many leopards does the world need? How many do we need? The minimum for leopards to exist? How many cranes? one thousand, ten thousand, a million?"

"How do we save them?"

"Buy all the land," he mumbled before going to sleep.

That afternoon, they went for a walk.

"I notice you frown a bit as you look at those hawks," he probed.

"Yes, I hate hawks, they kill the good birds."

He raised one eyebrow.

She continued, "I raised four bluebirds last year. Two didn't come back one day. The next day I was feeding Fric and Frac—grasshoppers, they ate grasshoppers—when they both flew off in fright, one south, one north. Then I heard a small squawk, and saw two hawks flying north, a bird in one's claws. Fric never came back; Frac hid for six hours, and blamed me; he blamed me!" Her shoulders shook with the memory.

He hugged her with one arm. "Beauty feeds on beauty," he said softly.

"No! It doesn't!" she snapped, more harshly than she wanted to.

"Hawks are no less wonderful and beautiful than bluebirds," he explained, "lions no less than antelope, tapeworms no less than bears."

"And what feeds on hawks. It isn't fair."

"Parasites feed on hawks, and eagles, humans. Even bluebirds feed on bugs and insects. You fed grasshoppers to them. Was it fair to the grasshopper? Isn't the grasshopper as beautiful in its way."

"The grasshopper doesn't feel as much."

"Then probably the bluebird doesn't feel as much as the hawk, or the hawk as much of the human."

"But why do they need to kill? Why not all live on grass?" she questioned.

"Because they don't. They learned to feed on other animals. Death is what makes beauty. Beauty communicates to the hunter, the victim, it camouflages or warns. The beauty of elk would fade quickly without wolves. The bluebird would not even fly without hawks. Death makes beauty and diversity. Without death all life would convert light to sugar in green ponds. No running, no flight, no trees, no flowers," he wandered off into thought.

She thought, and said, "I do not think so."

He wondered to her, "Why do women identify with herbivores, with the large-eyed and peaceful?"

"And why do men identify with predators, the mean-eyed and violent? As the mirror of their nature?"

"Yes, perhaps; and perhaps women identify with the young features in any animal, with babyness and motherhood, men with adulthood."

"Do you identify with hawks and lions?" She snorted.

"Yes, but also with raccoons and flies, buzzards and mountain goats," he reflected, thinking that it was more fun to fly than to wriggle, more appropriate to him to hunt than be hunted, although he had been killed by sharks and virus. He measured her words.

"What you love is an ideal," he judged. "The wolf in the zoo, eating steaks, not the wolf pulling at a rotting carcass; the eagle catching 'eagle bits', not scavenging on a bloated fish. There never was a bambi or a big, bad wolf; lions are not noble; sharks are not vicious."

"That's not true!" she protested.

"But it is. You have told me that people don't have the right to kill any animal. But they do; they are animals and they need to eat. What it isn't wise for them to do is kill the earth they live on."

Helen sputtered, but walked on.

The reverend lay down for his nap, but couldn't sleep. His robe was unfolded. And he thought that Satan had founded this very religion, basing it on man's pride in building, on the erroneous thought that man must earn God's acceptance, when he need only wish it in his heart. Why else would religion foster such pain and suffering for thousands of years, why else, but for vanity, pride, and hatred of truths which could tumble the whole human structure? Why else? But was he strong enough to say this? To follow his own way, giving up the comforts of the body, and respect of other men? Why even ask these painful questions? He knew he could not leave the mother church. Why do we feel guilty after we acknowledge our sins and are forgiven, he asked? Satan? Or because we wonder why it is so easy? He felt tears move slowly down his cheeks, and wondered if he had ever felt that part of his body so gracefully. Would he be strong enough to resist temptation? Surely he cried from stress and not from weakness, not from fear of losing his soul, just from human doubt and pride. Shehan knew that he must have strength; he would pray for strength and for guidance. Even if it meant giving up all he had or knew.

He felt his muscles pull in sequence as he moved down the old skid trail, leaping snags gracefully. He enjoyed the feel of the muscles pushing against his hide. Every motion was articulated. He determined his direction by keeping the warm light on the side he lay on. He stopped at a bower of lodgepole pines and sniffed the layer of pine needles. His smell was on them. He moved through clouds of scent into the open of the clearing. A beaver had built a small dam in front of the small stream, making the clearing in the process. He could hear the low sounds as the stream fell in several places. He sniffed the lady bird beetles on the seedlings. He lapped from the pond. He smelled the ground. Porcupine and coyote had been here. Then he dived in and wallowed, sitting with only his erect head above water. He got out and shook. Then he chased his tail, his long tan tail with the black tip.

Chapter 16. Symbiosis with Puma

Morgan Turner had hoped to see a bear. He had been hiking for two hours. He had found deer, bear, and coyote scat. Now, there were strange sounds coming through the trees, from below. He investigated cautiously. Approaching through the trees, he saw the motion before he identified the animal. It was tan, and moving toward him. He froze. It wasn't moving towards him. He stepped carefully to the edge of the clearing. Puma, it was a puma chasing its tail. *Felis Concolor.* No one had sighted one around here since—when? He didn't remember. He stood absolutely still.

Then time accelerated, causality shorted out. At least that's what he would conclude later. The puma darkened until it was green, then spun out like cloth. There was a woman in green silk dancing in the meadow faster and faster until her entire body was converted to the energy of the dance. Her face wrinkled with exertion, her limbs grew thinner. Her look became glazed, she struggled, then collapsed, but before he could move to her, something rose out of her back—a fir tree. Offering apples, oranges, figs, grapes, cherries—he couldn't see what else—and in the elbows of the branches, pineapples. An orange fell, but before it struck the ground, it burst open, and a yellow butterfly fluttered upward until it resembled a cloud pushed by the wind over the horizon. He relaxed, just as he felt the earth shaking from the ridge where the butterfly had disappeared.

Earthquake! He dived to the ground and covered his ears. The ground shook. He felt himself lifted several feet. The dirt beneath him shrunk and hardened. He lost his grip and fell off a smooth surface. He was back on the meadow looking up at a quartz platform six feet high. Particles dropped from it until the figure of a man was revealed in crystal. The crystal softened; he discerned lights within. The top darkened to brown; the crystal was the figure of a man. The eyes wide and wondering, a perfect hand extended. Each finger articulated perfectly. The lips moved slightly, as if to speak. A red dot appeared in the center of the chest. Red lines pushed out to the extremities, then purpled back to the center. The eyes stared in horror at some unimaginable distance. The spine became twisted; clumps of hair fell, down the shoulders, scratching the skin. The eyes bulged to the sides, as if offended with each other, but limited by the misshapen skull. The lips pulled back in a grimace, framing foam between long yellow teeth. The gesturing arm fell loosely to its side, shaking the suddenly pendulous chest, blotchy with scabs.

Morgan's eyes locked on the apparition with a horrid fascination. A gurgling moan came from the creature as it collapsed on bare granite.

He bent towards it, then stopped; only a pull at his own heart let him approach this—thing. The odor of decay forced him back. He regarded the deformed figure, noting the caked excrement around the buttocks, the wax on the ears, the mucus from the nose and mouth. There was expectation leaking somewhere, too; he could not leave, but didn't know what to do, either. It seemed stable, now; real. Its expression hadn't changed. It had not moved for a minute, or an hour, whatever. He bent over to reach for the wrist to see if it was alive. It was a delusion, he knew, a drug reaction. Ignoring the crazy pandemonium of roof-chatter in his brain, he touched the wrist. It was warm.

The body rolled on its back, the spine straightening, the hair smoothing, excess fluids and hair absorbed into the skin. The features seemed less ugly, but not perfect. The lips released a sigh and relaxed. Tears crept from each eye and ran down the high cheeks. The eyes opened and met his. They were calm and warm; he did not question their existence. They were blue, and alive.

"I'm sorry," the words were carried on the most wonderful voice, "I didn't know you were here." The voice had transformed his image of the body before him, to a beauty perfectly controlled.

Morgan managed a nod, hoping that his head wouldn't fall off. Harmony, that was what the voice conveyed; harmony with the meadow. He wondered if gods had come again. Who—what—was this, was happening.

"I am Silenus," the being spoke, "a spirit of wild nature." He sat up, unconscious of his nudity, but conscious of the discomfort of his listener. "You will not tell anyone," he stated easily. "I can show you."

Show me what, Morgan thought; he still could not speak. He felt serene; the meadow was serene. Another dimension had opened quietly. He was aware of everything: the spring violets, the smell of wet wood—he didn't know what to say.

"Nothing, is the proper answer. The earth without humanity is in harmony," Silenus stated.

Morgan didn't want to contradict directly, so he prefaced his comments with 'I think' or 'I heard that' or 'But.' "But isn't life a struggle?"

"Yes," Silenus shrugged, "a struggle. But not unfair. You think of animals as alone against the world; Tennyson's poetic image of nature red in tooth and claw, where Keats saw every maw the greater on the lesser feed."

"You're saying that wolves don't feed on antelope? That sharks don't kill flounder? That hawks don't—"

"No, but I'm saying that the elk work together with wolves, that the elk need wolves to be healthy elk, since wolves kill the diseased, the weak, young and old. Hungry wolves make a bond with the elk. They won't attack unless the elk agrees."

"Why would the elk agree?"

"Because it's inevitable; the elk knows it and accepts it. Eye contact is made between the lead wolf and the victim."

"How would you know?" Morgan asked boldly.

Silenus paused, remembering. "I watch. Wolves eat more mice than elk. Tell me, do you kill mice in your house? Do you eat them or put them in the garbage?"

"Well, yes," Morgan admitted, "but they spread disease."

"So do other humans. Do you kill them and put them in the garbage?" was the swift response.

"No, but that wouldn't be right." Morgan felt the argument getting out of control; people weren't animals. "People aren't animals. No one I know would savagely kill an elk and chew on its bones."

"No," Silenus reflected, "they would cleanly kill it with a gun, chop off its head for a trophy, gut it and leave the guts for coyotes, cut off some steaks for the freezer, and dump the remains in the garbage."

"That's not true!" Morgan heated up. "No good hunter would—"

Silenus leaned towards him, "No? If you don't believe me, take a tour of the dumpsters and landfills between here and Moscow next fall. I've seen headless gutted deer in them." Silenus paused and straightened up.

Morgan looked horrified but said nothing.

Silenus continued, "Wolves are good mates and good parents. They are loyal and caring, playful and responsible. They kill because they are hungry, because they are wolves, not warriors, religious fanatics, or psychopaths." Silenus wanted a challenge. Could he convert an average, unaware human to a knowledge of the earth?

"Most of nature lives in symbiosis with other species. Symbiosis is a word from the Greek, meaning 'living together.'" Silenus anticipated the question. "Examples are everywhere. The oncideres beetle in Texas lives on mimosa trees. The female climbs a tree, lays her eggs on a good limb, then girdles the limb by chewing around it for seven or eight hours. The limb dies and falls; the larva prosper—they cannot live in live wood."

"So what does the tree get?"

"Long life. Unpruned mimosa live for twenty-five years; pruned, they live to be one hundred. Consider other examples. The coral crab carries sea anemones on each claw for protection. The anemone has tentacles that can stun or kill anything interested in eating the crab. The crab is protected and the anemone has a much wider range in which to filter its own food.

"Cattle egrets, a small species of heron, hop around the feet of zebras, eating grasshoppers kicked up; they land on the zebras back to eat parasites. The egret will warn a zebra of the approach of a lion by hopping up and down on the host's back, calling and flapping its wings; if the host is too slow, the egret will hop onto the head and peck at the skull, usually producing the desired result—running. The oxpecker takes up a permanent residence on an African buffalo, courting, eating, mating, and sleeping on their host. Before nesting on the ground, the bird will even remove hairs from the mane and tail for its nest. Their diet includes flies, ticks, and necrotic skin—they ignore insects on the ground."

Morgan saw the images on the grasslands as Silenus spoke.

"The Egyptian plover grooms the Nile crocodile. The carp cleans the mouth of the hippopotamus. "The impala antelope prefers living in large herds close to water holes, which also attract baboons, jungle cats and dogs. The antelope are a favorite food of lions, leopards, cheetah, hyena, and wild dogs. Baboons like to live near the water and will associate with herds of antelope. The antelope alert the baboons to danger; the baboons frighten away most predators, including lions.

"Then, of course, bees, butterflies, moths, and humming birds associate with specific plants, and are often necessary for the pollination and existence of those plants. Lichen is a species formed by the symbiotic action of two unrelated species, algae and fungus. Lichens grow on trees

305

and rocks. Forest lichen may live to be 200 years old; arctic lichen may make it to 4,500 years. Lichens are incredible. They are dormant when dry, but are reanimated by moisture. They do not need soil; they are not susceptible to drought, or to extreme heat or cold. They erode rock. Reindeer eat them; humans use them for dyes and pharmaceuticals.

"Herbivores—horses, cows, sheep—cannot digest grasses. The digestion is done by intestinal bacteria. Without sheep, goats, horses, antelopes, most carnivores would have no food. Some rodents and monkeys would not exist either. The bacteria break down cellulose into molecules that can be absorbed by enzymes in the intestine. Peas and beans need different bacteria to convert nitrogen into nutrients. Without them, the plants would wither away. Trees depend on fungi in their roots to draw water and nutrients from the soil. Without fungi, dense forests would not exist; the fungi increase the actual root area for each tree. Fewer trees mean less oxygen recycling.

"Bacteria in the human gut may be responsible for vitamins. Many domestic foods are symbiotic with man: corn, cows, hens, for instance. Rats depend on humans, for food and entertainment. Cats and owls live in close association with humans; they eat rats. Coyotes and bears depend on garbage. You see where I'm leading: all life depends on other life, even human. Even air and water depend on life."

Morgan was looking at one of the seedlings covered with lady bird beetles. He watched as one lifted off.

Silenus explained: "Her spotted red wing covers, elytra, lift to 45 degrees, allowing her membranous hind wings to press down. During flight, the elytra are held at 45 degrees and act as fixed airfoils to increase lift. The wing tips go backwards and up, then forwards and down, to the plane of the body, then backwards and down, to the nadir and forwards and up to the body again, making figure eights faster than your eye can track them."

"And what good are lady bugs?" Morgan asked curiously.

"They eat aphids."

"And what good are aphids. They kill crops."

"No, not exactly. They remove surplus sugar from plants; the honeydew they excrete increases soil fertility." Silenus went on, "If they kill crops it's because we kill the lady bird beetles with chemical biocides, which were developed to save the crops in the first place. No, imbalances with crops are usually our own fault."

"Are you saying that aphids wouldn't ruin crops if we left it up to the bugs?" Morgan was incredulous.

Silenus considered, "No, the bugs would probably take a percentage of the crops, anyway, say 10 percent, but that's less than the usual loss."

Morgan asked, "Wouldn't the lady bugs eat all the aphids?"

"No, aphids reproduce faster. Besides, ants protect aphids, sometimes." When Morgan looked puzzled Silenus went on, "Ants are attracted to the honeydew. Some species of ants are so entranced that they keep domesticated aphid colonies."

"Domesticated? No?"

"The ants search for aphid colonies, capture as many aphids as they can, bring them back to the ant nest, and build mud shelters for the aphids. Warrior ants are left on duty to protect them. Aphid eggs are carried inside the ants nest in the winter. Ants round up aphids in the morning and take them out to graze, like sheep, returning to the nest at the end of the day. Ironically, honeydew has limited food value, even for ants. It isn't essential to their diets. It may be the equivalent of a treat, like a sugar donut for a snack.

"What about maggots?" Morgan mentioned the most disgusting insect he could think of.

Silenus responded, "Blow fly and bluebottle females lay eggs in decaying meat, usually corpses, sometimes wounds. Wounds are favored. When the larvae hatch, they feed only on necrotic tissue and pus, not on the healthy tissue; the dead tissue is a much richer source of plasma and red blood cells. Their excretions act as a disinfectant. Flies may often save the host's life. In fact, blowflies were used in American hospitals in the 1800s as wound cleaners. Like this: infected wounds were sealed up with fly eggs. When the nurse heard a buzzing inside, the bandages were removed and the flies released; the infection was usually gone."

Morgan was quiet.

Now, Silenus was watching the lady bird beetles crawl over one another. He picked one up, looked at it closely, and put it back on the needle.

"Then everything is symbiotic?"

"Not exactly. Let's say that no animal lives entirely alone. That even the lives of coral and chalk are part of the interaction. Geological cycles, and weather—" Silenus wandered off.

"What shall I do?" Stuart called after him.

"Revere the earth!"

Morgan noticed that Silenius had a tail like a puma. He sat for a while. Then carefully left in the opposite direction.

When he stopped wandering, he found himself with blanks in his memory and working another job, as a part-time auto mechanic at Baker's.

"My car won't start," the voice on the phone complained.

That always threw him. Cars were supposed to start and then break down, not just refuse to start. Well, it couldn't be helped. Walker asked, "Where are you ma'm?" As she explained the directions to her house, he wondered if it was going to get colder. "I'll be there in five minutes," he promised. "Thank you for calling Bakers." Then he hung up and shouted back to Gus, "Gus, I'm taking a truck!"

The answering shout came, "Take Betsy!"

Betsy was hard to start. It must have gotten below zero last night. Hard February weather. Why did they always neglect their own trucks? Five minutes later, he was with Mrs. Custer's chevy. Looking under the hood. He inspected the battery for corrosion and water level. The started hadn't turned for him either. The battery looked okay. He went to the starter motor and solenoid, connecting a jumper from the battery post of the solenoid to the starter post. There was no response, so he knew the solenoid was bad.

"You have a bad solenoid. I'm going to check something else. Why don't you go inside?" he suggested.

"No thank you. I'll watch," she sniffed.

Must be watching pennies, too, he thought. Good girl. He checked the ignition switch with a jumper wire and test lamp. It looked okay, so he returned the high tension lead to the coil.

"I can get it started for you, but the next time you turn it off, it will stay off, like this time," he explained. "If you follow me to the shop, I can fix it in ten minutes."

"How much will it be?" she inquired.

"Just the solenoid? I'm not sure." He assured her that it wouldn't cost much, thinking that he would be late with the valve job on the Galaxy.

"What's so important that you need to kill yourself?" Helen asked. Walker looked up from his bath. The bubbles had almost all disappeared. He looked around for more.

"I said, what do you need all the money for, that you have to work another job?" Helen repeated from the doorway.

Walker gave up looking for bubbles and gestured at her. She shook her head.

"Land," he said. "I want to buy some land here."

"Why?"

"Basically, so no one else will get it, and turn it into condos or a junk pile or ski resort. I want to set it aside."

"That's a very noble idea. Can I help?"

"Sure," he blew a bubble at her and stood up, "You buy some land and dedicate it to preservation."

"But preservation is so static. Conservation would be better," she reasoned.

"That's because you misunderstand the concept. I'm not talking about the preservation of every life form on it. I mean preservation from interference. From premature destruction. I wouldn't protect it from wind or gypsy moths—just humanity. Could you get me a clean towel, please?"

"Only if you cook something good for dinner," she bribed.

"Tomato Quiche okay?"

"For that, you can have a large towel, even," she teased. She thought these normal days might be ending—he was gone so often. She had to ask Marie if he had found an animal spirit or at least try to find out what was happening.

Later, while she was cooking, she offered, "We could buy some land together, as business partners. What do you think?"

Walker nodded, slicing tomatoes.

"I know of a place that might be for sale, a few miles from Marie."

Walker smiled and nodded.

It had taken him ten minutes to climb the pine. He sat unmoving while he scanned the lower hills. He leaned forward and pushed off with both legs, arms straight ahead, body opening like a knife blade. His head back, body arched. The arms swept to the sides. The face hardened.

She made several powerful strokes to accelerate her fall; then, with wings outstretched, she glided in a straight line, dropping through a gully parallel to the squirrel. She was not seen by the squirrel, who was eating in a small clump of grass a hundred yards from its rocks. She came up over the lip of the gully low and fast. When she spotted the squirrel again, she drove her wings harder, abandoning the approach glide. The squirrel ran several steps when it saw her, then stopped and headed back. She was now too high and fast to hit the squirrel. She fanned her wings and tail, body vertical and legs hanging down, as if to land. But she turned and dropped, legs extended ahead, talons aimed at the back of the retreating squirrel. She folded her wings and dropped. The squirrel lunged for the rocks as the shadow eclipsed him. She hit him in the rear, her momentum tumbling him several feet, before the claws locked into the fur. She carried him to the same rocks; his eyes seeing the haven again. She tore ribbons of flesh with her beak, her wings spread over the warm body.

A rabbit crouched near a hole, twitching his nose. Her head was turned so that a penetrating yellow eye could regard its target. Her interest was keen and unblinking. She turned her head to watch with the other eye. Had the rabbit noticed the intensity with which he was being studied and appraised, he would have bolted back into the hole. Everything in her field was considered by one of those eyes before being marked, or dismissed. Her feathers were dark brown with golden highlights. She took oil on her beak from the base of her tail and rubbed it through her feathers. Each feather required preening regularly to remain straight and functioning. The leg feathers were straight cuffs above the yellow plates of her feet. Each talon was like a sharp finger, precisely manicured, black and polished with a fine patina. She regarded her talons. Noticing a small tuft of white down under the curve of one talon, she caught it in her beak and shook it off. As it was carried in the wind, she followed its movements.

She pushed her wings down, jerking the body upwards. As her wings raised, the leading edge was tilted upwards, creating more lift, directed backwards. The hand of each wing was rotated 180 degrees during the upstroke, bending it backwards. The primary feathers spread apart so that air could pass between them, each feather helping to lift. A wind helped her up. She gained altitude. At a reasonable height, she glided downwards for speed, then curved up again. As the air streamed faster over the wings, pressure was reduced on top; the pressure underneath pushed the wings up. She passed the butte, air streaming through the wings with a rustling sound. She dived again, adjusting the long flight feathers. The terminal feathers, which looked like slotted margins, were spread to reduce drag. She wheeled and banked away, soaring over the valley. The flat planes of the wings were now rigid, like walnut plank. Flight was effortless and joyful.

She soared in large circles, searching for the lifting air currents. She could see the warm air rise from the ground in large bubbles that men called thermals. She circled to five hundred, then seven hundred feet on the edges of the bubbles. Up a few thousand feet, the wind was 150 knots. Her wingspread was almost eight feet. From the rabbit's hole on the ground, she appeared as a large, dark bird. The dark brown body and underfeathers contrasted with the lighter brown wing and tail quills. Her wings bent slightly at the wrists, halfway between the tips and her body. The wings were wide most of their length. The golden leading edge of each wing showed as she banked to stay by the bubble. She adjusted the spacing between feathers in response to turbulence. Occasionally, she twisted her tail to catch wind currents. Once, falling off the thermal, she positioned the leading edges of her wings to the left and tilted her tail down and to the left to slip sideways back to it. To find another thermal, she flew with the wind, and then turned to face the wind. She was gliding between thirty and forty miles per hour. Sometimes she threw a barrel roll or other aerobatic stunt exuberantly.

Stan was medium height; his bright blue eyes were set in a confusion of small wrinkles at the corners of his eyes. He was weathered.

"That's two today, ain't it?" Stan confirmed the count.

"Yea, slow day," Jim answered in disgust.

"Is she loaded?" Stan gestured to the gun. Jim patted the sawed-off shotgun and nodded. Both of them ruminated.

Jim observed, "Just ain't as many sheep-thumpers up here in Snakenavel," homesick for the Trans-Pecos mountains of Texas.

"Used to get thousands of the chingaladdos."

"Gettin any mud on your turtle, tonight?" Stan turned the topic to sex.

"Gonna give her some wall-to-wall counseling, an hammer her into the springs, headfirst," Jim boasted.

"Don't wanna mess with her, boy," Stan warned. "She's the stud duck's black widow. I'll stand ya a glass of calf-slobber when we're earthborn."

Maybe he'd better get knee-crawling drunk, he guessed, squeezing his fingers into her big ass in his mind's eye. He listened as Stan explained how they would come out of the sun and with the wind to give them two advantages for the kill. They had seen the black dot on the horizon enlarge to an eagle. Sheep-thumping eagles were what they were after.

She had been tracking their course as soon as she had heard the faint buzz and seen the moving dot. The course and speed were constant. When the plane angled out of the sun, she stared straight into the glare, never leaving the object.

When he was within a couple hundred yards, Stan lowered the Piper Cub to 1200 feet.

Her wings furled, she plunged into a steep dive.

"Let's follow it!" Jim shouted.

Stan opened the throttle and moved the stick forward. She was pulling away, so Stan opened it all the way. Only when he went over 120 miles per hour did Stan start to pull closer. But they had to pull out of the dive to keep from crashing.

She spread her wings and reversed direction ten feet above an outcropping. She began to climb again in the opposite direction from the plane.

Jim cracked the window and stuck the shotgun barrel out. They were several hundred feet higher than the eagle, who was still climbing. As they dropped parallel, she banked and reversed directions. She was moving east with strong, regular wingbeats.

"Let me try something," Stan suggested. He turned the plane and started descending above the eagle, coming down fast in an attempt to strike her with the undercarriage.

She folded her wings again and dropped. The plane followed, roaring its intention. As the plane accelerated towards her, she rolled on her back; the wings now added a downward pull to the pull of the earth. The talons opened for combat; locked the axle. She arched and plunged downwards, locked to the plane.

Stan fought for control, unable to see or understand why he hadn't pounded that dirty bitch out of the air. The plane slew sideways in a dive, accelerating. Jim pulled his gun in. The scream of defiance told them it was the eagle, but both of them were too fascinated by the angle of the plane to search for the source of the scream. Stan regained control a hundred feet from the ground.

He cursed. "Get gun ready. I'm gonna cut that bitch from asshole to appetite."

"Ya know," Jim started, "back when snakes used to walk, eagles used to attack planes, throwin 'emselves at it."

She drove her wings furiously, climbing with sheer power. At eight hundred feet, she folded her wings; the shape of a golden droplet, she dived towards the earth. The angle was too steep. Air buffeted her feathers violently. She felt several pulled loose. At five hundred feet she extended her legs, talons open.

Just as Stan was turning the ailerons up, a dark bomb struck the right wing tip. The plane rolled out of control, spiraling towards the rocks. Stan fought to get the nose up. Then they crashed.

She kept plunging towards the rocks. At the last moment, the wings shot out full. She beat the air before her. Then she struck the ground, quickly drawing in her wings.

The shotgun had landed forty yards from the wreck. She stood up and let the wind rustle through her feathers.

"Chief, I've got that list for you," Ted Jensen offered.

Packard looked up from his journal. "Oh, thanks. Now, I want a list of all convicts released in January through May, this year. Then I want a list of animal welfare organization members who have been arrested—for anything."

The chief intended to investigate all of the conservation and preservation group memberships. He couldn't tell who else would kill a researcher, unless it was an animal welfare person. But, he didn't see how it could be one of them.

"It has to be one of them," Ted said.

"Look, Ted, they may be a bit foamy at the mouth, but it aint because they're rabid," he paused, "no, they've just been rode hard and put away wet. It's got to be something else, something personal. Someone who just hated him."

Ted Edelman raised his eyebrows in disagreement. Pursing his lips he said, "Chief, I just don't buy it."

His whole relation to the earth changed. His muscles became gravid with power, warping the thick bones. He seemed to draw mass from the air. The muzzle pushed forward. He lifted up against a Douglas Fir, his torso lengthening, the claws reaching toward contact. He ripped down through the bark leisurely. He chewed on a chunk of bark as he walked away, satisfied with its sweet taste.

He was foraging peacefully. After making sure that the berries had all been stripped from their bushes, he started digging up roots to chew. The bear was low-slung, thick-set, and very muscular. His legs were short and stout, and strong; the claws on the front feet were longer than the ones on the rear. The outer dark brown fur was frosted with silver. The burly neck supported a heavy head, long with a high forehead and a concave face. He chose a ridge with a view to rest on; a place where he couldn't be surprised. At night he wasn't as selective, and just flopped down anywhere.

He had established his territory already. Although no others of his kind were around, there were cousins. There was an information place to the north, where one could find news of other bears or enemies. He had visited it once. Coyotes, skunks, and deer had been visitors before him.

Teddy Maitlack sat at the foot of the pine. He chose that place because of the 300-foot shooting lane at the base of the slope. He was sure that it was a trail; he had seen paw prints there. He gripped the fore-end of the .30/30 Winchester—his father's gun—and waited. He would add some memories to the gun. He might even get himself a trophy. More, he was providing a public service; he had been told that bears emerged from their winter seclusion hungry and smashed into peoples woodland homes, looking for canned goods or flour. He knew that the landowners breathed easier, knowing the population of bruins was culled. As a forester, he knew that these same bears killed plenty of good, marketable timber with their teeth and claws. He was protecting the trees, also. The terrain was hilly, with close growing conifers and thick brush. The floor was mossy and heavily needled. Old snow covered the north slopes; by April it would be gone. It would be hard to hear an approach. Bears were wary; their hearing was as good as a deer's, their nose better. The way they used shadow and cover—just let them appear—without ever coming.

The slope was still snowy. He approached, sniffing. Then he sat down on his haunches and pulled himself forward with his front claws. He started to coast and put his paws on his knees. Soon, going too fast already, he reached one paw behind; when this didn't slow him down enough, he rolled on his belly, scattering ice crystals, and dug in with both paws. After he had slowed down, he sat on his haunches again and pushed with both paws. This time he got going so fast that he lost control and began rolling and tumbling. Almost to the bottom, he rolled over a small pine that slowed him, scattering snow from the branches. He stopped just before the bottom. Sighing contentedly, he started to climb up the slope.

Two hours earlier, Teddy had loaded the 180-grain hollow point. He was cold and tired. His camouflage clothing, in green and brown, was not quite heavy enough. Then he saw the bear.

'Jesus!' it was a grizzly, a monster—just what he was after. It was playing. At first, he couldn't comprehend that—playing. Like a kid, sledding. Then he realized what he had thought. He raised the rifle, momentarily unable to find his target in the scope. He followed it down the lower half of the slope, deciding to wait until it reached bottom and stopped. He planned the shot. Then the bear was heading right back up the slope. He decided to try the shot, although the bear was getting out of his line. Must've seen him. He held his breath and released it slowly. Then squeezed the trigger. The report filled every space in the woods. He was momentarily blinded by the muzzle blast. Then he saw it galloping back across his line, with that strange rolling gait.

He followed it at a safe distance. There was still good snow cover between the trees. He hadn't found any blood, but that didn't mean that he hadn't hit it. The bear made such strange turns and jumps that following was not easy. He finally followed it to a log that had fallen over a stream. 'Blow down,' he cataloged it. The tracks indicated that the bear had crossed on the log and jumped into bushes on the other side.

Its tracks looked smeared, as if it was walking funny. It might be wounded and waiting for him. He had to be careful. Expecting to find tracks on the other side, he detoured around a hundred yards. When no tracks were found, he came within ten yards of the brush. He dug a few small stones out of the ground and lobbed them into the brush. Nothing happened. He resorted to yelling, trusting that the bear's sensitivity would make him charge out into his ready gun. Nothing happened.

Feeling a little foolish, he tracked back downstream a ways, then back up to the log, finding no tracks. He went up to the log and inspected it carefully. He followed the tracks into the leafless brush, destroying them as he stalked. A twig snapped. He fired! The echo was even louder in the trees. He listened; nothing. He found the end of the tracks. It looked like—the bear had backtracked! If so, then it went far downstream or upstream. It must have jumped from the log. He decided to track upstream to save time. He walked by willows and tangled pines, not finding any tracks for over a mile. He crossed to the other side.

He was back at the log. He didn't know where to go next. On a hunch, he went back upstream on the first side. This time he noticed a patch of crushed willows twelve feet from the center of the stream. Tracks led north from the other side. That damned animal must have jumped from the stream into the willows. If he hadn't investigated it, he would have ended up miles downstream. Meanwhile, he had wasted time on false scents. His anger was mixed with just a little concern.

He followed the trail back north, towards the slope where he had first fired on it. The trail was not disguised, now, nor as circuitous. He had heard from another hunter that a grizzly was reluctant to leave his territory, often doubling back two or three times in five miles. That gave him an advantage. He smiled. After four miles or so, he lost the tracks on bare rock. He wondered subconsciously if the bear had come to the rocks to lose him. He took off his gloves and rubbed his hands together for a while; he'd be by a warm fire soon enough. He put on his gloves and moved back out into the snow. He began moving east in a large circle. After 140 degrees and another mile, he found tracks leading west. Another half hour behind. He wished he had a helicopter. He thought of his father: 'If you wish in one hand and shit in the other, guess which'll fill up first?' He felt a little better.

The tracks veered once to a spruce with old claw and tooth marks; that tree was untouched recently, but a bite had been taken out of one nearby. Edging back west, the tracks led him to a deer carcass. Apparently killed by coyotes, it had been partly eaten by the bear—but not today. He's still running. He must be hours ahead by now. Several more miles, over a ridge, he found blood on the snow. He was hit. Then he saw the woodchuck hole. No, stopped for dinner. He hurried, guessing that the bear was close ahead. He loped in the tracks. Then he saw the dead-end canyon ahead, surrounded with scrubby timber. He made sure the tracks were leading in. He followed carefully, stopping to listen every couple of yards.

Looking around by chance, he saw the bear come out of the woods a hundred yards behind him. His heart started pounding—you never knew what it was going to do—but he forced himself to go slowly, as if he was not aware of the bear behind him. He concentrated on the tracks before him. After a nine or ten steps he noticed that the tracks were slightly broader, indicating that it had backtracked him again and circled back. He would look at them later. When he paused, he noticed out of the corner of his eye that the bear had paused, also, and was watching from behind a tree. It was time to turn the tables on it.

As soon as he was out of sight behind a bush, he crouched and ran toward the rim of the canyon and back toward the entrance. After a half mile or so, he was confident that he was now several hundred yards behind the bear. He started to move in, wanting to catch it before it found his cut-back. He was considering his shot when he saw the bear's shadow cover his. He turned immediately, but slipped, firing accidentally. On his seat, he levered a shell into the chamber, aimed, and fired. The bear went down. He breathed again, but couldn't stop shivering. He was lucky that bears were easy to shoot. This one had evidently figured out the circle gambit and arranged an ambush of its own. Damn, there was no game as smart as a grizzly. This one was too far south, but that would make his conquest all the better. He wished he had a map of their chase. He could see blood staining the snow. Grizzly was not a difficult animal to kill, if you hit a vital spot—heart, brain, spine. He advanced within a few feet, thinking 'better not try to skin it before it's dead.' He prodded its side with the end of his rifle barrel.

The bear jack-knifed up, knocking him backwards. Tearing the cloth and skin from Teddy's right thigh. By a miracle, he had held onto the gun. But the bear grabbed his shoulder in his mouth, shook him, and dropped him. The gun fell. The bear caught him up again, face between the tusks, shook again and dropped again. The bear clawed him up a third time, by the chest, shook him and dropped him on his back, then reared back and snorted, teeth clacking. Teddy gazed up at it, thinking that he could reach his gun and kill the sonofabitch. He couldn't be badly hurt, since he didn't feel any pain. But he could see his own blood flowing down his face, and from his arm, leg, and chest. He was tired and decided to rest a moment before reaching for his gun.

The bear hooked a claw into the trigger guard and dropped the gun over the inert body. He ran east, stopping occasionally to lick the two wounds. After an hour he stopped at a meadow, and began tearing it up for mice. Thirty one mice later, he decided it was time to sleep and entered a clump of bushes up the hill a ways. It would be dark soon. The air and silence were all so clean and wonderful. Tomorrow he would visit the tree, again.

Chapter 17. Enantiodromia

After the hunter was found, other hunters declared an open season on bears. They didn't find any grizzlies, but managed to kill sixteen black bears. Black bears, which may be colored brown, white, or cinnamon, may have been mistaken as brown bears. Walker felt sick. He had not foreseen the human over-reaction. And his short-sightedness had resulted in more deaths, instead of fewer. One hunter had been shot accidentally, but he didn't care about that; people were always shooting each other, accidentally or not. He could not kill again, as an animal, even to save other animals. He was suffering. He had to run until he was out of breath, just to avoid screaming. He could not live with the responsibility, just as he could not live hearing the voices of existence snuffed out by human greed. There would have to be another way. He needed time to think. He spent more time running and just being. He raged against the theft of life, of intelligence, of choice, by the mindless corporations from the people, from animals, from the earth itself. Venting his rage on fools did no good. Then, suddenly, he had a chance to present it to one of those corporations.

There were thirty people in the room. None with a title less than Vice President. The room was paneled in walnut; heavy draperies closed out daylight. It was equipped with an excellent air conditioner and soft lighting. The twenty nine men and a woman sat around a horseshoe table covered with green baize. It was from this room that Cyril Drake was dispatched to a field assignment in northern Idaho. As Executive Engineer and Vice President, Drake often had to lay the groundwork for another World Amitec conquest. It was the part of his job that he relished the least. Placing his mineral water back on the tabletop and setting his nameplate straight, he agreed to preview the operation of his heliblimp for the logging operation south of Sandpoint, in nowhere

Idaho. He took the elevator to the top of the building and the waiting helicopter. The empty seat of the blue swivel armchair was particularly noticeable to Eric Cargen, who wished he was out in the field in Drake's place. He sighed and brought the meeting back to order. Brazilian beef was next on the agenda.

Drake unlocked his briefcase and began the familiar rundown of operations for the Amitec Idaho wood products subsidiary. Since the clone forest had not reached financial maturity, yet, the test cut with the heliblimp would be a thinning operation. The last herbicide spraying should have wiped out the junk trees months ago, so he wouldn't have to look at them. He scanned the planting and fertilizing schedules for the holdings. Then, he went over the future acquisitions schedule. The owners of lands as far south as Coeur d'Alene should have received their brochures by now. He wondered if he could make any profit on a separate operation. He closed his eyes until the helicopter landed.

The crews had turned out full force for a VIP landing. Drake was hustled out immediately to the site. The crews followed at a distance. Drake noticed one logger prying into the bark of a clone pine. He excused himself from his underlings and went over to investigate. If there were bark beetles, he'd have somebody's balls for a necklace.

"Hey, tell me that's all right," he addressed the logger, who turned and cut him off at the knees with an ax. There was a sharp pain, then a long ache. Drake looked up speechless. His limbs were trimmed, the ax left in his chest—the screaming started and stopped abruptly, and the logger disappeared into the forest—before anyone reached him.

Nothing helped—he was being consumed by memories of his ugliness—he was a rapist, killer, but most of all a failure whose powers only resulted in more suffering and death. At least he had bought land. He had to go away.

Walker prepared a resume and sent it off to clinics and schools in

New York and Massachusetts. His lectures became uninspired again. He started to miss some of his 5-9:00 a.m. shifts at Baker's. He got a letter from Boston, asking him to come for an interview. He asked for, and received, a telephone interview.

Two days after the interview, they called him back and offered him the job in mental health. He accepted the position, to begin in July, at a starting salary of $25,300. He would give a month's notice at the college, and still have over a month to get there and take up residence. The next day he gave his notice at the college—Busby was quite rude about the prospect of finding someone to teach the last week. He would miss some of his students; he relented and promised to work the final week. Busby was civil again. The following morning, he gave his notice at Baker's. Baker didn't take it hard.

"I like you, George," E. K. preambled, "I like your work fine, but you never make me any money at it. You are just about the slowest thing without flippers I ever see'd. So now I can hire a high school kid with quicker hands and a slower mind. Hope you do well for yourself. You buy that land? Wanta sell it?" Walker had never heard E. K. string so many words together without a few days in between.

"Can I get you a coffee, E. K.?" he offered.

"Never turn down a free coffee," E. K. bumbled, wanting to show George that he liked him, anyway. All four of them on duty went over to the Rexall for coffee. E.K.'s wife stayed to guard the place like a sphinx, deferring any customers by asking them questions and riddles until they dropped. They talked baseball. He would miss them all more, Walker decided.

The last two weeks were a form of Purgatory. Walker invited Helen over for dinner, intending to tell her about his plans.

"What is that noise?" she asked querulously.

"Cage," he answered.

"Modern music, huh? I thought so. The twilight of great music can be traced to Darwin and Freud, to the analysis of mystery—the merciless spotlight of science probing into every hidden dimension. Some things should be left hidden."

At first, Walker was at a loss for words. "No, I don't think modern music is that much less than classical. Light only deepens mystery, not eliminates it. Light—"

"If knowledge is a room, then light eliminates mystery," she pressed.

"True, but if knowledge is a sphere in space, the more it expands, the greater the surface area touching the mystery outside." He took a sip from his glass. "Besides, modern music is more sophisticated; it incorporates more noise—"

"More noise, all right. I'll change it."

He watched her as she got up and sorted through the albums. She put on a Bruckner.

"I'm leaving," he blurted out.

"Music is indispensable, for health, for mystical experience, for soothing shocks—why?" her voice broke.

"Something went wrong. All I did—everything I did—nothing came from it, but pain and suffering. '—behold, all was vanity and vexation of spirit,' there was no profit," he mumbled off, thinking that there may have been a false prophet. Ecclesiastes had been right.

Helen was angry with him. She had told him that he now registered under two 'gants.' He knew that she would be all right, but he didn't know what to say.

"What happened?" she asked.

"I—I cannot say, exactly," he protested.

"Have you contacted a power, is that it?" she guessed. "Does Marie know? What?"

"No, I cannot tell her."

"She can help you. See her," Helen urged.

"I am Jagganath. I must—I—"

"Jagganath? For Christ's sake, don't be incoherent. Do you have an animal power, yet?"

"No," he answered. He certainly couldn't tell her the truth. And she knew that he certainly was not telling the truth.

"Are you lying?" she accused.

"No," he said. "I am telling the truth, but not being completely honest."

"I suppose you are going to tell me the difference?" she sneered.

"Yes, honesty has to do with facts. Truth has to do with facts and feelings in a context. I am telling the truth, but I can't tell you all the facts. Please be satisfied with that."

"All right," she sniffed, "we all have secrets, and keep them." She didn't think it could be too bad. People who conversed on Mozart could not be evil.

"I signed over the land in your name. If you can't keep it, give it to some conservancy group."

"You can fight it here," she suggested.

He shook his head. Things had gone too far. He would never be able to stand it. He reached for her, to express something without words, but she turned and went outside.

It was easy to begin traveling. Filling up at the Chevron station, he turned on to Interstate 90, which would take him through Chicago and into Boston, bypassing almost every other large city. The freedom was exhilarating. And traveling is a temporary freedom. He felt turned loose to adventure, hurled by chance into unexpected situations. Subconsciously, however, he remembered why he was leaving.

Nightmares, death, violence—all linked to his changes and his desire and actions to save his animals, his nature—

[End of Cycle 231]

About the Author

Marcus Rian had a normal and exciting childhood playing baseball and exploring forests. Although slow to learn and slow to awareness, he eventually became interested in dead languages, dead insects, and old coins. He was not interested in school and did not do well in it. After his release from the Air Force, he started writing this novel. Later, he was able to take some university courses in Latin, astronomy, and architecture. After getting a high school equivalency diploma in New Mexico, he took more university courses in physics, chemistry, philosophy, gymnastics, swimming, biology, psychology, geography, art, anthropology, and economics. Although his interests were broad and deep, they never fit the requirements for a formal degree.

Starting as a newsboy, then lifeguard, Rian created his own local businesses selling wild berries and filling ice cream machines. To support himself while he pursued his interests, he worked at many different jobs including artist's model, truck driver, dishwasher, ditch-digger, gardener, bank messenger, bookstore clerk, library supervisor, gymnastics teacher, printer, book editor, opera set painter, animal hospital attendant, television repairman, auto mechanic's apprentice, and computer engineer. He began working with a local veterinarian on animal rehabilitation and the reintroduction of exotic pets into their natural habitat. Since then he has studied wild canids all over the world, proposing an international northern hemisphere wolf path.

When not engaged in professional activities, Rian enjoys walking, swimming, horseback-riding, reading, and drawing, at a ranch in central Florida. He participates in volunteer programs with Greenpeace, Save the Children Federation, and Move-On.

Finding that his experience followed Auden's prescription for poets, he has written in poetic and scientific, forms. Recently, he has worked only on book-length themes. He continues to work hard to keep to the dictates of Wordsworth and Novalis to be a good poet.

About the Book

Synopsis

George Walker is an unemployed astronomer, oblivious to himself, others, and his environment, living in his own ideas. Slowly he acquires self awareness; he indulges his selfish wants, at the expense of others. With little understanding and little power, Walker starts changing. He can swim faster and heal faster. He can become like animals in some ways. He starts to believe that he is more than human, but then he is humbled by those who are more practiced at violence. He reads about the archangel Lucifer and fantasizes that he might be a reincarnation. He gleefully speaks and does evil things, returning violence for violence.

However, as he understands more of the Lucifer story, he develops characteristics and emotions that do not seem to be evil. Gradually, his awareness includes the suffering and joy of others, and he becomes more compassionate. He questions whether he has reached the end of his madness or whether this is merely a deeper evil, the expression of the essential Lucifer. Then He learns the value of having a sense of humor; he takes joy in living, playing and dancing. But, he cannot stop being violent, and now he cannot ignore the effects of violence on things he has come to love. He chooses a voluntary exile, for a while.

Author's Note

Like D. H. Lawrence's novels, this novel is symbolic and moral. It offers a little teaching, as well as a little entertainment. The author is not trying to shock or convert, but, like all good preachers, to save. We have deep-seated human problems, of image, of consumption, of exploitation, and of destruction. The world is unhealthy—it is wobbling and falling apart. How can one really write about it without lamentation and sorrow? As a sermon rather than a paean? As a fictional story rather than a lecture?

Colophon

The display and text type is Goudy Old Style
using Indesign on Macintosh G5
near Lower Lake Myakka
before the gazes of a thousand alligators.
Book cover and design by RianGarciaCalusa.com
Sky-diving angels on back by AM Caratheodory and Merissa Depasse
Cover photograph of Swan Point Cemetery by Merissa Depasse

www.ingramcontent.com/pod-product-compliance
Lightning Source LLC
Chambersburg PA
CBHW061537170626
46811CB00001B/7